FACING
A CRUEL
MIRROR

FACING
A CRUEL
MIRROR

+ + +

Israel's Moment of Truth

Michael Bar-Zohar

Charles Scribner's Sons • New York

Charles Scribner's Sons
Macmillan Publishing Company
866 Third Avenue, New York, NY 10022
Collier Macmillan Canada, Inc.

Library of Congress Cataloging-in-Publication Data
Bar-Zohar, Michael, 1938–
    Facing a cruel mirror : Israel's moment of truth / Michael
Bar-Zohar.
        p.   cm.
    ISBN 0-684-19194-6
    1. Israel—Boundaries.   2. Israel-Arab War, 1967—Influence.
3. Israel—Politics and government.   I. Title.
DS119.65.B37   1990
956.9405—dc20   89-70080   CIP

10 9 8 7 6 5 4 3 2 1

Printed in the United States of America

To the memory of
DAVID BEN-GURION

Contents

FACING
A CRUEL
MIRROR

The Spark

In the late afternoon of December 8, 1987, an Israeli truck driver lost control of his vehicle on the Gaza–Tel Aviv highway. The truck, carrying a heavy container, was on its way back from the occupied Gaza Strip to Israel. It skidded across the road and rammed into a Peugeot sedan with Gaza plates coming from the opposite direction. The Peugeot was crammed with Palestinians returning from work in Tel Aviv. The huge truck smashed the Peugeot; four Arabs were killed, a few others wounded.

The bloody accident took place close to the Erez roadblock commanding access to the Gaza Strip. Scores of Palestinians, returning by car or bus to their homes in Gaza, saw the collision. In less than an hour the news had spread all across the 140-square-mile strip, traveling with lightning speed throughout the crowded souks of Gaza, the miserable refugee camps surrounding the city, the impoverished villages scattered along the coast. Fueled with swelling hatred, the rumors said the Jewish driver had killed the Palestinians in cold blood to avenge the death of Shlomo Sekel.

Forty-five-year-old Sekel, an Israeli sales agent for a hardware company, had been a familiar figure in Gaza. A few days before, as he was about to enter a store at Palestine Square, an Arab terrorist had jumped him from behind and cut his throat, then vanished in the crowd.

The truck driver, the Gaza grapevine reported, had come to Gaza seeking vengeance. It was even rumored that the man was Sekel's own brother. That was untrue, of course.

The next morning a crowd of thousands assembled in the Jebalia refugee camp, near Gaza, waving Palestinian banners, brandishing clenched fists, chanting anti-Israeli slogans. After a while the crowd stirred and moved forward, an angry human torrent streaming down

Jebalia's dirt-paved streets. Youngsters rushed to the front lines of the spontaneous procession, covering their faces with their checkered kef-fiyehs. Many of them had picked up stones and debris in Jebalia's alleys.

As the throng reached the camp's center, they came upon a squad of Israeli soldiers, reservists in their thirties who were grudgingly serving a thirty-day period in the strip. The youths stormed them with a hail of stones. From a narrow alley another group of Palestinians emerged, cut-ting off the Israelis' escape route.

After the first stones the teenagers started throwing Molotov cocktails at the soldiers. Rudimentary firebombs made of bottles filled with gas-oline, they were ignited by a burning piece of cloth. The Israelis started firing, first in the air, then at the approaching mob. A seventeen-year-old Palestinian, Hatem Abu Sissi, was killed; sixteen others were wounded. One of them, twenty-year-old Ra'd Shahada, was to die the following day.

The violence spread like brush fire throughout the Gaza Strip, then swept the West Bank and Jerusalem. Everywhere spontaneous protests formed. Crowds numbering thousands, waving flags, throwing stones, setting rubber tires on fire and erecting roadblocks on the main streets, advanced upon the Israeli soldiers. The small army units in the occupied territories were at a loss as to how to control the huge crowds.

Superior officers and political leaders interviewed the same day ex-pected the outburst of violence to subside quickly, like so many other disturbances over the past twenty years. They were wrong. The protests of December 9, 1987, were the beginning of a long turbulent insurrection that was to engulf the occupied territories and turn into a nightmare for both Israelis and Palestinians.

A nightmare indeed; nobody would have imagined, in those first days of December 1987, that two years later the revolt still would be raging throughout the occupied lands. But as 1989 neared its end, the protests, the violence, the fury still inflamed the West Bank and the Gaza Strip. The number of Palestinians killed during the uprising was approaching six hundred; about 20 percent of them were teenagers and children. Scores of Israelis had been killed, some burned to death by firebombs in their cars, some kidnapped and savagely assassinated, others stabbed in the streets of Tel Aviv and Jerusalem, or slain in a bus driven into an abyss by a Palestinian.

During those bitter years the violent scenes of Israeli soldiers clashing with angry crowds of Palestinian women and youngsters became a permanent item on evening newscasts around the globe. A number of Israeli soldiers and officers were thrown in jail, while others were dishonorably discharged from the army for maltreating or killing Palestinians. Israel was severely condemned by international human rights organizations; a U.S. diplomat bluntly said that Israel had become "a damn nuisance."

The insurrection had turned into a tragedy for Israel and the Palestinians. For two years it had consumed the energy of both nations; it had disrupted the Israeli economy and brought disaster upon the Palestinians, whose standard of living had plummeted sharply.

In 1987 we couldn't foresee the sudden threat to our personal security, either. Israel, whose army was the strongest in the Middle East, had difficulty protecting its civilians from the threat of individual Palestinian terrorists. More than one hundred thousand Arab workers crossed from the West Bank into Israel every day to work in the different sectors of our economy; it was practically impossible to prevent an attack on innocent civilians by a fanatical Palestinian determined to kill as many as he could, to become a martyr of the insurrection.

Foreign observers could not or did not want to understand this unique characteristic of the Palestinian uprising: The West Bank was not Vietnam or Algeria. It wasn't a foreign land to the Jewish people. It wasn't separated from Israel by seas, oceans, and continents. The uprising was happening in our own courtyard, twenty minutes from Tel Aviv, two minutes from the Jewish quarters of Jerusalem. At times it invaded our cities and villages. And many of us listened with concern to the muffled rumble rising from the Israeli Arab community; we knew that our Arab citizens couldn't remain indifferent to the desperate confrontation between their own Palestinian brothers and Israeli Jews. The uprising, therefore, directly affected the security of Israel and its citizens.

The revolt of 1987 troubled us deeply by suddenly exposing this intense hatred that had been simmering in the hearts of the Palestinian people; this determination of an entire nation to fight us with stones, knives, axes, and firebombs; this ugly violence, and the deadly dangers it suddenly brought to our very doorstep.

But the uprising also raised a cruel mirror to our faces. And many of us were shocked by the grim image that we saw.

We saw Israeli soldiers beating up and firing at youngsters, jailing thousands of Palestinians, blowing up houses, harassing and humiliating civilians. We read about the swiftly rising number of people killed, wounded, expelled, or imprisoned as the revolt continued. We learned about the tough measures our army was applying in its harried efforts to crush the uprising. Many of us reacted angrily to the administrative arrests, the curfews, the closing of schools and universities, the brutal treatment of Palestinian suspects.

Many of us were exasperated by a government that refused to realize that we would have to leave most of the occupied territories if we wanted to preserve our Jewish identity, our moral society, and our democratic regime. Many Israelis recoiled from the extremist declarations of right-wing leaders who formulated inhuman solutions to the Palestinian problem, and before their insensitivity to the bloody toll of the uprising.

But we were also shaken by the blindness of some left-wing leaders who, steeped in self-hatred, justified—and in certain cases even glorified—the violence and murder practiced by Palestinian extremists. And we were appalled by Israelis who would harshly criticize our army and our leadership while lauding PLO chief Yasser Arafat and the leaders of the revolt, the very people who ordered the firebombing of civilian cars, the kidnapping, mutilation and murder of children, and the stabbing of old men in the streets of our cities.

The dark mirror held up to us by the Intifada mercilessly reflected the weaknesses of our society. We saw to what point the state built by David Ben-Gurion and our founding fathers had changed during the forty years of our existence. We saw how the values of Zionism—pioneering, labor, and the dream of a moral and just society—had been eroded throughout the years. The cautious, moderate policy of a past generation had given way to the right wing's rigid, ambitious doctrine of a Greater Israel—a doctrine that produced, along with fiery speeches and pompous declarations, a disastrous policy of unlimited settlement in the West Bank and a blunt refusal to trade even one square inch of land for a peace treaty with our neighbors.

We saw how Israel, so united in the past in front of our enemies, had turned into a nation deeply divided. Our society had become polarized by the conflicting influences of extremist forces: religious intolerance, territorial dreams, the cult of military might on one side; and on the other, defeatism, a questioning of our very right to exist, and even the idealization of our enemies.

Still, it was not only shadows we saw in our mirror. It also projected the tremendous effort of Israeli society to preserve its moral values. The Israeli army adhered to its codes even at the cost of much-publicized trials, and severely punished soldiers and officers who had broken the law. At the very apex of the insurrection, when passions in Israel were running high after several vicious murders of Israelis by Palestinians, we were offered a unique item on the evening news: the general in charge of the West Bank coming to the television studio to express his concern and sorrow for the wounding of a Palestinian baby by one of his soldiers. I don't remember any such apology by French, American, or British officers after far more revolting acts committed by their soldiers during recent African and Asian conflicts.

The Israeli parliament, the Knesset, thwarted all efforts to introduce the death penalty for terrorists. Freedom of speech was fiercely protected: Palestinian leaders were interviewed daily on Israeli and foreign television, and West Bank figures were invited to lecture throughout the country. In university auditoriums in Jerusalem and Tel Aviv, panels of Israeli and Palestinian scholars civilly debated possible solutions to the conflict.

Israel's democratic foundations were not affected by the uprising. Democratic nations often curtail their freedoms when fighting for survival. We remained a free and open society in spite of being engaged in combat on several fronts, each vital to our existence. Besides striving to bring the uprising under control, we were fighting a daily battle along our northern border against Palestinian terrorists; and at the same time we were struggling against the fanatical Hizballah, the "Party of God." We also had to cope with extremist Arab states like Libya, Syria, and Iraq that were building an arsenal of chemical and biological weapons after their attempts to develop atomic bombs had been thwarted.

Used to fighting a perpetual war of survival, Israel carried on as normally as possible. Our cultural and scientific life went on unperturbed; theater festivals, concerts, art exhibits, and book fairs continued as in the past. Amos, a communications satellite, was launched in space. Tourists, reluctant at first, returned to the holy sites and the golden beaches of Israel; our relief mission was among the first to reach earthquake-stricken Armenia.

Still, we couldn't ignore the drama unfolding around us. The Palestinian insurrection had created a new reality. It was the catalyst that had sped up the long invisible processes evolving deep under the surface of our society. It had made us face up to our true image and answer questions that many of us had tried to ignore since the Six-Day War in 1967. It forced a soul-searching upon us, a reappraisal of our goals, our values, and our society. The insurrection urged us to seek a solution to the Palestinian problem, which had lain dormant at our doorstep for twenty years. Slowly, painfully, Israel realized that after the outburst of the Palestinian revolt it would never be the same again.

But on December 9, 1987, nobody understood that the protests in Gaza and the West Bank heralded a long bloody conflict. Foreign Minister Shimon Peres was on an official visit to Argentina; Defense Minister Itzhak Rabin was on his way to an official visit to Washington. They both refused to cancel their visits, convinced that the "disturbances" would quiet down in a day or two, like so many in the past.

They couldn't have imagined that the Intifada, the Palestinian uprising, had just erupted.

Chapter 1

Triumph

We had been waiting for the Palestinian uprising for twenty years and six months, since the Six-Day War of 1967. Those twenty years were the most intensive and dramatic of my life. I had made my first steps in politics shortly after the war ended; my writing career had barely started three years before. As it has been for many Israelis who have taken part in the wars and the political struggles that shaped our destiny, my personal life was closely intertwined with the dramatic events of those tumultuous years.

I cannot look back at those chapters in my life without referring to the violent history of the region that served as an ever-present backdrop to each personal event. Likewise, I am unable to describe our confrontations with the Palestinians, our experience of war and peace with our neighbors, without recalling so many episodes of my life, in uniform and out of it; without being assaulted by a host of images from my past, such as the desert battlefields of the Sinai and the blood-soaked land of Lebanon, the fiery party debates, the violent street protests, the angry confrontations on the Knesset floor.

In 1967, I was twenty-nine years old. I had spent most of the preceding eight years in Paris. Born in Bulgaria, I had emigrated to Israel at the age of ten and grown up in a poor neighborhood in Jaffa. After obtaining a degree in international relations at the Hebrew University, I had pursued my studies in Paris. I had worked my way through school as a correspondent for several newspapers and a radio station. In 1963, I got my Ph.D. in political science; my thesis dealt with the secret alliance between France and Israel that led to the Suez war.

My thesis was published as a book that became a bestseller in France and Israel. All of a sudden I was well known and was awarded important prizes; reporters interviewed me, asking for my views on issues I didn't know much about, diligently printing my answers in their papers. Perhaps it was hubris that made me turn to Ben-Gurion, whom I had never met, and offer to write his biography. Yet when the founder of Israel agreed in November 1964, no one was more surprised than I.

I would devote most of the following nine years to researching Ben-Gurion's life. I spent much of my time beside Ben-Gurion, delving into his personal papers, interviewing him at length, meeting his closest friends and greatest opponents.

One of the young leaders Ben-Gurion liked most was Moshe Dayan. I met Dayan several times, but we didn't become close until I returned to Paris for a short period in 1966. One day he telephoned me from Tel Aviv, bitterly complaining about the Israeli embassy and all the other Israeli representatives in France who had failed to get him an appointment with André Malraux, the celebrated French writer who was then minister of culture in De Gaulle's government.

I happened to be a close friend of Malraux's personal assistant. Within minutes of Dayan's call I phoned him back. "Moshe," I said, trying to sound casual, "how would lunch with Malraux next Monday suit you?"

Dayan was stunned. That day he decided I had extraordinary powers, and I decided to do my best to protect that flattering, although utterly unmerited reputation.

In May 1967, I returned to Israel and to my research on Ben-Gurion. Three weeks later the Six-Day War erupted.

I participated in the campaign on the Sinai front, reaching the Suez Canal with the armored division of General Israel Tal. As soon as the fighting ended I was recalled by Moshe Dayan, who appointed me press secretary to the minister of defense. I remember his first words when I stepped into his office the day after the cease-fire. Instead of discussing my new job, Dayan had some advice for me: "Michael, take your car and go see the West Bank before the revolt begins!" The defense minister was certain that a Palestinian rebellion against us was only a matter of time.

I followed Dayan's advice and, together with thousands of elated Israelis, set out to discover the West Bank. But in Hebron and Nablus, in Jericho and Jenin, in the picturesque villages and the grim refugee camps, we didn't encounter the bold, defying spirit of upheaval. We met a subdued, desperate nation, paralyzed by fear of Israeli military might, stunned by a crushing defeat—a broken people, unable to digest the fact that the last six days had destroyed their world, their leaders, and their aspirations.

Only a week before, the entire Arab world had been in ecstasy, fore-telling the imminent collapse of the Jewish state. In Cairo, Damascus, and Old Jerusalem, huge crowds were dancing in the streets, waving flags and slogans. Their hero was Egypt's president, Gamal Abdel Nasser. In a sudden succession of dramatic coups, Nasser had shattered the ten-year calm on his border with Israel. Breaking the agreements negotiated by the United Nations in 1957, Nasser dispatched his army into the Sinai Peninsula, expelled the U.N. peacekeeping force, locked the straits of Sharm el-Sheik to Israeli shipping, and threatened to destroy Israel. In a meeting with exhilarated pilots at the Bir Gafgafa air base, Nasser openly defied the Jewish state: "If Israel wants war, we say: 'Welcome.' We are ready!"

Faced with that challenge, Israel was slow to react. Prime Minister Levi Eshkol, a good-natured, moderate man, seemed to hesitate; rumors spoke of a veritable revolt in the Army General Staff against his lack of resolve. Eminent Israelis demanded that eighty-one-year-old Ben-Gurion replace him as prime minister and lead the country in the forthcoming confrontation. A group of women protested in the streets of Tel Aviv, calling for the appointment of Moshe Dayan as defense minister.

Emboldened by Israel's distress, Egypt, Syria, and Jordan signed a military agreement, joining forces to crush the Zionist state once and for all. Winds of defeat swept Israel, the specter of a new holocaust rising to haunt the tiny nation. Israel's foreign minister, Abba Eban, flew to Paris, London, and Washington to seek help. Gas masks were urgently shipped from West Germany. In Tel Aviv, high school students dug trenches in the city's shady boulevards; teams of rabbis marched through public parks chanting prayers, thus consecrating the areas as emergency cemeteries.

Israel, its back to the wall, had no choice but to meet the challenge. Prime Minister Eshkol formed a National Unity government in which Moshe Dayan became minister of defense; the leader of the right wing, Menachem Begin, was invited to join the government after a lifetime in the opposition.

On June 5, Israel launched an air and land offensive against Egypt.

Syria joined Egypt immediately. Levi Eshkol sent an urgent message to King Hussein of Jordan, asking him to keep out of the war and guaranteeing Jordan's territorial integrity. Hussein hesitated for three hours, then threw his forces into the battle. From the hills surrounding Jerusalem, Hussein's artillery shelled the Jewish part of the city; from the heights of Kalkiliya, in the coastal plain, long-range cannon opened fire on Tel Aviv. A wave of unprecedented enthusiasm swept the Arab states. The time had come to avenge the humiliation of 1948.

The euphoria, however, was premature. On the very first day of the war, Israeli air strikes destroyed on the ground the air forces of Egypt, Jordan, and Syria. In a three-pronged attack, Israeli armored forces penetrated deep into the Sinai, annihilated the Egyptian divisions, and reached the Suez Canal. In the West Bank, Hussein's army suffered heavy losses and hastily retreated across the Jordan River. In the last two days of the fighting, Israel dislodged the Syrian army from the Golan Heights.

Six days after the first shot had been fired, hostilities ceased all over the Middle East. The Arab world woke up to a cruel reality: Israel had single-handedly won a tremendous victory. The defeat of the Arab states had been even more humiliating than the 1948 debacle. The armies of Egypt, Syria, and Jordan were on their knees; their air forces had ceased to exist. The Palestine Liberation Organization, headed by Ahmed Shukairi, and his much-publicized Palestine Liberation Army, based in Gaza, had been wiped out by the war.

Israel had taken the Sinai and the Gaza Strip from Egypt, the Golan Heights from Syria, the West Bank and Jerusalem from Jordan. It had conquered an empire, a territory of 26,476 square miles, 3.3 times larger than its original size. It controlled a population of 6,396 Arabs and Druze in the Golan, 33,441 Arabs and Bedouin in the Sinai, 356,261 Palestinians in the Gaza Strip and 666,234 more in the West Bank. More than half of the Palestinians in Gaza and a fifth of those in the West Bank were refugees from the 1948 war, living in misery in squalid camps.

The military victory elevated most Israelis into a state of euphoria from which they were to emerge only six years later, with the outbreak of the Yom Kippur War. The forces of light had conquered the forces of darkness. We had achieved a wonderful victory. We were heroes. The whole world was against us, and still we had triumphed.

We basked in the world's admiration and in our own. Writers and poets extolled the magnificent Israeli soldier whose heroism was equaled only by his moral and humane values. Generals stated that our wonderful army could have crossed the Suez Canal and conquered all of North Africa, stopping only at the shore of the Atlantic (to refuel). Politicians and intellectuals, even some well-known left-wing leaders, flocked to the newly formed councils, leagues, and associations for a Greater Israel; they eagerly explained to foreign correspondents that Israel had reached its natural borders, liberated the historic homeland of the Jewish people, removed forever the Syrian threat, and turned the Suez Canal into a genuine international waterway. The new map of the Middle East, they solemnly declared, was in the best interests of both Jews and Arabs.

The staunchest allies of the annexionists turned out to be the Arab leaders. The Israeli government kept a cool head and tried to use most of the newly acquired territories as assets that it could trade for peace. On Moshe Dayan's initiative, the National Unity government officially proposed to give back the Sinai and the Golan Heights in exchange for peace; on another occasion Dayan declared that he was expecting a phone call from King Hussein.

But King Hussein didn't call. Neither did President Nasser nor any other Arab leader. Instead, Nasser convened an Arab summit in Khartum, where the Israeli peace initiative was rejected. Khartum unanimously adopted the formula of the three "no"s: no to the recognition of Israel, no to negotiation with Israel, no to peace with Israel. "What was taken by force will be retrieved by force," Nasser declared.

In the absence of a partner for peace, Israel was left alone to deal with the occupied territories and determine their future. The Sinai and the Golan didn't raise any particular problems. They were very sparsely populated and could be administered easily, even incorporated into Israel without raising any demographic problems. They had no sentimental or historic significance for the Israelis; their main value was as security buffer zones that would protect Israel's vulnerable territory. Even the establishment of Jewish settlements in the Sinai and the Golan wouldn't prevent a territorial compromise if one day the Arab states agreed to make peace with Israel. In the opinion of most Israeli leaders, such settlements, whose ties to the land were not religious, could be removed if that was the price to pay for a peace agreement.

The West Bank was totally different. That was the historic Judea and Samaria, the ancient cradle of the Jewish nation. That was the very Eretz Israel, the Land of Israel. Wherever we turned, we saw one of the landmarks of our history: Hebron, where the biblical fathers of Israel were buried in the Patriarchs' Cave; Nablus, the capital of the ancient Kingdom of Israel; Bethlehem, where Rachel's tomb still stands; Jericho, whose walls had fallen before the trumpets of Joshua; Shiloh and Anathoth, Mounts Gerizim and Ebal. For any religious or nationalist Jew, this was the Holy Land that couldn't be negotiated or abandoned.

And of course, there was the crown jewel—Jerusalem—the eternal symbol of the Jewish people, the site of the two Temples, King Solomon's capital. When we stood, deeply moved, before the Wailing Wall, when we climbed on Mount Scopus and the Mount of Olives, when we walked around the ramparts of the Old City or toured the ruins of the old Jewish Quarter, we knew deep in our hearts that we would never abandon this place.

A few weeks after the Six-Day War, Jerusalem was annexed to the State of Israel by an unanimous vote of the Zionist members of the Knesset. But what about the rest of the West Bank? "We returned to those places, never to leave them again," Dayan declared. But those places were also the national home of the Palestinians, densely populated by a nation that hated us, considered by the world as a part of the Kingdom of Jordan. And there lay the heart of the Palestinian problem: Should we annex the West Bank? Or should we keep it out of bounds for Israelis? Should we settle in the midst of the Palestinian population? Should we try to coexist with the local Arabs or remove them from that coveted land?

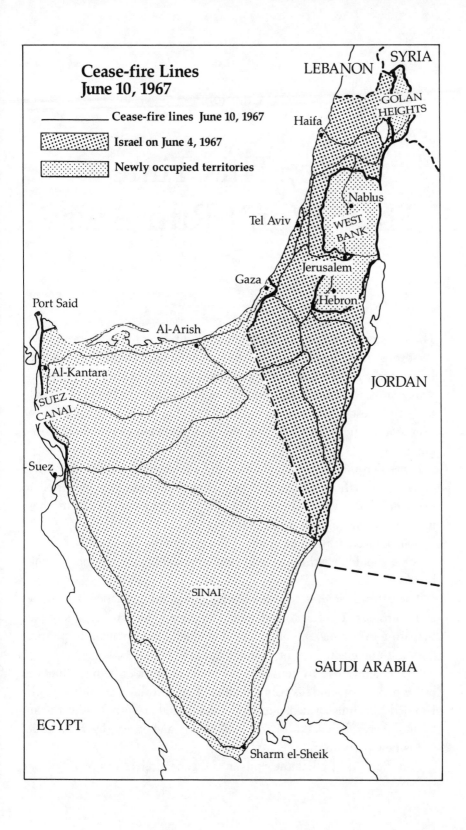

**Cease-fire Lines
June 10, 1967**

—————— Cease-fire lines June 10, 1967

▨ Israel on June 4, 1967

▧ Newly occupied territories

LEBANON

SYRIA

GOLAN
HEIGHTS

Haifa

Nablus

Tel Aviv

WEST
BANK

Gaza

Jerusalem

Hebron

Port Said

Al-Arish

JORDAN

Al-Kantara

SUEZ
CANAL

Suez

SINAI

SAUDI ARABIA

EGYPT

Sharm el-Sheik

Chapter 2

No, This Time
They Won't Run Away

The unexpected victory of 1967 triggered a tremendous emotional outburst throughout Israel, turning cool heads, igniting fertile imaginations. I was deeply involved in the impassioned debate about the future of the West Bank. My recent appointment as Dayan's aide allowed me to observe the most dramatic events since 1948 from the inside, and for the first time in my life to step into the political scene, even though in a minor role.

It was Ben-Gurion who had unwittingly infected me with the political virus. One night in 1965, like countless times before, I had tried to persuade him to write his memoirs. "No," he had said. "I am too busy in politics. I have no time."

"But Ben-Gurion," I protested, "you must write history."

"One shouldn't write history!" he said forcefully. "One should make history!"

These words impressed me deeply; despite my influence as a writer and journalist, I began to feel that politics was the only means of participating in the making of history. I gradually got involved in politics, hoping to be elected to the Knesset one day.

One couldn't live in Ben-Gurion's presence without being influenced by his personality and his political ideas. While working on his biography I joined his circle of dedicated followers; together with Moshe Dayan, Shimon Peres, Itzhak Navon, Chaim Herzog, and others, I was a founder of his new party, Rafi.

Rafi didn't do well at the polls in the general elections of 1965. We

won only ten seats and felt condemned to a long period of barren opposition. But two years later came the Six-Day War that shook the
political establishment and brought about a change in our leadership.
Moshe Dayan emerged as Rafi's leader. Ben-Gurion's moral influence
remained immense; he was viewed as the Father of the Nation, and his
leonine head, with its pugnacious features and its halo of white hair,
had become the symbol of Israel's rebirth. Still, I saw Ben-Gurion gradually retiring from active politics and, like the old soldier in the legend,
slowly fading away.

After the war, some of Ben-Gurion's most devout admirers joined the
annexionist camp. The West Bank and Jerusalem hadn't been occupied, they said, but liberated; they claimed this was also Ben-Gurion's
view, and they were closely following the concepts of Israel's founding
father.

From my long conversations with the Old Man, and from his letters
and diaries, I knew that they were right, but only up to a point. It is
true that Ben-Gurion had been a staunch supporter of a Greater Israel
for many years. I found out, however, that he went through a profound
metamorphosis in the mid-fifties: his courage and realism had triumphed
over his emotional attachment to the ancient boundaries of his homeland.

In his youth Ben-Gurion had dreamt of a Jewish state stretching on
both sides of the Jordan River, like the ancient Kingdom of Israel. The
boundaries of Palestine, as defined by the League of Nations after the
First World War, matched that concept. In 1920 the San Remo Conference entrusted Great Britain with the Mandate over all of Palestine.
A year later, though, His Majesty's colonial secretary, Winston Churchill, tore the eastern part of biblical Palestine from the promised national
home and created the artificial Emirate of Transjordan. Churchill had
to fabricate a substitute kingdom for the Hashemite Prince Abdullah,
Lawrence's friend and Britain's wartime ally. Abdullah had remained
crownless after the cynical partition of the Middle East between England
and France. Ben-Gurion gradually resigned himself to that new reality
and limited his territorial sights to mandatory Palestine—the lands
stretching west of the Jordan.

Then, in 1937, a British Royal Commission of Inquiry, headed by
Lord Peel, proposed a partition of mandatory Palestine into a large Pal-

estinian state, a British enclave (including Jaffa and Jerusalem), and a tiny Jewish state, limited mostly to the coastal plain. And to the stupefaction of his activist friends, Ben-Gurion publicly endorsed the partition plan.

They couldn't believe it. The militant Ben-Gurion, the dreamer of a large Jewish state, had deserted his friends and allies—Tabenkin, Berl Katznelson, Ben-Aharon, Golda Meir—and joined the meek, moderate group he disliked, people like Weizmann, Sharett, Locker, and Goldman. He was assailed by criticisms and attacks, mostly from within his own camp. "Why, Ben-Gurion?" they would write to him or shout at him in public meetings. "How could you?"

But he wouldn't answer. He would tell no one the reasons for his change of mind. Nobody but his son Amos. "Amos was the only one who knew the truth," he told me years later. Amos, who was eighteen years old at the time, had written a letter of protest to his father. "I don't understand you. How could you, the supporter of Great Zionism and Great Israel, agree to the partition?"

Revealing his secret design, Ben-Gurion wrote back: "A partial Jewish state is not the end, but only the beginning. . . . We shall bring into the state all the Jews it is possible to bring. . . . We shall organize a modern defense force, a select army . . . and then I am certain that we will not be prevented from settling in the other parts of the country, either by mutual agreement with our Arab neighbors or by some other means. I am not in favor of war . . . [but if] the Arabs behave in keeping with [their] barren nationalist feelings and say to us, 'Better that the Negev remains barren than that Jews settle there,' then we shall have to speak to them in a different language. But we shall only have another language if we have a State."

In other words, Ben-Gurion saw in the amputated Jewish state a springboard toward a Greater Israel. He hadn't abandoned his dreams, only decided to achieve them in stages.

At the beginning, a tiny Jewish state would be created, and Jews from all over the world would return to their homeland. In a second stage, a formidable Jewish army would be raised. And then, in a third stage, the Jewish state would expand its territory, with the Arabs' consent or without it. (Today, fifty years later, the Palestinian nationalists follow the identical step-by-step approach. According to PLO public declarations, their master plan is based on several stages: first, the creation of a small

Palestinian state in the West Bank, then the return of the Arab refugees from their diaspora, and finally the armed liberation of all of Palestine. The resemblance is blood-chilling, at least for the Jews.)

In 1937 the partition plan of Lord Peel failed, but ten years later Ben-Gurion accepted the partition plan of the United Nations. He hadn't changed his mind, and his territorial goals remained the same. He defined the partition borders as "ridiculous," but accepted them, expecting that the Arab states would reject the plan, which they did. They invaded Palestine, giving Ben-Gurion the pretext for expanding the territory of the Jewish state. During Israel's Independence War hundreds of thousands of Palestinian Arabs fled in panic before the advancing Israeli army, and Ben-Gurion actively encouraged that exodus. In his diary I found several entries about his territorial goals. The army should liberate the entire West Bank, he wrote, and reach the Jordan River, "which, after all, is our natural border."

Still, when the war ended in 1949, Ben-Gurion hadn't achieved his territorial dreams. A large portion of the West Bank, including the cities of Hebron, Nablus, Jericho, and East Jerusalem, remained in the hands of the Jordanian army.

My friend, the writer Chaim Gouri, told me he had asked the Old Man a few days after the end of the war: "Ben-Gurion, why didn't you liberate the entire country?"

Ben-Gurion had replied: "There was a danger of getting saddled with a hostile Arab majority . . . of entanglements with the United Nations and the big powers, and of the State Treasury collapsing. Even so, we liberated a very large area, much more than we thought. Now, we have work for two or three generations. As for the rest—we'll see later. . . ." The realist in him had triumphed over the visionary; the statesman had gained the upper hand over the conqueror.

Still, he hadn't fully relinquished his dream.

A few months later he traveled to the south, to visit the newly liberated port of Eilat, on the Red Sea. As the convoy passed through the Jordan Rift Valley, Ben-Gurion got out of his jeep and gazed at the Edom mountains beyond the Jordanian border. Next to him stood the young and handsome General Yigal Allon, one of the heroes of the Independence War.

"How would you take those hills?" Ben-Gurion inquired, pointing at the jagged peaks veiled in a purplish haze.

Allon began to analyze the problem, explaining the route he would take and the forces he would use. Suddenly, he stopped and asked in astonishment: "Why do you ask? Do you want to conquer those hills?"

Offhandedly, the Old Man muttered: "I? No. But *you* will conquer them."

Nonetheless, Ben-Gurion kept hoping that the occasion would arise when he would be able to liberate the rest of Palestine. In his archives I found abundant proof that during the first years following the establishment of the State of Israel, he continued to secretly plan the next stage, in which he would achieve his territorial ambitions. In 1956 he went so far as to submit to his French ally, Prime Minister Guy Mollet, a plan for the reshaping of the Middle East "in the best interests of France, England, and Israel." The plan included the removal of Egypt's President Nasser; the dismemberment of Lebanon, its south going to Israel, its eastern provinces to Syria, and the rest becoming a Christian state; and finally, the partition of Jordan. The West Bank would be annexed by Israel and the East Bank by Iraq.

I learned that Ben-Gurion's dramatic change of mind occurred a few weeks later, at the end of the Sinai war. During the weeklong war, in October 1956, the Israeli army launched a lightning offensive against Egypt, occupied the Gaza Strip and Sinai, and reached the banks of the Suez Canal. But when the triumphant Ben-Gurion visited the Arab cities and refugee camps in the Gaza Strip and Northern Sinai, he came face-to-face with a new reality that shook him deeply: the Palestinians hadn't fled before the approaching Israeli army as they had in 1948. Knowing that Israeli soldiers were civilized people, and not the murderous monsters they had believed them to be in 1948, the Palestinians barricaded their doors, raising white flags as a sign of surrender.

Ben-Gurion understood that he would have to cope, now and in the future, with a new reality: the Palestinians wouldn't flee anymore. Which meant that if Israel ever occupied the West Bank, it would be faced with a population of one million or more hostile Palestinians. And by their sheer number, those Palestinians might one day tip the delicate balance between Arab and Jew, bringing an end to the Jewish majority in the Land of Israel, and consequently, to the Jewish state as well.

Ben-Gurion as I knew him was an audacious man who drew his lessons from reality, as unpleasant as they might be. That winter day, while

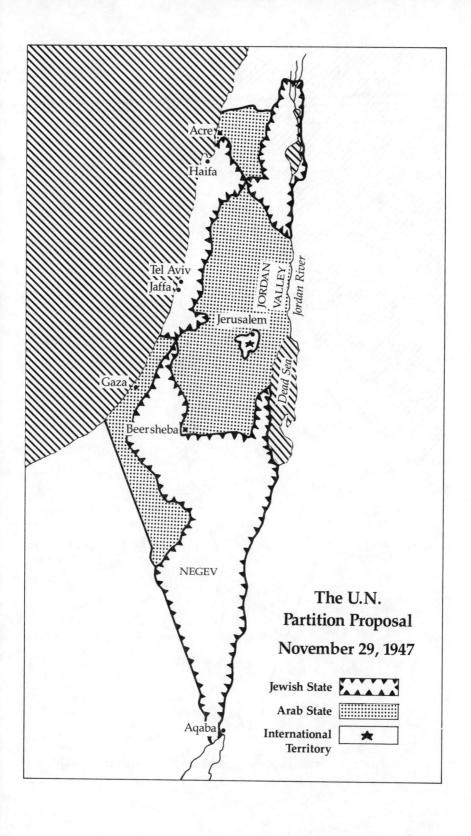

Acre

Haifa

Tel Aviv
Jaffa

JORDAN VALLEY

Jerusalem

Jordan River

Gaza

Dead Sea

Beersheba

NEGEV

Aqaba

The U.N.
Partition Proposal
November 29, 1947

Jewish State

Arab State

International
Territory

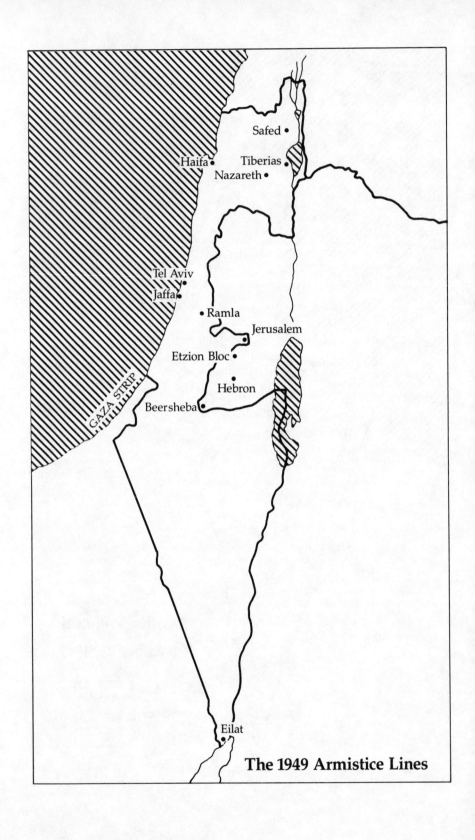

The 1949 Armistice Lines

Safed

Haifa • Tiberias
Nazareth

Tel Aviv
Jaffa
• Ramla
Jerusalem

Etzion Bloc •
Hebron
Beersheba

GAZA STRIP

Eilat

touring the refugee camps in the Gaza Strip, watching the huge crowds of Arabs clinging to their barren, miserable piece of land, he understood he had to give up his dream for a Greater Israel. "This time they [the Palestinians] won't run away," he said to his friends. This was to become his personal slogan. In the future he would concentrate his energy on preserving what he had acquired and in bringing more Jewish immigrants into the country.

Several times in the years following the Sinai campaign, his young aides, Dayan, Laskov, or others, would come to him and say: "Ben-Gurion, Hussein's throne is shaky. Now's the time to take the West Bank," or "Ben-Gurion, Iraq's regime has been overthrown, Syria is in deep domestic trouble. Now's the time for us to advance to the Jordan River." But his response was always the same: "No, for this time they won't run away."

He remained faithful to this conviction even in the intoxicating atmosphere of elation and self-confidence that swept Israel after the Six-Day War. After the astounding victory, many of Israel's leaders took to borrowing their speeches from the Bible and haranguing the crowds with slogans about the sanctity of the Land of Israel, and the West Bank "from which we would never part."

But the Old Man, whom so many treated as "senile" and "out of focus," kept a cool head. "For a real peace," I heard him say in 1967, "we should give up all the occupied territories, except for Jerusalem and the Golan Heights."

He had dreamt, indeed, of a Greater Israel. Nevertheless, having to choose between a large country and a Jewish majority, between the Jewish land and the Jewish state, he chose the Jewish majority and the Jewish state.

But in 1967, Ben-Gurion was a very old man who had returned to his kibbutz in the Negev, far from the spheres of national leadership. Two other men were to shape the future of Judea and Samaria—two men who were friends and rivals, comrades in arms and political foes, who deeply respected and bitterly criticized each other. These two men, both aspiring for the leadership of Israel—and bound to lose it because they hadn't learned the art of joining forces—were Moshe Dayan and Yigal Allon.

Chapter 3

Who Wants an Empire?

In 1938, a year before the Second World War, a snapshot was delivered to Dr. Chaim Weizmann, president of the World Zionist Organization. The photograph was of Itzhak Sadeh, commander of the Hagana, the Jewish defense underground. A tall, broad-faced man in shorts, Sadeh grinned confidently at the camera, warmly hugging two young men.

Two handsome youths they were, clad in khaki clothes and proudly displaying their rifles. The one on the right had the passionate face, clear forehead, and rebel locks of Lord Byron; he was Yigal Allon. The one on the left had a finely carved face and a crooked, slightly defiant smile. He hadn't yet lost his eye and acquired the black patch that would make his pirate's features famous all over the world. He was Moshe Dayan.

Weizmann turned the photograph over and proudly wrote on its back: *L'Etat Major,* which in French means "The General Staff."

History would prove him right. Nine years later, Itzhak Sadeh commanded the glorious Seventh Brigade in the Independence War of Israel. Yigal Allon would even outdo his tutor and become the best general of the Israeli army in that war. Moshe Dayan's maturing genius, a few years later, would make him famous as the victorious Chief of Staff of the Army in the Sinai war of 1956, and the minister of defense who crushed the entire Arab coalition in 1967.

A strange relationship developed between the two heroes. I knew them well and felt that they had a lot in common: They were both born and raised in the north; they were both farmers, Allon in kibbutz Genosar, Dayan in the cooperative village of Nahalal; they both lived among the Arabs, understood them, spoke their language and respected them; they both were charismatic leaders admired by large segments of Israel's younger generations; they both were born fighters who rose quickly in the ranks of the Hagana and its commando unit, the Palmach; and both had far-reaching political ambitions.

Still, they went through life fighting an endless duel. Allon's dream of becoming Chief of Staff of the Army would never be realized. Four years after Allon, disappointed, retired from active duty, Dayan got the job. The reason was mainly political: Allon was a member of the left-wing Ahdut Haavoda Party; Dayan was one of the young leaders of the Mapai Party, whose founder was David Ben-Gurion.

In later years they both became ministers, but their old rivalry continued to erupt until it reached its peak on the eve of the Six-Day War. Levi Eshkol, who combined the offices of prime minister and minister of defense, was forced by public pressure to abandon the Defense portfolio and entrust it to somebody younger and more competent. Eshkol's choice would have been Allon; public pressure forced him to appoint Dayan. And Dayan reaped all the laurels, on June 10, 1967.

Working at Dayan's side after the Six-Day War, I witnessed the courage and wisdom he showed in some of his major decisions. As minister of defense, he was in charge of the occupied territories and of their 1.1 million Arab inhabitants. He had to give Israel the means of ruling over a hostile and bitter nation without turning the Israelis into oppressors. He was soon to prove that he was the right man for the job.

The shooting was barely over when he took his first step. Disregarding the advice of the army, which feared a bloodbath, Dayan removed all the barriers between the Jewish and Arab sectors of Jerusalem, and let the masses intermingle freely. This symbolic unification of the city turned out to be a tremendous success.

Dayan's second step was at least as controversial. Hoping to defuse Palestinian frustrations by improving their living standards, Dayan opened Israel to scores of thousands of workers from the occupied territories. The resulting prosperity in the West Bank and Gaza was unprecedented; it definitely blunted the Palestinians' bitterness and eroded their motivation to revolt against the Israeli occupation.

In a third, highly unusual measure, Dayan opened our eastern border as well. Striving to create a climate of cooperation with Jordan, despite the occupation of the West Bank, he inaugurated the policy of the "open bridges" over the Jordan River. Every day since 1967, hundreds of trucks have been crossing the cease-fire line between two warring nations, Israel and Jordan. They carry out a flourishing trade of produce and other food, manufactured goods, and equipment between Israel, the West Bank, Jordan, and the entire Middle East.

Dayan also opened the bridges for free travel, enabling the Palestinians to go to Jordan, and henceforth to any other country in the Middle East; allowing their families to come and visit them each summer; and inaugurating a route of pilgrimage to Mecca, which in the last few years has also been used by Israeli Arabs.

Still, we were an occupying force. We never forgot that even the most enlightened occupation is an occupation all the same. We had no handbook on occupation methods; the best we could learn from other nations' experience was what not to do. When the first general strike in the West Bank occurred, at the end of the summer of 1967, thousands of Palestinians closed their stores and shops. I was at Dayan's office when the army generals came and declared that they were going to open the stores by force. "We'll smash the padlocks, and the damn shopkeepers will be back in minutes."

"Nobody touches any padlocks," Dayan snapped, and asked to meet with the Palestinian notables. The meeting was set for the following afternoon. When we arrived, a large crowd dressed in Arab galabiehs and dark European suits was waiting.

"I am the defense minister of Israel, not of the West Bank," Dayan told the assembly. "What matters to me is the defense of Israel. All the rest doesn't concern me. If you want to close your stores, close them. I couldn't care less. These are your stores. If a woman from Tel Aviv wants to buy some elastic band for her panties in Ramallah, where it's cheaper, she'll be disappointed and will have to go to a Tel Aviv store. Big deal. Close your stores, open your stores, I won't interfere.

"You don't like our soldiers patrolling in your cities, stopping you, searching you, lining you against the walls, making your life miserable. I can understand you. We'll do our best to take as many soldiers as we can out of the cities.

"But if your people threaten our security, I'll bring the army back. If your children throw stones at cars, I'll close the schools. If you build roadblocks, I'll impose a curfew.

"It's up to you," Dayan concluded.

In a few days, the strike was over.

*   *   *

During the first few months after the Six-Day War, we traveled exten-
sively throughout the occupied territories, met with thousands of
people—mayors, intellectuals, blue-collar workers, farmers, sheiks, religious leaders, refugees; Dayan also talked to teachers, poets, journalists,
and political leaders. The Palestinians, even the most radical among
them, were deeply impressed by Dayan's genuine interest in their problems and his willingness to listen to their opinions. "I never expected
'Mussa' Dayan to show me such respect," a West Bank mayor admitted
to me. I think Dayan understood better than anybody else the reality in
the West Bank.

But when asked how he envisaged peace with the Palestinians and
Jordan, he was unable to conceive of a viable solution.

Dayan had a realistic, incisive mind, capable of coldly analyzing any
situation. But strangely, he lacked the ability to formulate a clear, solid
response to problems. His assessments of the situation in the West Bank
were the best I'd ever heard. But when he started speaking about solutions, he would suddenly become nebulous, at times even contradictory,
and outline something unclear about Jews and Arabs living together,
about not deciding now what the definitive solution should be, about
practical, temporary arrangements.

At times he spoke of unilateral autonomy or a "functional compromise"; sometimes he preached joint rule of Israel and Jordan over the
West Bank, and recommended Jordan's sovereignty over the inhabitants
and Israel's sovereignty over the land.

Dayan had a fertile, unconventional mind that was able to produce
countless original concepts and bold new approaches. His main concern
was to avoid the danger of becoming the prisoner of any clear-cut, rigid
plan; instead, he strove to find practical answers, leaving the future
vague, and progress step-by-step toward a solution that wouldn't imply
the evacuation of the West Bank. He objected fiercely to the annexation
of the West Bank to Israel, and as fiercely opposed the idea of full or
partial withdrawal from the West Bank. Perhaps his attachment to the
historical cradle of our people was so deep, so intense, that he couldn't
utter the formula of territorial compromise—or even think of it.

A close friend of Ben-Gurion had said to me once: "The two men
who inherited Ben-Gurion are Moshe Dayan and Shimon Peres. Moshe
received the charisma; Shimon got the vision."

That was true in many respects. Dayan's charisma was overwhelming; Peres's vision would emerge at a crucial point in history, as we'll see later in this narrative. But the first to make a brilliant display of vision vis-à-vis the Palestinian question was Dayan's old friend and rival, Yigal Allon.

I knew Yigal Allon well from the time I had been Paris correspondent of *Lamerhav*, the newspaper of Allon's party. Allon wasn't less hawkish, or less attached to the biblical Land of Israel, than Moshe Dayan. For years he had been a supporter of Greater Israel and had dreamt of enlarging our eastern borders to the Jordan River. After the Six-Day War, eager to prove he was at least as patriotic as Dayan, he made one major mistake: he pressured the government into building a Jewish city—Kiryat Arba—on a hill overlooking the city of Hebron, where Abraham is buried in a shrine holy to both Jews and Arabs. Kiryat Arba was to become a source of trouble, as many of the most extremist Jewish settlers made it their home.

But with the exception of Kiryat Arba, Allon didn't let his feelings blur his thinking, and he showed more courage and insight than all his peers in drawing the political conclusions from a deeply complex situation.

In the summer of 1967, when the victory-intoxicated nation was walking on air, Ben-Gurion was the first who spoke about withdrawal from the occupied territories in exchange for peace. Neither Dayan nor Peres spoke like him. Among the outstanding Israeli leaders, Yigal Allon was the only one who thought in a pattern close to Ben-Gurion's, and conceived a peace plan between Israel and Jordan.

In 1967, Allon was no longer the handsome, dashing general of 1948. Many of his dreams had ended in disappointment. Bitterness had left its mark on his character. His face had been ravaged by a disease that affected his facial nerves, causing a spasmodic twitching that deeply embarrassed him. But his mind was clear and imaginative, as his plan was to prove.

The Allon plan was based on two assumptions: the first was that we should give back to Jordan most of the territory we had conquered in the Six-Day War; the second was that we couldn't return to the former situation, when the Jordanian army was so dangerously close to our densely populated areas. Therefore, Allon envisaged a solution in which no Arab army would be permitted to enter the West Bank, and the defense border of Israel would be set along the Jordan River.

I remember the first time Allon briefed me about his plan, in the winter of 1967. He was then minister of education and we met at his office in the seedy ministry building in Jerusalem. It was a bitterly cold winter, and Allon kept on his old trench coat made of a rough tan fabric. He spread the map I had brought on his desk and pointed at the West Bank.

The occupied lands were a large enclave engulfed on three sides by the territory of Israel. Their boundary was marked by a sinuous green line, the pre-1967 frontier. (The term "green line," borrowed from the color of the boundary line on high school maps, has since become the popular Israeli expression for the 1967 border.) The enclave's fourth boundary was marked by the Jordan River. The enclave had roughly the shape of a kidney, its curved side bending around Jerusalem, its straight side following the river.

Allon explained which parts of the West Bank we should keep in any case: Jerusalem, of course; the Etzion Bloc (a region south of Jerusalem which was a Jewish settlement area before the Independence War and had been conquered by Abdullah, Hussein's grandfather); the northern shore of the Dead Sea, and a band of territory along the Jordan River.

While talking, he traced the line of the new borders on the map. The line cut several portions of the kidney but left most of it intact, held by a pair of crablike pincers from the north and south. The pincers came together but did not touch on both sides of the city of Jericho. Allon pointed at the Jordan valley. "The Israeli army will be positioned here," he said, "to prevent any Arab army from crossing the river."

"Yigal," I asked, "what about the connection between the West Bank and Jordan?"

"Here." Allon stabbed his pencil at Jericho, roughly sketching a corridor across the river. "Territorial continuity," he explained, "and yet, screening by our forces along the security line."

I had to admit Allon's plan made sense. I wholeheartedly agreed with it. I continue to believe that it was, and is, the best possible plan, with one significant change: the West Bank shouldn't be returned to Hussein but made part of a Jordanian-Palestinian federation.

Dayan squarely rejected the plan. He couldn't agree to any form of

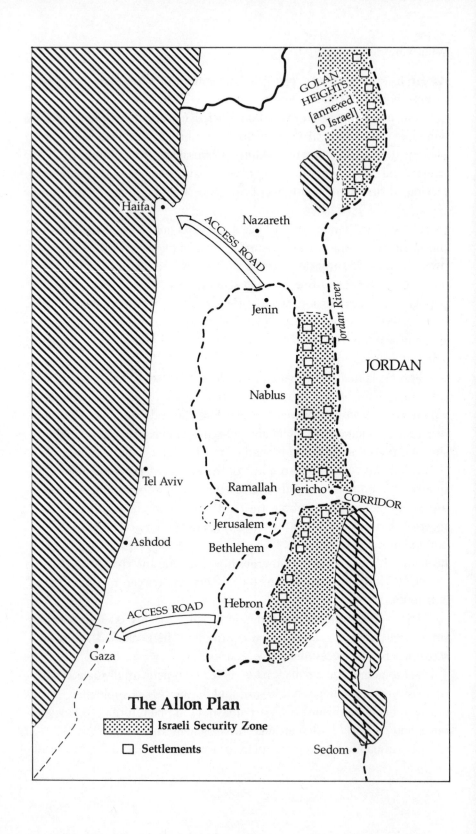

GOLAN
HEIGHTS
[annexed
to Israel]

Haifa •

Nazareth •

ACCESS ROAD

Jordan River

Jenin •

JORDAN

Nablus •

Tel Aviv •

Ramallah •

Jericho •

CORRIDOR

Jerusalem •

Ashdod •

Bethlehem •

Hebron •

ACCESS ROAD

Gaza •

The Allon Plan

▦ Israeli Security Zone

□ Settlements

Sedom •

territorial compromise. He found an unexpected ally across the Jordan River: King Hussein. When he was offered the Allon plan at one of their first meetings, the king said coldly, "Totally unacceptable," and kept rejecting it till it was too late.

The Allon plan, or any other form of territorial compromise with Jordan, was to become the main subject of the longest peace negotiation ever—the secret negotiation between Israeli leaders and King Hussein, which stretched over more than twenty years.

I believe that King Hussein could have been the first Arab leader to make peace with Israel, were it not for the weakness of his desert king-dom, for in spite of his sincere willingness to reach an agreement with us, Hussein had first of all to survive. That he has is one of the miracles of the twentieth century.

During my military service I devoted a long time to the study of King Hussein. Nobody ever augured a long life to this short, wiry, deep-voiced Hashemite. Many ridiculed him because of his playboy image, his pretty American wife, and his penchant for European nightclubs, ski vacations in St. Moritz, fast planes, sleek yachts, and flashy uniforms that made him look as if he had emerged from a Middle European operetta. The world press for years mocked the King of Jordan, branding him "the little King," "the cardboard King," the "puppet"; I once read an article in which he was referred to as "the Mickey Mouse King."

Strangely enough, "the Mickey Mouse King" turned out to be a great survivor, second only to Emperor Hirohito. The man nobody believed would sit on Jordan's shaky throne for more than a year or two has remained there for more than thirty-six years and doesn't seem on the verge of retirement yet. The man whom assassins have stalked since his coronation, whose life was saved in 1958 by British paratroopers deployed on the roof of the royal palace, whose piloting skills saved him from a couple of Syrian MiGs that tried to gun down his personal plane, who crushed the PLO in Jordan in 1970, and stood defenseless in front of a Syrian armored column headed for his capital—this man has become one of the most stable and respected monarchs of our time.

Kassem of Iraq, Sadat of Egypt, and Bashir Gemayel of Lebanon were assassinated during Hussein's reign; King Faisal of Iraq, King Saud of Saudi Arabia, Nasser of Egypt, Ben-Gurion, Sharett, Eshkol, Golda Meir, Dayan, and Allon of Israel have all died, and he has retained control over his small, beleaguered country, resented by the Palestinians, fiercely admired by the Bedouins, cordially hated by the leaders of the hard-line Arab countries.

After the Six-Day War he was the first to whom Israel turned.

Since June 1967 almost every self-respecting Israeli statesman, and quite a few high officials, have met secretly with King Hussein. These scores of unpublished meetings are a unique phenomenon in international relations: the leaders of two nations at war repeatedly meeting over more than twenty years, in a frank and trusting atmosphere.

Actually, Israel's secret negotiations with Hashemite royalty had started long before the Independence War and had reached their dramatic peak on the eve of our declaration of independence, on the night of May 11, 1948.

That night Golda Meir, dressed like an Arab woman, secretly traveled to Amman and sneaked into King Abdullah's palace for a conversation that, had it succeeded, might have completely changed the fate of the Middle East. But Golda's mission failed: the king refused to make peace with Israel and joined his Arab brothers in the invasion of the newly born Jewish state. I remember Ben-Gurion describing to me Golda's return from Amman and her grim report of the king's army thrusting toward Tel Aviv.

The negotiations with Abdullah were resumed after the war, with the purpose of achieving peace between the two nations. In 1950 a tentative agreement was reached on the draft of a nonaggression pact between Israel and Jordan; but in July 1951, when the king walked out of the al-Aqsa Mosque in East Jerusalem after the Friday prayer, he was assassinated by a Muslim fanatic. That was the end of the peace initiative.

A sixteen-year-old boy walking close behind Jordan's monarch had seen the old Abdullah die for his courage. Twelve years later, the youth—Abdullah's grandson and now King Hussein of Jordan—asked to meet with representatives of Israel and renew the dialogue that had been cut short by the assassin's bullets.

My friend Moshe Zak, a former editor of the *Maariv* daily, thoroughly researched the story of the secret Hussein meetings. The first meeting took place in 1963, Zak told me, in London; Hussein met with Dr. Jacob Herzog, director of Prime Minister Eshkol's office. The king wanted to obtain U.S. assistance and asked for Israeli diplomatic help in Wash-

ington. The discussions were fruitful; they also produced an understanding for the distribution of the Jordan waters between the two countries.

Further meetings followed: in 1965 with Golda Meir, in 1967 and
1968 with Ministers Abba Eban, Yigal Allon, Moshe Dayan, and Chief
of Staff Chaim Bar-Lev. In later years Hussein was to meet with Prime
Ministers Meir, Rabin, Peres, and Shamir and many of their aides.

Two meetings had been held in Paris; several others took place aboard
a ship in the Gulf of Aqaba, at deserted spots on both sides of the Israeli-
Jordanian border, even in a secluded guesthouse near Tel Aviv.

But the preferred place was London. After a couple of meetings at the
Dorchester Hotel, the Israelis found a Jewish doctor who would put his
clinic at their disposal. The Israelis would be the first to arrive and wait
in a side room; then the king would come, leave his Scotland Yard
bodyguards in the waiting room, enter the doctor's office, and walk into
the room where the Israelis expected him.

Only vague and inaccurate reports, which were categorically denied,
leaked to the media. Some well-informed friends gave me colorful de-
scriptions of Golda Meir serving coffee to Hussein in a house north of
Tel Aviv; of the antique sword Hussein gave to Allon; of Hussein's
present of a gold pen to Abba Eban (who promised to sign the peace
treaty with it); of the Israeli-made Galil rifle Hussein received from Prime
Minister Itzhak Rabin.

Eyewitnesses told me how Hussein once piloted an Israeli helicopter
to Tel Aviv and was overtaken by his emotions while flying over Jerusalem. As a guest of Itzhak Rabin, he was driven along Dizengoff Street,
Tel Aviv's favorite playground, to sample the sight of young Israeli men
and women out for a night of fun.

The meetings in Israel and Jordan could be effectively concealed from
indiscreet witnesses, but the doctor's clinic in London was different. The
Jordanians and the Israelis couldn't fool the British forever, as Prime
Minister Harold Wilson revealed when he quipped to an Israeli minister:
"I hear you and King Hussein have got the same doctor. How funny."

The Israeli-Jordanian negotiations started in that cloak-and-dagger
atmosphere. In several articles and research papers that he put at my
disposal, Moshe Zak reconstructed the story of the secret negotiations,
down to the smallest detail. In July 1967, barely three weeks after the
Six-Day War ended, Hussein met in London with Dr. Jacob Herzog,

Eshkol's special envoy. (Dr. Herzog, a brilliant man, was the brother of our current president, Chaim Herzog. When his brother Jacob met with Hussein to talk of his lost territories, Chaim Herzog was the military governor of the West Bank.)

There was something poignant in the London meeting: Hussein admitted his fatal mistake in joining Egypt and Syria against Israel, and expressed his regrets for getting carried away. "I warned Nasser," he said. "I told him the Arab summit conference had concluded that our armies were not ready for a new war, but he would not listen. What could I do?"

In the following meetings Israelis and Jordanians started talking about a peace settlement. In 1967 quite a few Israeli leaders opposed it. Menachem Begin, who refused any territorial compromise, was then a minister in the National Unity government; he gave his consent to a meeting between Allon, Eban, and Hussein, only "to clarify the King's position." Dayan openly objected to the Allon plan, and was quite content to learn that the king and his prime minister had rejected Allon's proposals.

On August 27, 1968, Hussein met with Eban, Allon, and Herzog in London. Allon had already convinced the Israeli government to authorize the establishment of the first settlements in the Jordan valley, according to his concept. Now, as he faced the king and his prime minister, Zaid al-Rifai, Allon unfolded a large map and explained his plan. According to Allon's map, 70 percent of the West Bank would be given back to Jordan.

"I know how hard it is for Your Majesty to resign yourself to the loss of such important territory. But when we reach peace . . . the Hashemite Kingdom will actually recover almost a hundred percent of the population that was under its control."

Zaid al-Rifai interrupted him. "Your plan of annexing thirty percent of the territory is totally unacceptable to His Majesty." Hussein nodded.

"But you can get the Gaza Strip in exchange for the Jordan valley," Allon offered.

"We'll get Gaza eventually," Rifai said. "Anyway, the discussion on Gaza can only complicate the problem, as it would compel us to involve the Palestinians in the negotiations."

Rifai made clear that peace would be reached only if Israel returned to the borders of June 5, 1967.

At the next meeting, on September 29, the king said to Allon: "If

Israel insists on keeping all of Jerusalem then the Arabs, and all the Muslims, will do everything in their power to achieve your withdrawal." It was a hint that, under these conditions, a new war was inevitable.

The first round of the London talks ended in failure. But this was only the beginning.

The meetings continued throughout the years despite the War of Attrition along the Jordan valley, sporadic clashes between Jordanian and Israeli units, and retaliatory raids of the Israeli army on terrorist bases in Jordan. Often, following those meetings, Israeli ministers would discreetly advise the United States to grant assistance to Jordan. Once Abba Eban had to deliver a confidential message from Hussein to President Lyndon Johnson and was forced to ask everybody else—including Israel's ambassador in Washington, Itzhak Rabin—to leave the Oval Office.

Moshe Dayan told me once about a late-night conversation in which he promised Hussein to evacuate the region of Safi in Jordan, southeast of the Dead Sea. The Israelis had seized Safi from a terrorist unit that used to fire on the Israeli Dead Sea Works. The Israeli army did indeed withdraw from Safi. Hussein, wearing combat fatigues, arrived on the spot a couple of hours later at the head of a Jordanian brigade. At a press conference he announced he had defeated the Israelis and driven them away from his territory. Hussein's story wasn't denied by Israel.

Other important results were obtained throughout the years, but on the main question of territorial compromise, no progress was achieved. Yet, while the talks didn't result in a peace treaty, they at least created a de facto peace along the border and permanent consultation on many delicate issues.

Still, an Israeli-Jordanian peace agreement that might have been achieved immediately after the Six-Day War became a faraway dream within a couple of years. A new power had emerged in the Middle East, totally changing the rules of the game. It was Yasser Arafat's PLO.

For years, the Palestine Liberation Organization, the supreme representative body of the refugees, had been identified with a foul-mouthed braggart, Ahmed Shukairi. Shukairi, an Acre-born Palestinian, was a mercenary diplomat. He had been the ambassador of Syria, then of Saudi Arabia, to the United Nations. In 1964, when the PLO was created, Shukairi became its chairman. Heavily relying on Saudi subsidies, Shukairi also created the PLO military branch, the much-publicized Palestine Liberation Army. Based in Gaza, the formidable Palestinian battalions were poised to wipe out the Zionist state when the hour of reckoning finally came.

But the Six-Day War wiped out Shukairi, his army, and his organization. The only survivor was the Fatah, a rather insignificant guerrilla group with a long record of ineffective acts of sabotage carried out in Israel. It was headed by a small, round man with a balding head, a short grizzled beard, and quick, keen eyes. His name was Yasser Arafat.

A member of the famous Husseini family, Arafat was a Cairo-born Palestinian. When studying engineering in Cairo he founded a Palestinian students' union, but had been jailed by the Egyptians because of his connections with the fanatical Muslim Brotherhood. After his release he had become a successful entrepreneur in Kuwait, then the editor of a Palestinian weekly in Beirut. Until 1962 he had spent much of his time in Algiers, from which he would make secret visits to China and North Korea. In 1964 he had formed the Fatah, in cooperation with Syria.

Arafat wasn't a war hero, although in later years he tried in vain to fabricate a tale of his military feats in Israel and the West Bank. He wasn't a charismatic leader, either, and his personality lacked power and determination. But he was an excellent underground operator, a shrewd navigator between warring factions and clans, a smart politician, and a man totally dedicated to his goals. Those traits made him a respected and popular leader, and the unifying link between many groups. Arafat never married. "Palestine is my wife," he used to say with an uncertain smile.

Adopting the war name Abu Amar, Arafat launched the first operation of the Fatah inside Israel on January 1, 1965, a stillborn attempt to sabotage the huge pipeline carrying water from Lake Tiberias to the Negev desert. Subsequently, Fatah terrorists infiltrating from Syria and Jordan blew up telephone poles, water towers, generator shacks, and other isolated, unguarded structures in Israel, most of them close to the border. In a few cases the operations brought about the deaths of Israelis, mostly civilians.

Israel retaliated with heavy raids on Jordan; King Hussein promptly dispatched his tough Bedouin soldiers to the border areas and blocked the access routes of the guerrillas. As a result, the activities of the newborn Palestinian organization were severely limited. This didn't prevent the Fatah leaders from bragging about imaginary valiant acts of heroism inside Israel.

Then came June 1967. Following the Arab debacle, Yasser Arafat had a brilliant idea that engendered a dramatic metamorphosis within the Fatah. Arafat realized that the Arab defeat had transformed the consciousness of the Palestinians. Israel's overwhelming victory, the blatant humiliation inflicted upon the Arab nations, and the shattering of their dreams had rekindled hatred and lust for revenge in the hearts of millions of Arabs, most of all the Palestinians.

For the Arabs of Palestine, as for all the Arab states, any dialogue, negotiation, or compromise with Israel was taboo. In the fanatical climate of the Middle East, the only acceptable form of struggle to the Arabs was the bloody total annihilation of the Israelis. Killing Jews—even children, old people, or women—was considered a further step toward victory. This barbaric war knew no laws, no principles. It was based on a primitive concept of retribution: the Jews took our land, and in order to recover that land, we must kill the Jews.

"When you want to understand the soul of a nation," Dayan once told me, "go to the poet, listen to his verses." And in the fiery verses of the popular Palestinian poet Fadwa Tukkan, I discovered the all-consuming hatred of the Palestinian people for the Israelis:

> The hunger of my hatred
> opens his mouth.
> Nothing but their livers would satisfy the hunger
>   that dwells in my flesh.
> Oh, my insane, stormy rage!
> They murdered the love inside me.
> They turned the blood in my veins into gall and
>   melted tar.

The Arabs cried out for revenge. But the Arab armies had been wiped out. Since June 10, 1967, there had been nobody left to resume the battle against Israel—nobody but the Fatah.

Arafat understood that if the Fatah resumed the battle immediately, even against all odds, it would soon become the spearhead of the Arab struggle. It would become the living proof that the Arabs had not surrendered to Israel; it would emerge as the source of pride for the millions who were still dazed by the June humiliation.

Therefore, Arafat immediately started dispatching small groups of Fatah guerrillas across the narrow Jordan River into the Israeli-occupied West Bank. Laden with explosives, Soviet-made Kalashnikov submachine guns, pistols, and grenades, the guerrillas were ordered to hit the Israelis as hard as they could, mostly by carrying out acts of sheer terrorism against the civilian population.

This they did. A mine would explode under a civilian Israeli vehicle, killing or maiming its occupants. Soviet-made Katiusha rockets fired from a nearby hill would land in the middle of a settlement or devastate an apartment building. An ambushed school bus would turn into a gory spectacle of carnage. Smuggled explosives would blast a supermarket or spray death in a crowded square. These acts metamorphosed the PLO into one of the ugliest national movements in modern times. Nobody in the Fatah regretted that the victims were civilians, women, and children. Each death was hailed as a superb act of heroism, and the Fatah guerrillas would sing a hymn of praise for their Kalashnikov guns, which they called "Klashin":

> Klashin makes the blood gush in torrents.
> Haifa and Jaffa are calling us.
> Commando, go ahead and do not worry:
> Open fire and break the silence of the night!

By the time news of the attacks reached the squares and souks of the Arab cities, they were transformed into epic victories. In the Fatah press releases the dead were counted by hundreds. Any civilian car would be described as an armored carrier; a sabotage in a department store would become a surprise attack on a military base. And the dead, civilian or military, children or soldiers, would boost the morale of millions of Arabs. A growing flow of cash streamed into the Fatah coffers from the Arab capitals, to finance more arms, more training, more incursions of the guerrillas.

As time passed, the Marxist elements inside the Fatah and its satellite organizations grew, and an acute anxiety seeped into the palaces of Arab kings and princes. They needed the Fatah against Israel, but they feared it might turn against them one day. They therefore doubled and trebled their subsidies to Arafat, and they willingly contributed to the legend of the indomitable Fatah guerrillas fearlessly avenging the tarnished honor of the Arab nation.

But this situation did not continue for long. Quickly and efficiently, the Israelis sealed off the Jordan valley. I recall the meetings at the Defense Ministry when the master plans for the protection of the Jordan valley were systematically worked out. Fences, patrols, minefields, ploughed strips, and sophisticated electronic devices detected almost every Fatah guerrilla who crossed into Israel. The army dispatched its toughest fighters—the paratroopers and the elite commando units—to hunt down and annihilate the terrorists. The scorching hot canyons and wastes of the barren Judean desert, the thick vegetation along the river, the cave-riddled yellow hills dominating the stifling valley were soon to become a death trap for the Fatah. Hardly anybody who crossed the river came back alive. Most of the projected operations were never carried out. Still, Israel paid its toll in blood; some of my best friends, mostly paratroopers, were killed in the cruel firefights with Fatah terrorists.

The most deadly weapon of the Israelis was their Intelligence. A few months after the start of the Fatah war, they succeeded in penetrating the organization to its highest echelons. In many cases, they knew in advance who was going to cross the border, and when and where the incursion would take place. Many of the coups were smothered at birth: Fatah agents in the occupied territories were arrested, and the few units that succeeded in crossing the Jordan were hounded to their deaths long before they could reach their targets.

The Fatah was in deep trouble. And for the first time, while Arafat's men were staggering from failure to defeat, other Palestinians were emerging in the limelight. On July 23, 1968, three Arab terrorists successfully hijacked an El Al aircraft, Flight 426 from Rome to Tel Aviv, and forced the pilot to land at Algiers. This was the first hijacking of an Israeli plane, and it augured a new stage in the war between Israel and the Palestinians.

The hijacking had been carried out by a splinter terrorist group, the Popular Front for the Liberation of Palestine. The PFLP was an extreme left-wing organization whose leader, gray-haired, arrogant George Habash, preached not only the destruction of Israel but also the toppling of the conservative Arab regimes and Marxist world revolution. Together with some other small terrorist organizations like the Syrian-backed El

Saiqa—the Thunderbolt—and the Iraqi-sponsored Arab Liberation Front, the PFLP was a member of the newly remodeled PLO, headed now by Arafat.

But George Habash rejected Arafat's doctrine that Israel should be destroyed by guerrilla warfare and popular uprising inside the West Bank. He preached violent terrorism against Israel and the West all over the world, transferring the battle to airports, embassies, synagogues and other Jewish institutions, and attacks on well-known Zionists. A successful act of terrorism in Europe or America, Habash claimed, would help bring the Palestinian cause to world attention much more than any Fatah incursion into occupied Palestine.

To one journalist Habash frankly stated that he would not recoil even before the danger of a Third World War. This new kind of all-out, unrestrained terrorism won Habash the support of a rising leader who was to become the world's number-one terrorist: Libya's young dictator, Colonel Muammar Qaddafi.

In the summer of 1968, Habash dramatically proved he was right. While Arafat's guerrilla war in the Jordan valley was stagnating and his commandos were being slaughtered on the Israeli border, Habash's air piracy yielded results. The hijacked El Al plane and passengers were held in Algiers, while Habash blackmailed Israel into surrender. Israel reluctantly agreed to negotiate and, after prolonged talks through third parties, exchanged a group of terrorists held prisoner in its jails for the kidnapped Israelis.

At Habash's headquarters, the PFLP leaders rejoiced. The air war was now on. Planes were an easy prey. On December 26 a PFLP commando attacked another El Al airliner while it was about to take off at Athens airport. A passenger was killed. Israel retaliated violently: since the PFLP commandos had set out on their raid from Beirut, helicopter-borne Israeli paratroopers landed at Beirut airport and blew up thirteen Arab aircraft.

In the meantime, Israel was feverishly building up its defenses against the air pirates. Security officers, armed with .22 pistols, were posted aboard all El Al planes. The flight deck was isolated from the passenger compartment by armored doors. The crews underwent special training. An array of sophisticated security devices was planted aboard the aircraft. El Al planes were turned into veritable flying fortresses, and hijacking became practically impossible.

So Habash's unrestricted air war branched out in different directions.

His men attacked El Al offices in Greece, Belgium, West Germany, Iran, and Turkey. They set fire to a Jewish Home for the Aged in Munich, and seven people died. A Swissair plane headed for Tel Aviv was blown up in the air by a "smart bomb," activated when the plane reached cruising altitude over the Alps. All forty-seven passengers and crew members were killed. In an attack on Israeli passengers in the El Al lounge of Munich airport, one person was killed and eight were wounded. Hanna Maron, one of Israel's most popular stage actresses, lost her leg in the attack.

The terrorist organizations had indeed become the spearhead of the Arab combat against Israel. Emerging from the underground, Arafat had been elected chairman of the Palestine Liberation Organization. The PLO had adopted an extremist national charter defining, as its main goals, the liberation of all Palestine and the destruction of Israel; the only way to achieve those goals was by armed struggle. Arafat's Fatah had swelled to many thousands, and Arafat's guerrillas had gradually gained control over a large part of Hussein's Jordan, rapidly transforming it into Fatahland.

Still, Habash was the one who continued to carry out the most spectacular coups. On September 6, 1970, the PFLP sent its terrorists into action. In quick succession, four airplanes were attacked on takeoff from various European airports. The attempt to hijack an El Al plane over Amsterdam ended in failure, but it was the only hijacking that misfired.

A Pan Am jumbo jet, successfully taken over by PFLP terrorists, was flown to Cairo. The passengers were hastily evacuated down the emergency chutes, and the jet was blown to pieces by the terrorists. A worse fate awaited the passengers of the other two hijacked planes, belonging to TWA and Swissair. They were landed on a disused World War Two landing strip at Zarqa, a sunbaked spot in the middle of the Jordanian desert. On the ground, the Fatah and other terrorist groups enthusiastically joined the operation.

In the sweltering summer heat, 425 men, women, and children were held prisoner in the planes, which turned into veritable furnaces under the rays of the desert sun. The planes were surrounded by hundreds of elated guerrillas, toting their Kalashnikovs, threatening the passengers, ripping open their suitcases, and planting explosives aboard the planes.

Meanwhile, their leaders were calmly negotiating with Western governments for the exchange of the hostages for a large number of terrorists imprisoned in Europe and Israel. Both planes were subsequently blown up by the wildly excited guerrillas.

From Amman, King Hussein was helplessly watching the metamorphosis of his kingdom into a pirates' refuge governed by Arafat and his henchmen. Since 1967 the remains of Jordan had been gradually taken over by the Palestinian guerrillas. At first, the Fatah was content to control the refugee camps; but later, getting bigger and stronger, it gradually took over towns and villages close to the Israeli border, participated in the administration of daily life in Jordan, and stopped recognizing the king's authority.

Armed guerrillas freely circulated in Jordanian cities, behaving like the real masters of the land. They issued vehicle registration plates, collected taxes, and openly defied the government. Jordanian ministers and high officials were constantly threatened, and couldn't step out of their offices without the protection of bodyguards. The PLO even strong-armed the royal family; once they prevented the king and his brother, Prince Hassan, from entering one of Amman's sections that was under their control.

The Jordanian army, composed of Bedouin tribesmen absolutely loyal to their king, pressed Hussein to act against the terrorists, but in vain. Hussein was shocked when he toured an armored regiment and saw a brassiere flying from a tank's radio antenna.

"What does this mean?" he demanded angrily.

"That means that we are women," the tank commander replied insolently. "You won't let us fight."

No, Hussein could not let them fight, as the eyes of the whole Arab world were upon him, and any attempt on his part to restrain the terrorists would be regarded as betraying the Arab cause. But in those September days, even the cautious king understood that the guerrillas had gone too far. They had turned Jordan into an outlaw state; they had usurped his power and posed a threat to his throne and his life. Sooner or later, they would turn against him and topple his regime. To save his head he had to act fast.

In utmost secrecy, the chiefs of the Jordanian army were summoned to the king's palace in Amman. Quietly, the army took up positions at all the strategic points of the kingdom, discreetly surrounding refugee camps and guerrilla bases, headquarters and ammunition dumps. They waited a few days, until the negotiations between the terrorists and the

European governments were concluded and most of the hostages hijacked in the TWA and Swissair planes were released.

On the next day Hussein gave the green light to his generals. And the Bedouins, giving vent to the fury that had been building up inside them for years, launched the bloodiest assault ever against the Palestinian guerrillas.

That was how the last month of the violent summer of 1970 became, for the Fatah, Black September.

On the night of September 17, Hussein let loose his restive army. The confrontation soon turned into a massacre. The Palestinian guerrillas were no match for the regular Jordanian army. Hussein's soldiers pursued and shot the guerrillas in the streets; they slaughtered them mercilessly, mutilated and burned their bodies, dragged suspected guerrillas in front of firing squads without any trial.

Many of the guerrillas found shelter in the refugee camps, but the Jordanian army hunted them down. The royal artillery shelled the camps, often using phosphorus shells, killing or burning their victims. Thousands of guerrillas fled to Syria and Lebanon; others went as far as crossing the Jordan River and surrendering to the hated Israelis, to escape the living hell behind them.

How many were massacred? The most conservative accounts place the number of guerrillas who died at around two thousand. Others say anywhere between four and ten thousand.

It was a terrible blow to the PLO, the Fatah, and Yasser Arafat. While the Arab world watched in horror, Syria, the closest ally of the Palestinians and the vilest enemy of Israel, decided to intervene, rescue the guerrillas, and bring Hussein down. A task force of three hundred tanks was dispatched into Jordan, while other armored columns massed hastily along the border.

Suddenly, the tables were turned. Hussein's regime now seemed on the verge of total collapse. The Jordanian army could easily crush the Fatah terrorists, but could not resist the Syrian elite units. It was only a matter of days before the Syrians, sweeping through the desert, would get to Amman and annihilate the Hashemite dynasty. Hussein's life, like so many times in the past, again hung on a thread.

The desperate king turned to the United States for help. The United States was indeed willing to rescue his moderate, pro-Western regime.

It had already dispatched the Sixth Fleet and the superb aircraft carrier *John Kennedy* to the eastern Mediterranean. The Eighth Infantry Division in West Germany and a crack paratroop division in the United States were rushed to military airfields, ready to be airlifted to the Middle East.

But all those units, even if given the green light, could hardly reach Jordan in time to save Hussein. On the other hand, the intervention could seriously undermine the U.S. position in the Arab world. There was only one power able to save Hussein, and the United States appealed for its help.

In a dramatic meeting between Henry Kissinger, the national security adviser to President Nixon, and Itzhak Rabin, the Israeli ambassador in Washington, the White House asked Jerusalem to move swiftly to deter the Syrians.

A few hours later, huge armored units converged on all Israeli roads leading to the northern frontier. The Israeli army, which usually made its moves in secret, was pushing its elite tank divisions to the Syrian border in broad daylight.

The Syrians grasped the threat immediately. They could not afford a showdown with Israel. On September 22 the first Syrian tanks crossed the border back into their own territory. Two days later, not one Syrian tank was left in the Kingdom of Jordan. Hussein's life and regime were saved.

In small groups, the remnants of the Fatah guerrillas flocked into Lebanon. They were still stunned by the terrible fate that had befallen them, but most of all they were obsessed with an all-consuming lust for revenge.

For the time being, Arafat was out of the game, while Hussein had won back his kingdom, his army, and his freedom of action.

Chapter 4

Lady of Iron

After Black September the talks between Jordan and Israel resumed. Their main subject was a possible interim agreement.

At a meeting outside Tel Aviv, Golda Meir received Hussein flanked by her team—Allon, Dayan, and Eban. She offered Hussein a plan to transfer the Gaza Strip, including the port, to Jordanian rule, and give Jordanian citizenship to the Gaza Strip inhabitants. The plan also included joint economic undertakings to be carried out with European assistance: the building of a railway from the Aqaba-Eilat region to the Dead Sea, a huge housing project to assuage the misery of the refugees in the West Bank. In return, Israel would keep its military bases in the West Bank and Israelis would have the right to settle there, without expelling any Arabs.

The Israelis offered reciprocal measures: Arabs of Jordanian nationality would be allowed to reside in Israel, and a battalion of Jordanian soldiers would be stationed at the Kishon port, near Haifa. The question of Jerusalem, which was a major stumbling block, should be left open.

It appears, though, that the Israelis spoke in several voices. Allon was trying to press for his plan, while Dayan remained faithful to the vague, fluid outlines of his "functional compromise" concept. "You don't have to concede one inch of your soil," Dayan said to Hussein. "Let us have our settlements and military positions necessary for our security without your giving up land. Call it whatever you like, foreign presence or not. We are not interested in ruling over your people."

Hussein rejected the offers. He was ready to sign a peace treaty, he said, in return for all his territories, and nothing less. Still, he was ready to consider an interim agreement if Israel would agree to withdraw from an eight-mile-deep band of territory along the Jordan River. Israel countered with the proposal of a corridor in the Jericho region that would link Jordan to the West Bank; that way the king would have a direct involvement in the West Bank. The corridor was to follow the main lines of the Allon plan.

But the king stuck to his demand of withdrawal along the Jordan, and the talks failed.

I don't know if there was a real possibility of reaching an interim agreement at that time. King Hussein is known for his cautious policy, his hesitations, his tactics of one step forward and two steps backward. Still, I have the feeling that if Israel had tried harder at that moment, some agreement could have been achieved between the two countries.

From Israel's point of view, that was the opportune moment for a settlement. Israel had never been stronger. It had won the War of Attrition against the Egyptians and the Soviets on the Suez front, and against the PLO in the Jordan valley. The PLO was almost nonexistent after the Black September massacre. Nasser was dead, and his successor, Sadat, appeared to be a rather pitiful figure, desperately trying to fill the shoes of his magnetic predecessor. Hussein felt stronger, having won his country back from the Palestinians. In Washington, President Nixon was a devoted friend of Israel. Menachem Begin had left the National Unity government and wasn't breathing down Golda's neck anymore.

We couldn't expect the Arabs, particularly Hussein, to take the initiative for a peace agreement. But we weren't the Arabs. We genuinely wanted peace, even at the price of painful concessions. And at that propitious moment, when we were victorious, we should have emerged from our complacency.

A peace agreement with Jordan was perhaps out of the question at that time: Hussein's life wouldn't be worth much if he signed a treaty leaving a part of the West Bank in the hands of Israel. Yet a serious effort to reach an interim settlement, inspired by Allon's general concept, might have been fruitful. Hussein might have been less adamant in objecting to a temporary settlement, leaving the definitive solution for a later date. But such an initiative implied breaking some taboos inside Israel, the greatest of which was the taboo on territorial compromise. This kind of concession could have been possible only if Israel had had a strong, imaginative, and determined leadership.

It didn't. The leadership crisis that was about to haunt Israel for the next twenty years made the peace initiative its first victim. Ben-Gurion, who could have courageously seized such a unique historical opportunity, was an old man quietly writing his memoirs. Levi Eshkol, who had died in March 1969, hadn't been known for his bold initiatives; anyway, he had been a prisoner of the National Unity government and of Menachem Begin, whom he had thoughtlessly ushered into the Israeli cabinet. And Golda Meir, who had taken over as prime minister after Eshkol's death, was the opposite of what Israel needed. She was strong and determined, indeed, but mostly determined to do nothing.

I strongly believe that Israel began sliding downhill under the charismatic leadership of Golda Meir. The contradiction in this phrase is only illusory. Golda Meir was one of the most charismatic leaders Israel ever had. Her contribution to Israel's survival during the Independence War and the first years of the Jewish state was enormous. Still, she played a tragic role in the later stages of Israel's history and is responsible for many disasters that befell the nation in the seventies.

What charisma, indeed! Golda seemed to have everything—an unbending character, a tremendous willpower, a total identification with her nation, a sublime indifference for what people might think of her, an absolute certitude in her righteousness. And a magnetic presence. She was far from being pretty, her taste in clothes was pathetic, she was poorly read, her vocabulary was limited. Still, people were thrilled by her very appearance on a podium; her audience drank in her speeches with quasi-religious abandon. In the Labor Party she wielded more power than Ben-Gurion at his peak.

Golda had the gift of the simple, touching phrase. "We'll never forgive the Arabs," she said during the War of Attrition, making headlines all over the world, "for forcing us to kill their sons." At the party meetings we used to joke that if Golda decided to read aloud the telephone directory, instead of deliver a speech, people would be spellbound from A to Z.

Nobody dared to interrupt her. Moshe Dayan never contradicted her. Peres and Allon behaved like lambs in her presence. She was the absolute ruler of the Labor Party, which had been created after the Six-Day War by the fusion of Golda's Mapai, Dayan's Rafi, and Allon's Ahdut Haavoda. I remember how Golda lashed out at me once, in the spring of 1977, when I criticized Labor's leadership for stubbornly ignoring the angry upheaval in Israeli public opinion. I warned the Central Committee that the newly formed Movement for Change was going to win the support of many of our traditional voters.

Golda wasn't prime minister anymore, but when she stepped on the podium a hush fell over the large auditorium. "You think so, Bar-Zohar?" she thundered at me. "You think people are going to vote for them? You think people like them? Perhaps you like them, too, Bar-Zohar. Perhaps you don't like us, perhaps you don't like me. Perhaps you should join them, if you think they'd win."

Nobody dared to utter a word in my defense and Golda Meir easily carried the subsequent vote. (A couple of months later, at the May 1977 election, the Movement for Change achieved a tremendous success, capturing fifteen of our seats in the Knesset and opening the way for Menachem Begin to the prime minister's office.) I couldn't blame my friends, though. Golda seemed to simultaneously enthrall and frighten everybody, including Harold Wilson and Richard Nixon. Even today she remains tremendously popular in Israel and the United States, a symbol of toughness and strength. The Iron Lady of 10 Downing Street seems to us Israelis a sweet country aunt compared with our Golda.

Yet Golda wasn't Wonder Woman. She totally lacked political imagination and a statesman's insight. She was unable to conceive a policy in any field, and her use to Ben-Gurion in the past had been as a devoted aide who loyally executed his instructions. Golda stubbornly refused to recognize facts that she didn't like; she furiously denied the existence of a Palestinian people. "I am a Palestinian myself," she once snapped at a meeting of the Labor Party bureau and went on to crucify the leaders of the party's Young Guard for thinking otherwise.

Golda rejected any initiative that might result in her surrendering a portion of the territories occupied in 1967. It was not because she was an annexationist. She was not. She had inherited an empire from Eshkol and was determined to keep it, even if it meant sinking into absolute immobility and totally freezing any diplomatic activity. She didn't feel she had the right to give up something that had been bequeathed to her by her predecessors. She merely entrenched herself in her positions, enclosed all of Israel's conquests with her strong arms, and didn't budge.

That was why she bluntly rejected the Dayan plan of 1972. After the failure of several peace initiatives, like the Gunnar Jarring U.N. mission and the Rogers plan, a new, more modest proposal was worked out by

Moshe Dayan. Dayan told me that the idea was to restore the normal routine to the Suez zone, and remove the causes of friction and fighting.

His plan called for an Israeli withdrawal to a new line twenty miles to the east of the canal, the reopening of the canal to international shipping, and the rebuilding of the cities along the waterway. Most Egyptian cities, like Ismailia, Suez, and Kantara West, had been devastated by Israeli artillery during the War of Attrition. Finally, Dayan said, a token force of Egyptian policemen should be allowed to cross the canal and establish its headquarters on our side, as a part of the normalization process.

Dayan spoke of his plan to several American leaders, who found it encouraging. His close confidant, Knesset member Gad Yaacobi, traveled to Washington to sound out Undersecretary of State Joseph Sisco and several other leading American policymakers about the concept. The response was very favorable.

But then the plan was submitted to Golda, and she had it shelved at once. That was a tragic mistake. According to many observers, if Golda had accepted Dayan's proposal, the Yom Kippur War might have been averted.

Golda also failed to realize that Israel was changing, and major social revolutions were taking place before her eyes. The power of the Histadrut, the huge federation of labor, was eroding steadily; the first wildcat strikes that paralyzed the port of Ashdod and Lod International Airport occurred while Golda was in office.

She also didn't grasp the significance of the fact that Sephardic and Oriental Jews were soon to outnumber Ashkenazi Jews. She didn't understand either that a new kind of Oriental Jew was emerging in Israel: the Sephardis of the first generation had been subdued and docile people who passively accepted the Israeli political hierarchy, but the younger generation, raised in Israel, was confident, aggressive, and starting to claim its rights.

Golda's social insensitivity broadened the rift between Sephardic and Ashkenazi Jews in the early seventies. "He who doesn't speak Yiddish would never understand the soul of the Jewish people," she once declared on the state radio, deeply offending half of Israel's population. When an Israeli Black Panther movement emerged, representing the frustrated second generation of Oriental Jews, she dismissed the young radicals by simply saying, "They aren't nice," an expression that still triggers bitter reactions in Israel.

A woman of strong emotions, Golda didn't forget or forgive easily. She had dramatically broken her relations with Ben-Gurion when he had seceded from their party, the Mapai, and formed his own splinter party, Rafi. Golda nourished a deep resentment toward Ben-Gurion's followers who had joined him in the ill-fated Rafi. Among them were Moshe Dayan, Shimon Peres, future Presidents Itzhak Navon and Chaim Herzog, Gad Yaacobi, and myself.

She didn't forgive us, but most of all, she couldn't forgive Ben-Gurion; for many years she refused to make up with her former idol. When I wrote my biography of David Ben-Gurion, only two people refused my requests for an interview: Menachem Begin and Golda Meir.

The tragedy of Israel was that when it most needed an inspired, non-conformist leader, a sort of new Ben-Gurion, he was nowhere to be found. In the mid-sixties, after Ben-Gurion's departure, the country had been left in the hands of the Old Guard—Eshkol, Golda Meir, and others, who had been excellent aides and companions to Ben-Gurion, but lacked his foresight and imagination. In 1967 they didn't know exactly what to do with the territories Israel had conquered and didn't have the courage to adopt bold, unconventional initiatives like the Allon plan.

The younger leaders, on the other hand, were lacking in unity; besides, they weren't popular enough, or confident enough, to take the matter into their own hands. They remained the docile junior ministers in successive governments, even if they held key positions like security, foreign affairs, or deputy premiership. That's how the leadership crisis, which had been evolving secretly for years, burst into the open.

Ben-Gurion had done his best to prevent such a crisis. The Old Man believed in young people and wanted them to be active in the public arena when they were still in their prime. While at the command of his party, he had twice reached over the heads of his companions and picked younger men and women whom he deemed better qualified to run affairs of state. Levi Eshkol, Golda Meir, Finance Minister Pinhas Sapir, and others had been members of such a young team, promoted over the heads of Ben-Gurion's closest comrades.

In the mid-fifties he tried for the third time to select a younger leadership, looking for the best men available in his party. That's how he chose Dayan, Peres, Eban, Navon, Teddy Kollek, Avriel, Josephtal, and others. He assiduously courted Professor Yigael Yadin, the former Chief of Staff. At the 1959 elections he introduced into the Mapai Party list no fewer than seven young leaders, some of whom became ministers in his government.

That influx of "young Turks" deeply worried the Old Guard of the party. Here was Ben-Gurion passing the torch to those "youngsters" while they, his old and faithful companions, were still very much alive. For the first time in her life, Golda Meir openly opposed Ben-Gurion. And so did many other older leaders who saw their political futures in jeopardy. "We know about the old Eskimos who are taken out of the igloos by their sons to die in the cold," thundered Education Minister Zalman Aranne. "But we are not Eskimos, we've got teeth!"

The internal strife that devastated and finally split the Mapai Party between 1960 and 1965 was officially caused by the Lavon affair, a murky espionage mishap in Egypt. The "affair," though, had been nothing but a battlefield on which the war of succession inside the party was fought. That war ended with the defeat of Ben-Gurion and his young protégés and their departure into political exile, at the head of the small Rafi Party.

Still, a few years later, the younger leaders—Ben-Gurion's supporters as well as his opponents—were back in the government. Dayan was minister of defense, Allon became deputy prime minister, Eban was minister of foreign affairs, Peres became minister of transports and communications in 1970. And only when they reached such important positions was their inability to lead the nation publicly exposed.

There is no doubt in my mind that those young men were the best Israel could produce, a fine team of soldiers, builders, and pioneers. But they had all been affected by a terrible flaw that badly eroded their leadership capacities: they had grown up in the shadow of a powerful, charismatic leader.

Most of their adult life had been dominated by the towering figure of Ben-Gurion. He was a centralist leader, holding all the power in his hands and having the final say. His young aides knew well that they could count on his backing in whatever they did, but they could never do anything without his consent. They grew up around him like the children of a strong, dominant father who could never come completely into their own. At the age of forty, even fifty, they still had to wait outside Ben-Gurion's office until the Old Man reached his decisions; then they would execute his instructions to the best of their abilities. But they wouldn't be able to develop the backbone, the determination, and the self-assurance that make a powerful leader.

Even the most charismatic of the young Israeli leaders, Moshe Dayan, was affected by this deficiency. I worked with him when he was at the apex of his glory, after the Six-Day War. I was amazed to discover that the man, considered by many to be Ben-Gurion's successor, rarely made a decision without first getting the prime minister's approval. I found him one morning thoughtfully perusing a list of half a dozen names, all of them senior officials of the Defense Ministry. "I need a new head of the Storage and Maintenance Department," he mumbled. "Whom shall we appoint?"

I shrugged. "Who cares?" I didn't attach great importance to the job.

"Michael," he said, "ask my secretary to get Eshkol on the phone. Let's ask him."

I was stunned. "Why do you need Eshkol for that? That's your decision, an inside appointment in the ministry. That's not the prime minister's business."

Dayan looked up at me. "Michael, I'll give you a piece of advice, free of charge. Always ask the man upstairs. Always."

For that reason, Dayan didn't fight Golda on his Suez plan. He was convinced that the plan was good and could defuse the tension on the Israeli-Egyptian border. But the moment he learned Golda was against it, he dropped his support of the idea.

By the same token, he accepted the appointment of General David ("Dado") Elazar as Chief of Staff of the Army shortly before the Yom Kippur War. Dayan couldn't stand Dado, criticized his character, and vehemently opposed his promotion. He knew I liked the confident young general and told me openly: "He will become Chief of Staff over my dead body. This man is no good for the army."

But on finding out that Golda was in favor of Dado's appointment, not only didn't Dayan oppose it anymore, but he officially submitted his name to the prime minister. (Curiously enough, after the Yom Kippur War, a board of inquiry blamed General Elazar for the grave mistakes in the first days of the war and recommended his immediate dismissal. The board cleared Dayan, although public opinion bitterly accused him and eventually forced him to resign. Had Dayan opposed Elazar's appointment earlier, he might have emerged unscathed from the Yom Kippur War. But he didn't, and the war shattered his hero's image.)

Like Dayan, Yigal Allon didn't fight hard enough to have his plan adopted by the government, nor did any of the other young ministers push for innovative policy. In 1973 the Arab states still refused any peace negotiation with Israel, and on the Israeli side, all the projects for a solution or an interim agreement on the eastern or southern border had been disdainfully discarded by Golda Meir. Egypt and Syria, haunted by their 1967 defeat, were secretly plotting their next attack; Israel, lulled by an illusory feeling of invincibility, had fallen asleep on its laurels; and the Middle East was inexorably drawn into the tragedy of a new war.

Chapter 5

War and Earthquake

On October 6, 1973, the day the Yom Kippur War erupted, I was in New York for the world premiere of a film about David Ben-Gurion, *B. G. Remembers*, for which I had written the screenplay and supervised the filming on behalf of Ben-Gurion. I had come to the United States for only a few days; Israel was on the eve of national elections, and I was a member of the advertising committee at the Labor campaign headquarters. We met every morning at six and approved the next day's ads in the national newspapers.

A couple of days before I left Israel, I came back home to find my wife deeply upset. "Moshe Dayan has called three times," she said. "He asked that you call him back as soon as you return."

I didn't work for Dayan anymore. At that time I was teaching political science at Haifa University, doing rather poorly in politics, and researching my Ben-Gurion biography, but I kept in close touch with the defense minister. I rang his office and got him on the phone. "Michael, what is this stupid ad in the papers today?" he asked angrily.

"What ad?"

"About the Bar-Lev line."

That morning we had run an ad showing an Israeli soldier lazily stretching in a rattan chair by the Suez Canal, his automatic rifle lying on his knees. "Everything is quiet on the Bar-Lev line," the caption said, and in smaller print announced that under the Labor government Israel was more secure than ever.

"What about the Bar-Lev line?" I asked. The name of Chaim Bar-Lev, the former Army Chief of Staff, had been given to the fortified line of bunkers and fortresses that Israel had built along the canal. That line was said to be impregnable to Egyptian invasion.

"That's not the Bar-Lev line," Dayan furiously mouthed. "That's my line. That's my conception, and Bar-Lev has nothing to do with it."

I was surprised. Dayan had never before protested against the designation of the Suez fortifications as the Bar-Lev line. I managed to calm him down and make him drop the whole matter, but when I told the advertising committee about Dayan's complaint the chairman paled. "I don't want any complications with Dayan," he said.

The next morning, the ad ran in the papers under the caption: "Everything is quiet on the Suez Canal."

It was not so quiet, after all, I thought on the plane that carried me back from New York to Tel Aviv on October 7, 1973. According to the news, the Egyptian army had crossed the canal, broken through the Bar-Lev line, and advanced five miles into the Sinai. The Syrians had almost overrun the Golan Heights. The joint Egyptian-Syrian attack had taken Israel by total surprise. We had suffered heavy losses.

I doubted if Dayan would have phoned me or anybody else to rectify the mistake about the "Bar-Lev line" after October 6. His phone call was nothing but a trivial episode, of course; still, it indicated that Dayan was largely to blame for instilling the false feeling of security in Israeli society. I also remembered our last meeting, when he had told me there was no danger of Egypt attacking us this year. He was so confident that he didn't pay enough heed to the tremendous effort Egypt had invested in planning its revenge. When he sobered up, a few hours before the war started, it was too late.

The night I landed in Tel Aviv, I changed into my uniform and flew to the Sinai. I spoke to Dayan several times during the war from Sharon's headquarters in the Sinai, but we didn't discuss his responsibility. I joined my paratrooper brigade, and on the night of October 15 we made our move.

Under the cover of night, we cut through the enemy lines, using the gap the Egyptians had left between their Second and Third armies. We advanced stealthily along the "stitch" between the two Egyptian army corps; on reaching the Suez bank, we crossed the canal in rubber boats and established a bridgehead on the African side. That daring commando operation was the turning point of the Yom Kippur War on the southern front; soon we were joined by large armored units, and we struck deep into Egyptian territory, reaching a point sixty miles from Cairo. Simultaneously, our army in the north repelled the Syrian invasion and established a new front line barely twenty-five miles from Damascus. We failed, however, to dislodge the Egyptian army from our side of the canal.

When I returned home at the end of the war, I was among the Labor members who demanded the establishment of a board of inquiry. Twenty-seven hundred Israelis had been killed, the Egyptians had crossed the canal and thwarted our counteroffensives, and the myth of Israel's tremendous power had been shattered. We demanded that a judicial board of inquiry be created to establish who was responsible for the colossal mishap that could have had even more tragic consequences.

At first Golda and the party apparatchiks lashed out at all those who called for an investigation. "There's nothing to investigate," Golda snapped. For a while the party apparatus labeled us as "traitors" and "Israel's worst enemies." Then suddenly Golda gave in, the board of inquiry was established, and we were once again in good standing.

I went to see Dayan. "I think you should resign, Moshe," I said to him.

He was surprised and hurt. "The board of inquiry will clear me," he said.

"I'm sure it will. This doesn't change the fact that you failed as minister of defense. You made all of us think that an Egyptian attack would never take place."

"I happen to think otherwise," he said angrily, and there the conversation ended. We met only a few months later, when he finally submitted his resignation. As a token of reconciliation, he gave me a book of poems, prefaced by him, with a warm dedication.

The board of inquiry indeed cleared Dayan, but the people's verdict was different. Both Dayan and Golda Meir were forced to resign. And with them disappeared the entire traditional leadership of the Labor Party: Golda Meir, Pinhas Sapir, Yaacov S. Shapiro; even Abba Eban was removed from the scene. In a move rather similar to the presidential election of 1976 in the United States, the Labor Party elected as its leader an outsider, Itzhak Rabin.

Rabin was the only man who could not be held responsible in any way for the Yom Kippur debacle. He had served as Chief of Staff of the Army during the Six-Day War and later as ambassador to Washington. He hadn't even been a cabinet minister in 1973. And now, all of a sudden, he was prime minister.

Rabin carried about him the aura of the victorious Chief of Staff and the successful diplomat. During the War of Independence he had been an attractive blond, blue-eyed boy who distinguished himself in the elite Palmach corps under the command of Yigal Allon. The Labor Party clung to Rabin in despair, hoping that he would rescue it from its deplorable state.

But in politics miracles rarely happen. We soon found out that the blue-eyed boy was blue-eyed no more. Rabin had no political experience whatsoever; he was a rather cynical, aloof man, lacking warmth and patience with people, interested uniquely in foreign affairs and defense matters, obviously despising political activities and politicians. He lacked personal charm, was a mediocre speaker, and had little sense of humor. People soon discovered his major flaw: a strange insensitivity to human and social problems. Some of his rivals sarcastically labeled him autistic. Rabin's recent remarks in 1988 about the West Bank uprising, approving of "beating" and "wounding" the leaders of the violent Palestinian protests, derive from the same insensitive streak in his character. When asked by an aide why he approved of beating up the stone-throwers, he quipped: "Do you prefer shooting them?"

On the other hand, Rabin had a clear and orderly mind, although one that was conventional to the extreme; his admirers zealously praised his "analytical brain." He was frank and courageous in his public utterances, always speaking his mind and sticking to the truth, even when it was unpleasant. And together with his new defense minister, Shimon Peres, he succeeded in rebuilding the power and confidence of the Israeli army.

It was under Rabin and Peres, with General Mordechai ("Motta") Gur as Chief of Staff, that the army commandos carried out the famous Entebbe raid in Uganda. An Air France airliner that had taken off from Tel Aviv had been hijacked by Palestinian terrorists after a stopover in Athens. The terrorists forced the pilots to land at Entebbe. Uganda was then governed by the bloodthirsty dictator Idi Amin. Gur assembled a special task force that flew across Africa, landed at Entebbe twenty-five hundred miles away, and liberated the hostages, killing the terrorists. The leader of the commandos, Colonel Jonathan (Yoni) Netanyahu,

was killed during the operation. Yoni's brother, former Ambassador to
the United Nations Benjamin Netanyahu, is today Israel's deputy foreign
minister.

Rabin formed the youngest and the most "Israeli" government in the
history of Israel. Quite a few of the Labor ministers—like Allon, Peres,
Yaacobi, Yadlin, Ofer—had been born or raised in Israel. That was a
new leadership with a new mentality. Unfortunately, the flaws I pointed
out here in the previous chapter appeared much more vividly during
Rabin's term; and the emergence of the new leadership, which had been
hailed at first as the start of a new era, ended in disappointment. Neither
Rabin nor any of his younger colleagues could give Israel the confident
and resolved leadership it so badly needed. Soon a deep feeling of nos-
talgia for the founding fathers swept the entire country. It seemed a
symbolic act of God that David Ben-Gurion suffered a stroke during
the final days of the Yom Kippur War and died a few weeks after the
cease-fire.

Besides the poor image of the Rabin government, it was tainted by a
new rivalry, much worse than the Allon-Dayan sporadic confrontations.
That was the Peres-Rabin feud, which was to tear the Labor Party apart
for ten years and may still emerge from the shadows of our recent past.
Peres and Rabin were rivals for the Labor Party nomination to the premiership; their consecutive fights in 1974, 1977, and 1981 were often
ugly and disruptive. Their tense personal relations undoubtedly harmed
the functioning of the Rabin government between 1974 and 1977.

But it was this uninspiring government, acting in difficult conditions,
that paved the way to the first peace treaty in our history.

The peace process started with the agreements signed between Egypt
and Israel after the Yom Kippur War.

Nobody would have believed in October 1973 that the bloody Yom
Kippur War would produce real peace between Israel and Egypt. But I
have no doubt that the war did. I believe that we wouldn't have achieved
peace with Egypt without the Yom Kippur War and its inconclusive
ending. A partial agreement, yes; a temporary separation of troops according to Dayan's 1972 plan, certainly; but never a real and lasting
peace treaty.

After the war President Sadat admitted that he'd had very slight hopes
of conquering the Sinai. What he wanted to do, he said, was to "rock

the boat" and force the great powers to intervene in the Middle Eastern conflict. The world had got used to Israel's control of the Sinai and the Golan; only a major crisis, endangering world peace and affecting the oil supply, could shake the powers out of their lethargy.

Sadat was right: the great powers were shaken by the Yom Kippur War. Moscow and Washington forced a cease-fire upon the warring nations and convened an international conference in Geneva. Then U.S. Secretary of State Henry Kissinger flew to the Middle East and inaugurated his shuttle diplomacy. The result was an agreement of "disengagement," which was the first step in the direction of peace.

Sadat had certainly "rocked the boat," but he had achieved much more. For the first time in twenty-five years he had created a different climate between Egypt and Israel, a climate in which they could negotiate as equals.

Before the Yom Kippur War many of us had met with Egyptians in Europe or elsewhere and had heard from them the same words: "We cannot talk to you as losers to winners. First we need a victory, even a symbolic one. Then we'll talk as equals."

Did the Egyptians win in 1973? Looking back at the Yom Kippur War, I am convinced that Israel was the real winner. Furthermore, I believe that in 1973 we achieved our greatest victory ever. We had been attacked by surprise on both fronts and endured a double Pearl Harbor, not thousands of miles away, but frightfully close to home. And still, we had recovered in a few days, launched a double offensive, and were threatening our enemies' capitals at the end of the war. That was a splendid victory if there ever was one.

The Egyptian army, however, had even better reasons to be proud. On three previous occasions, in 1948, 1956, and 1967, Egyptian soldiers had scattered in panic before the advancing Israelis, discarding their shoes in the desert. During the War of Attrition, Israel had bombed, raided, invaded their country at will, landed in their territory, shot down their planes, calmly dismounted and carried away their most sophisticated radar station, ridiculed them in front of the entire world. In the eyes of the Egyptians we were supermen, mythological heroes whom nothing could defeat.

But in October 1973 the Egyptians crossed the canal and threw their pontoon bridges over it; they dug into the barren dunes of the Sinai and held up against all of Israel's counteroffensives; they took prisoners, shot down planes, and fought well. They ended the war feeling victorious. And that sensation of victory wiped out their inferiority complex, and allowed them to come confidently to the negotiating table.

That sensation was coupled with another conclusion derived from the Yom Kippur War. "What was taken by force will be retrieved by force," Nasser had said. But in its most successful attack, at the cost of many thousands of casualties, under the effect of total surprise, Egypt had managed very little. All its conquests amounted to a mere five-mile-deep strip of sand. Such a meager result after such a formidable first strike meant that Egypt would never be able to reconquer the entire Sinai Peninsula. Another war was now out of the question. The only way for Egypt to recover the lost land would be by negotiations.

Israel, on the other hand, had also been deeply affected by the war. The feeling of invincibility evaporated on Yom Kippur; the anguish caused by thousands of casualties proved that the nation was deeply vulnerable to losses in human lives. A much more sober and flexible Israel emerged from the fighting, an Israel ready to make territorial concessions for an interim agreement.

The disengagement in the Sinai, reached thanks to the clever, patient diplomacy of Henry Kissinger, actually meant a one-sided withdrawal of the Israeli army from the African bank of the canal, and later from the canal itself. It would have been unthinkable a few months before; now it was greeted with relief by most of the Israeli population, and was carried out in perfect order and general calm. In retrospect, there is no doubt that this was the first step in the direction of a comprehensive peace settlement with Egypt.

But Egypt wasn't ready yet. It was disposed to advance toward an understanding with Israel very slowly, one step at a time. The disengagement agreement was for Egypt a giant step in an unknown direction. It needed time, and more confidence, before abandoning Nasser's policy that rejected any settlement with Israel.

Israel's leaders turned again toward Jordan.

Shortly before Golda Meir resigned, King Hussein came to visit her in Israel. After the painful result of the Six-Day War, he had refused to join the Syrians and the Egyptians in their Yom Kippur attack on Israel. Now he asked for an interim settlement that would entail an Israeli withdrawal from a strip of land eight miles deep along the Jordan River.

He had made a similar proposal before the Yom Kippur War, but Golda had rejected it. She had proposed instead to open a "corridor" in the region of Jericho, according to the Allon plan. To make the king accept the future presence of Israeli soldiers in the West Bank, Golda's team had conceived a reciprocal arrangement: a Jordanian regiment would be stationed at Haifa, by the Kishon port. The king had refused.

When he came to see Golda at the end of March 1974, the king asked again for a partial settlement along the Jordan River, but called it "a disengagement," based on the model of the separation of forces between Israel, Egypt, and Syria. Golda disagreed. The disengagement with Egypt, she said dryly, was not from all of the Suez line, only from part of it. The king was deeply offended. "Did I have to fight you in the October war," he asked bitterly, "to bring you to a disengagement along the entire border?"

After Golda was replaced by Rabin, the meetings with Hussein were intensified. The king met at least eight times with Rabin and his team, which now included Defense Minister Peres and Foreign Minister Allon. The king criticized the Israeli leaders for having ignored his assessments before the October war and called for the Israelis to change their attitude.

The Israelis, though, couldn't accept a withdrawal along the Jordan River. That would mean they had to remove all the Israeli settlements from the Jordan valley and give up their "security border"; besides, such a step was a violation of the coalition agreement specifying that the Jordan River was Israel's security border.

Different solutions were offered by Israel: Allon proposed a token withdrawal in the Jericho area, others suggested an interim political settlement that would give Hussein political control of the West Bank even without an announcement of the end of belligerency. Hussein refused. He was ready, he said, to sign either a disengagement agreement, like the one with Egypt and Syria, or a full peace treaty, if he got all of his territory back, down to the last square inch. The Jordanian prime minister, Zaid al-Rifai, said bluntly to Henry Kissinger that in any interim agreement the bridges over the Jordan River must be under Hussein's control.

In August 1974, Allon met Henry Kissinger at Camp David and briefed him on his plan for a partial withdrawal in the area of Jericho. Kissinger advised him to wait. The Arab heads of state were to meet in Rabat,

Morocco, and he didn't want Hussein to be accused of separate negotiation with Israel.

But the Rabat conference, in November 1974, turned sour for Hussein.
He had expected the Arab heads of state to entrust him with representing
the Palestinians, but instead they recognized the PLO as the sole representative of the Palestinian people. Hussein was bitter and disappointed. When he next met with Yigal Allon in a trailer in the desert,
he let his prime minister vent his frustration. "You sign disengagement
agreements only with those who fought against you in the October war,"
Zaid al-Rifai said, and the king nodded in agreement. He felt that because
of Israel's intransigence the Arab leaders had lost faith in him and turned
to the PLO. Allon pointed out that the mayors in the West Bank are
PLO supporters and resent the king. "You'll see them all coming to kiss
his hand," Rifai said.

On another occasion, when Allon spoke of a territorial compromise,
the king said angrily, "We are out of the picture. Please talk to the PLO
and then we'll see."

A few months later, Henry Kissinger also accused the Israelis of in-
flexibility. "If you had come to the negotiation with Jordan bringing
concrete proposals, the PLO would have been stopped," he said to Yigal
Allon.

"We brought proposals," Allon said, "and the king refused."

"He refused because you insisted on the continuation of your military
presence," Kissinger retorted. In 1979, at a Washington party for a
departing Israeli diplomat, Kissinger was to admit: "My great mistake
was that I didn't pressure Israel to reach an interim agreement with
Jordan."

I doubt that he would have succeeded. Rabin's government wasn't a
strong one. According to the coalition agreement, any proposal for a
territorial compromise in the West Bank had to result in early elections.
Rabin wasn't ready to risk new elections for a partial agreement with
Jordan.

The situation on the southern border was different. The disengagement
agreement with Egypt was a first step toward the withdrawal from all of
Sinai, if Egypt was ready to talk peace.

But Egypt wasn't ready—not before a political earthquake shook Israel
and put an end to the thirty-year reign of the Labor Party.

                    *   *   *

Throughout his political career Ben-Gurion had feared that the right-wing Revisionist Party would one day defeat Labor and achieve control over the country. Ben-Gurion's fears didn't subside with the death, in 1940, of the party founder, Vladimir (Zeev) Jabotinsky, a gifted writer, fiery orator, and charismatic leader. The Revisionist Party spawned the Irgun underground that fought against the British Mandate by using methods that many labeled terrorist. In 1948, Menachem Begin, the leader of the Irgun, transformed it into a political party, renaming it Herut. (In the seventies, after fusing with the Liberals and some other groups, it became the Likud.)

Ben-Gurion's apprehensions only grew with the years. He viewed Herut as a populist party, drawing support from nationalistic, right-wing, and low-income classes, capable of tantalizing them with extremist slogans, demagogic promises, and cynical exploitation of their poverty. Herut seemed to him the only party in Israel that could wrench power from Labor.

Therefore, he took far-reaching measures. In a conscientious effort he managed to ostracize Herut and its leaders from public favor. He incessantly reminded the nation that Herut's clandestine predecessor, the Irgun, had rejected the authority of the organized Jewish community in Palestine in the dramatic years preceding Israel's independence. He reminded Herut's leaders that in their youth they had admired Hitler's brownshirts and had consciously built their party as a fascist organization. He accused the Irgun of almost setting off a civil war in 1948, when it brought an illegal shipload of arms to the newborn Israel in an alleged attempt at a coup d'état.

Ben-Gurion incessantly quoted from Menachem Begin's speeches praising the use of force and preaching for a war of conquest against Jordan, or threatening to rise up in arms when the government decided to accept indemnities from West Germany for the plundering of the Holocaust victims.

Ben-Gurion never missed an opportunity to ridicule and humiliate Begin in the Knesset. He avoided calling Begin by his name, addressing him as "the demagogue," "the Herut martyr," and even "the clown." He coined a phrase, "without Herut and the Communists," meaning that those two internal enemies of the nation, from the right and the left, would never be admitted into a government coalition.

And on the day he resigned from office, June 16, 1963, he described his fears of a Begin victory in his private diary. Shortly before his death, he showed me these passages. In the entry explaining the reasons for his resignation, he wrote of Begin: "The 'leader' [Begin] sensed his power growing, his audacity increased, and violence began to gain control of the Knesset, as was proved in the foreign policy debate and the pandemonium [Herut] provoked. . . . And only the blind do not see that this is the beginning of 'the leader's' takeover."

At the end of that entry Ben-Gurion predicted the establishment of "fascist rule" in the country.

In a letter to poet Chaim Gouri, the Old Man said that if Begin gained control of the country, "he will replace the army and police command with his ruffians and rule the way Hitler ruled Germany, using brute force to suppress the labor movement; and will destroy the state by political adventures. I have no doubt that Begin hates Hitler, but that hatred does not prove that he is unlike [Hitler]." These harsh, excessive accusations show how obsessed Ben-Gurion was with the real and imaginary dangers of a Begin victory.

The situation changed dramatically with Levi Eshkol's ascension to power. Eshkol was a good, warmhearted man, not a subtle and tough politician. He couldn't understand why Ben-Gurion had refused, for so many years, to allow the remains of Jabotinsky, Herut's founding father, to be interred in Israel. He assumed Ben-Gurion had acted out of petty hatred. Therefore, in a widely acclaimed gesture, in 1964 he authorized the burial of Jabotinsky's remains in Jerusalem and held a state funeral for the famous Zionist leader.

The good Eshkol didn't understand that Ben-Gurion's stubborn refusal of such a noble, humane gesture had one single goal: to prevent the legitimization of Herut. That was exactly what happened the day of Jabotinsky's funeral. For the first time hundreds of thousands of Israelis saw that their government was paying homage to Herut's founder. The man, therefore, couldn't be all bad. Menachem Begin walked behind Jabotinsky's coffin; if Jabotinsky deserved a state funeral then his pupil, Begin, couldn't be all bad either; and the Herut Party members, who participated en masse in the ceremony, were perhaps decent guys, after all.

Three years later the Six-Day War erupted. Five days before Israel attacked, Eshkol formed a National Unity government in which he included Begin. The unity government was totally unnecessary: Israel had fought before, in much more desperate conditions, without the support of a wall-to-wall cabinet. Eshkol had formed the unity government in order to save face, after bowing to national pressure and giving the Defense portfolio to Moshe Dayan. That way he could present his capitulation as a reshuffling required for achieving national unity.

Once again Eshkol was praised for his decision. But this second gesture of his was another step in the legitimization of Herut and Begin. The Ben-Gurion taboo—"without Herut and the Communists"—had been broken: Begin became a national figure, a senior minister in the war government; he was no longer an enemy of the people. He had at last been given official respect as an outstanding Israeli leader, a member of a victorious government, a statesman who had the right to reach for supreme power in the nation.

Still, Begin's legitimization wouldn't have produced any results if Labor hadn't collapsed under the weight of its own errors.

In 1948, Israel had a vast majority of Ashkenazi Jews; in 1977 there were equal numbers of Sephardis and Ashkenazis. The Sephardis, mostly from the Middle East and North Africa, were much more nationalist than the European Jews. They had lived among the Arabs for centuries and nourished rather harsh views of them. This made them more receptive to the hard-line slogans of the Likud. Furthermore, without being ultra-Orthodox, the Sephardi Jews had a profound respect for traditional values and religious practices. Labor's indifferent—often even hostile—attitude toward religion offended many of them, whereas Begin's meticulous observance of Jewish customs made them proud.

Those trends were even stronger in the young generation of Sephardis born and raised in Israel. Their parents, who had been flown to Israel from Yemen and Kurdistan, from the Atlas mountains and the city ghettos in Morocco, from Syria and Iran, from India and Libya, had been inspired by deep messianic feelings. For them the very return to the Land of Israel was a dream come true; they seldom asked for more.

Israeli democracy, with its mores and habits, was foreign to them, sometimes hard to understand; it destroyed their traditional form of society, shattered the father-dominated family cell, preached the discarding of their old clothes, food, folklore, professions, customs, even names. They accepted all of that meekly; they didn't question the hegemony of the existing political and social elite, creating what came to be known as "the Second Israel."

That meant another society, mostly living in immigrant camps, in tents, huts, pitiful houses built of asbestos or corrugated iron. They spoke different languages, didn't mix with the established Israeli community, took almost no part in the social, cultural, and political life of the country. The Second Israel was employed mostly in manual labor; its sons were rarely seen in good high schools, and very few of them graduated from a university. It emerged on the political scene only on election day and voted massively for David Ben-Gurion, the New Messiah, the King of Israel. It was almost as if the Second Israel was situated on another planet, so close to the white residential quarters of Tel Aviv and the sunny villas of Herzliya, and yet so far away.

But the younger generation revolted. The younger Sephardis grew up in Israel; they spoke and read Hebrew. They understood Israeli democracy. They bitterly accused the Labor governments of severing their ethnic roots and brutally destroying their heritage. They resented the condescending attitude of the Labor officials, who bossed them around, whereas the Likud politicians toured their neighborhoods, speaking of discrimination.

They failed to understand, and refused to embrace, Labor's socialist views. They didn't try to analyze the difference between Labor's humane, Western-oriented socialism and the tyrannical Soviet ideology. They hated the red banners and the socialist terminology the Labor Ashkenazis had imported from Europe; they disliked the Russian songs of Labor's youth movements; they knew the kibbutz—the crown jewel of Israel's pioneering socialism—as an employer, in whose fields, orchards, and chicken farms they worked as hired hands. For them the kibbutz was also an elitist society that wouldn't allow their children into its schools and their families into its swimming pools.

The resentment that developed in their hearts tore them away from Labor: some of them joined the religious parties, some of them formed short-lived ethnic Sephardic parties; but most of them flocked to the Likud. Most of the Soviet immigrants who started arriving in the early seventies also found their way into the Likud. Having escaped from the socialist paradise, they hated every political symbol or slogan that reminded them of the Soviet Union. Labor leaders sweated hard to explain the difference between Israeli and Soviet socialism. It didn't help. The red flag sent the Russians running to the Likud, which prided itself on the national blue and white colors.

The deepest crisis, though, and the least perceived one, was the ideological collapse of the Labor movement. Since the arrival of the first Aliya to Palestine in the nineteenth century, Labor held the monopoly on real Zionism. The Labor movement was building the country. Its pioneers created new kibbutzim and moshavim all over the land; they dried marshes and reclaimed barren soil; they planted trees, built roads, worked in factories; they settled along the borders; the youth of their settlements volunteered en masse for the commandos, the paratroopers, the Air Academy; they established the powerful Histadrut—a unique federation of labor that combined social security, trade unions, health, education, and ownership of one third of the nation's economy. Any Israeli who looked for a challenge, and wanted to do something for his country and contribute to its development, would naturally choose the path of Labor Zionism. Anyone who dreamt of a just and new society had to join the ranks of Labor. That was the "Pioneering Zionism," in contrast to the "Verbal Zionism" of the right wing.

But that was in the past. At the end of the sixties and the beginning of the seventies, the old challenges didn't appeal anymore. Settling on a kibbutz didn't seem a tremendous sacrifice nowadays; kibbutz life was quickly becoming a synonym for prosperity. The kibbutz pioneers were no longer drying out marshes and fighting Arab marauders during the day and dancing the horah around the campfire at night. Life in a moshav—a cooperative village—no longer had its allure. The return to the land, a sacred ideal of the past, had lost its magic.

Besides, the kibbutz and the moshav didn't seem vital to the nation's defense anymore. The army defended the borders, and Israel's security didn't depend on isolated frontier settlements. The Histadrut, too, had lost its monopoly on building the country. Private investors were also building cities and factories. The Histadrut had become a huge, powerful machine; after many years of boycott, the Likud had joined the Histadrut and was trying to conquer the Labor fortress from within.

Strangely enough, the only pioneering movement left seemed to be Gush Emunim—"The Bloc of the Faithful"—an organization of young religious Zionists whose goal was to settle all over Judea and Samaria.

They planned their operations with meticulous care, fought against the army and the government, and were mobilizing public opinion and the press on their side, as the Labor settlers had done under the British Mandate.

The Labor government and its kibbutz movements also created settlements in Gaza and the West Bank. But they acted according to rigid criteria, authorizing settlements only in the areas vital to Israel's security: the Golan, the Jordan valley, the Etzion Bloc, the southwestern edge of the Gaza Strip. The official settlement areas roughly corresponded to the Allon plan; there was a national consensus that even if a territorial compromise were achieved, they would remain a part of Israel.

Still, the government was too weak to effectively oppose the pressure by Gush Emunim. In several cases, Peres and Rabin capitulated before the skullcap-wearing pioneers who settled outside the authorized regions; in other instances, they even cooperated with the settlers, as did Allon himself, by helping to establish the township of Kiryat Arba.

Ben-Gurion, who had been a visionary, but had his feet planted solidly on the ground, knew that Israel's secret of survival was its capacity to meet new, inspiring challenges. During his reign he continued conceiving new goals: winning the War of Independence; doubling the population in four years; absorbing the new immigrants; transforming the Israeli army into a melting pot, to create one people out of the hundred-odd different communities; teaching the Hebrew language; returning city dwellers to agriculture; settling the Negev; developing the Lakhish region.

And so much more. It had been difficult, often painful, and the nation was always short of breath, perpetually galloping toward the next objective the crazy Old Man would indicate. But what satisfaction when a goal was achieved! What a sense of fulfillment at seeing this unique State of Israel flourish! And what pride in being an Israeli, despite all the dangers and vicissitudes.

But Ben-Gurion was gone, and there was nobody to raise the torch again. Of course, if Labor had kept conceiving new challenges and new goals—such as better education, high-tech industry, science, monumental projects on a national scale—it could still maintain its monopoly and attract masses of young people. But there were no new challenges. And in a society that had lost the pioneering spirit, Labor had little to offer that Likud hadn't.

* * *

Another political change with far-reaching consequences had taken place after the Six-Day War—the metamorphosis of the religious parties. The National Religious Party, the main religious political organization, had been a loyal ally of the Labor movement throughout the years. It had participated in practically all of Mapai's and Labor's coalitions. The religious leaders had given Ben-Gurion a free hand in the areas of foreign policy and defense as long as their demands in religious matters were satisfied.

Those demands were, in general, quite reasonable. Since the creation of Israel the relations between state and religion were governed by an agreement based on the status quo of 1947. Buses for public transportation continued to run in Haifa on Saturday, as they did before 1947, and didn't run in Tel Aviv, as they didn't before 1947. As in the past, pork wasn't (officially) on sale, but when the religious parties asked to prohibit raising pigs in the country Ben-Gurion refused, clinging to the status quo agreement. Civil marriage wasn't allowed for the same reasons. On the other hand, the religious parties didn't like the paragraph defining "Who is a Jew" in the Law of Return, but didn't even dream of changing it.

The National Religious Party was a very convenient partner for Ben-Gurion. He got their support, and they were rewarded with the benefits of power. They felt secure and serene in the Labor coalitions, in which they generally received the portfolios of Interior, Religion, and Welfare; they spoke warmly of the "historic alliance" between their party and the Labor movement.

Even after Ben-Gurion was replaced by Sharett, Eshkol, Golda Meir, and Rabin, the historic alliance seemed to stand firm. But the first cracks in this alliance appeared after the Six-Day War. All of a sudden the biblical Land of Israel had been liberated. To many religious Jews the land was holy; it had been given by the Lord to the Children of Israel. Didn't the Bible say so? They couldn't even think of giving it back to Hussein, or the Palestinians, or anybody else. They couldn't accept any negotiation that might result in the withdrawal of Israel from some of its holiest sites. For the first time since Israel was created, a large portion of Israel's religious Jews identified with the most extremist hard-liners as far as a territorial compromise was concerned. And the moderate National Religious Party wasn't moderate anymore.

At that time many of the old, sober leaders of the National Religious

Party were already leaving the political stage. They were replaced by younger and more radical leaders, some of them openly identified with Gush Emunim. Since 1969 the National Religious Party had agreed to join the Labor governments only on condition that the territorial status quo would be respected; any plan for the partition of the Land of Israel—meaning the relinquishing of the West Bank—would automatically imply the dissolution of the Knesset and the calling of new elections.

Finally, the younger generation of religious leaders was much more sensitive to the Labor leaders' attitude on religious matters. They disliked Rabin's apathy toward their concerns. In December 1976 a first shipment of U.S.-made F-15 jets landed in Israel after the beginning of the Sabbath. The religious ministers in Rabin's government revolted and abstained during a no-confidence vote in the Knesset.

Rabin, unaware of the change that had taken place in the National Religious Party, promptly resigned, calling for early elections. His admirers called his resignation "a brilliant maneuver." Rabin took his rivals by surprise, they said; neither Peres inside the party nor the Likud and the Movement for Change would have time to prepare their campaigns.

Within a few months Rabin's supporters were to find out that the "brilliant maneuver" had broken the historic alliance.

And that the religious establishment, headed by the National Religious Party, was already on its way to join that pious, God-fearing, observing Jew who had also sworn allegiance to the Holy Land of Israel, Menachem Begin.

The Likud also displayed another asset that Labor sadly lacked: leadership. Ariel Sharon, the victorious general of the Yom Kippur War, became a member of the Likud; Ezer Weizmann, the nephew of Israel's first president and the man who had built the best air force in the world, joined the Likud. Young leaders in their twenties and thirties, many of them Sephardic, running in mayoral races or for the Knesset, were encouraged to join the Likud. David Levy, Moshe Katzav, Meir Shitrit, and David Magen were only a few of them. At the same time, the Labor leaders, too deeply immersed in internal commitments, smothered any effort of younger party members to win a place on the party ticket. I was soon going to experience that frustration myself.

But the main leadership asset of the Likud was Menachem Begin.

When Ben-Gurion, Eshkol, and Golda Meir had led the Labor Party, Menachem Begin had paled in comparison. He even looked ridiculous and pathetic when they were around; his emotional speeches, his bombastic formulas, his theatrics, his exaggerated mannerisms of a Polish gentleman were the subject of constant ridicule.

But when Labor's founding fathers cleared the stage and left Rabin to face Begin, everything changed. Rabin was a poor speaker; he accentuated the wrong words in a phrase, and his intonations rang false; his speeches were boring, he seemed oddly detached and was unable to stir an emotional response. Compared to him, Begin loomed as a great orator, a master of the Hebrew language who spoke in images, quoting naturally from the Scriptures, lacing his diatribes with stinging sarcasm.

In the new setup of Israeli political life, the absence of the founding fathers had created a void. Begin was the only one who projected a father image; and many Israelis, disappointed with the leadership of Rabin and his younger ministers, nostalgic for the great old leaders of the past, naturally turned to Begin.

Besides, Begin couldn't be accused of the mishaps of the Labor administration. He had left the National Unity government long before the Yom Kippur War; he wasn't responsible for the inflation that swept Israel after 1973; and most of all, he was not corrupt.

Corruption was one of the key words in the 1977 election campaign. It caught the public eye when the newly appointed governor of the Bank of Israel, Asher Yadlin, was exposed as a thief who had been robbing the Histadrut for years. A witch-hunt started soon afterwards; its next target was Abraham Ofer, the minister of housing. Unable to withstand the ugly campaign, Ofer drove his car to a deserted beach and shot himself. The allegations against him were never proved.

The third case was the worst. An Israeli journalist, Dan Margalit, discovered that Itzhak and Leah Rabin kept an unauthorized bank account in Washington, in violation of Israeli law. The account was small and unimportant; still, the Rabins had infringed the law. The scandal exploded in April 1977, barely a few weeks after Rabin had won the Labor nomination for prime minister, defeating Shimon Peres by a narrow margin. The general elections were less than two months away. Mrs. Rabin was tried in a court of law, and Itzhak Rabin dramatically resigned from office.

Those scandals were followed by the exposure of other, rather minor affairs, like the sloppy administration of buildings and other properties belonging to the Labor Party. But the public got the distinct impression that the entire Labor hierarchy, from top to bottom, was rigged with corruption; people suspected many other dark secrets were lurking behind the party's facade.

Shortly before the election I met my friend, the poet Chaim Gouri. "Michael, we're going to lose the election," he said sadly. "The governor of the Bank of Israel is in jail, the housing minister is in his grave, the prime minister is on trial. How can we win?"

On May 17, 1977, the unthinkable happened. After thirty years in power, Labor suffered a tremendous defeat, losing nineteen of its fifty-one seats in the Knesset. Fifteen seats went to the newly constituted Movement for Change. The Likud won forty-five seats. The National Religious Party and the ultra-Orthodox Agudat Israel were ready to offer their sixteen seats to a Likud coalition.

The president of Israel called Menachem Begin to form the next government.

It was the end of an era.

Chapter 6

Peace Now

Many Israelis regarded Labor's defeat in 1977 as the worst disaster in the history of Israel. We saw in it the death of the Zionist dream, the beginning of the end. It was an act of folly, the mass suicide of the Jewish people.

Some compared it with the traumatic debacle of the Yom Kippur War. Others said the Jews should start packing. People couldn't believe that Labor wasn't in power anymore. The Labor hegemony was a synonym of eternity in the Israeli psyche. It was inconceivable that Israel could survive or even exist if Labor wasn't at the helm. I recalled an old electoral speech of Begin when he had unleashed his verve against the Labor fanatics. "They ask what will happen if Labor isn't in power anymore," Begin theatrically uttered. "And they think: the sun will not rise if Labor isn't in power anymore. The trees will not grow, rain will not fall, the moon will not shine, life will cease all over this land if Labor isn't in power anymore."

Begin didn't exaggerate. That indeed was the feeling of hundreds of thousands in the country when the Likud won the elections. The glorious State of Israel had fallen into the hands of a group of lunatics and demagogues. The Third Temple had collapsed. Many spoke openly of leaving the country; many felt that the last chance for peace with our neighbors had evaporated and foresaw the Likud expansionists triggering an apocalyptic war that would bring an end to the State of Israel.

Itzhak Ben-Aharon, a former minister and ex–secretary-general of the Histadrut, openly called on television for disobedience to the new government. Refusing to admit their own errors, the Labor leaders accused everybody else. Peres accused Rabin and Rabin accused Peres; both accused the party, and the party accused the Movement for Change, the

71

press, the Yom Kippur War, and, mostly, the nation. We sullenly
watched the leaders of the Movement for Change—our brothers who
had turned into our nemesis—join Begin's coalition and take the minister's oath at the rostrum of the Knesset.

But our trials had only started, for after losing power to the bunch of
warmongers of the right wing, we were to helplessly witness those warmongers making peace with our worst enemy.

Soon after his electoral triumph, Menachem Begin suffered a severe heart
attack. For several days he was in critical condition at Ichilov Hospital
in Tel Aviv. And it was from his sickbed, while still connected to
monitors and plasma infusions, that he announced the appointment of
Moshe Dayan as his minister of foreign affairs.

The astounding news caused bitter disappointment in the Likud, where
several leaders had been busy trying on pin-striped suits and tuxedos.
But that was nothing compared to the explosion of fury in the Labor
Party. Dayan had crossed the lines and joined the enemy, taking his
parliamentary seat with him. That was the worst act of treachery a
politician could commit.

That was my feeling, too; I abhorred Dayan's step and didn't speak to
him for a long time. But I understood his motives perfectly. During the
last three years, which Dayan had passed in semi-exile writing his memoirs, I often used to visit him. I found out that he had been deeply shaken
by the wave of resentment provoked by his part in the Yom Kippur
tragedy. "The Israelis love to worship living idols," his brother-in-law,
Ezer Weizmann, said to me, "but they also love to destroy them with
unrestrained zeal." The man who had been the national hero till yesterday
couldn't cope with the criticism and the accusations that rained on him
from all sides. "A woman spat on my car today, Michael!" Dayan said
to me once, deeply upset. "She spat on me!"

Most of the time he was lecturing me on the findings of the Agranat
board of inquiry and quoting long paragraphs that proved he was as clean
as the driven snow. He would comment angrily on articles in the papers
that kept blaming him in spite of the board's conclusions.

"Do you remember when we created Rafi?" I asked him once. "You
said then that Ben-Gurion was obsessed with the Lavon affair and didn't
care about anything else. You said you wouldn't join Rafi if the Old Man

kept driving us crazy with his demands for a judicial inquiry. Well, now you behave exactly like him!"

But Dayan was younger than Ben-Gurion. And after reading the drafts of his memoirs I understood that the man was determined not to end the story of his life with the Yom Kippur debacle. He couldn't bear the idea that his glorious autobiography would end with the sorry chapter dealing with the board of inquiry. Dayan wanted, at all costs, to add a chapter to his life story, to do something that would rehabilitate him in the eyes of history and of his nation.

That was what Begin shrewdly perceived. And by appointing Dayan minister of foreign affairs, he gave him the unique opportunity to add a major chapter to the book of his life: the chapter about the peace agreement with Egypt.

"Sadat is heading for peace," Dayan had been repeating since the Yom Kippur War. He was convinced the president of Egypt realized he had exhausted the military options and was determined to pay the heavy price of peace with Israel in order to recover his lost provinces.

Dayan didn't wait long to find out if his hunch was right. Wearing a golfer's visor cap and dark glasses, he secretly flew to India to convince its prime minister to mediate between Israel and Egypt. He failed, but didn't give up. On September 4 he took off again. Wearing a long beatnik's wig, a false mustache, and dark glasses, he flew to Europe, was hurled by Mossad agents into a waiting automobile, was driven in and out of several garages, changing cars on the way, and finally boarded a lavish private jet that brought him to Rabat, the capital of Morocco. There he asked King Hassan to arrange a meeting between him and a special envoy of Sadat.

Hassan agreed; a few days later he flashed a message to Dayan saying that Sadat had accepted his proposal. On September 16, Dayan again donned his wig, mustache, and smoked glasses, and repeated the James Bond routine in Brussels and Paris. His trip ended once again in Morocco. But this time, in the Royal Palace in Rabat, he shook hands with Dr. Hassan Tuhami, Sadat's deputy.

Both Dayan and Tuhami, as well as their host, were deeply moved by the historic encounter. Not long ago they had been the worst of enemies; now they were discussing the prospects of peace.

Tuhami emphasized Sadat's determination to make peace with Israel. "You (and Begin) are strong and brave leaders," Tuhami said, "and we believe you are capable of reaching fateful decisions that could bring real and fair peace. President Sadat didn't trust your former government, but he trusts you. . . . President Ceauşescu of Rumania asked him to meet with Begin, but Sadat didn't believe such a meeting would be fruitful. Now he has changed his mind, thanks to the mediation of the King of Morocco and his trust in Begin's government."

After these encouraging words Tuhami presented a set of rigid conditions to a peace negotiation. First, Israel had to declare it would withdraw from all the territories conquered in the Six-Day War. Only after such a declaration would Sadat agree to meet with Begin.

Dayan couldn't accept Tuhami's conditions, of course; even the Security Council of the United Nations, in Resolution 242, adopted in 1967, had asked Israel to withdraw from "territories" and not "the territories" conquered in the war. That meant the United Nations had conceded that Israel could keep some of its conquests. Still, Dayan considered Tuhami's demands only as an opening statement meant to achieve a bargaining position. He reached an agreement with the Egyptian official to exchange position papers on the peace issue and meet again after they had reported to their leaders.

But before their next flight to Morocco, an astounding event shook the entire world.

At the beginning of November 1977, Sadat flew to Teheran for a meeting with the Shah of Iran; he was then to visit Saudi Arabia. While flying over Mount Ararat in Turkey he thought of a dramatic move that might speed the peace process. He decided to call for an extraordinary conference of the Security Council permanent members in East Jerusalem. But on his way from Teheran to Riyad he changed his mind. Even if the representatives of the Five Powers came to Jerusalem, he thought, they might fail to reach an agreement.

He kept racking his brains for a solution, and the idea came to him during his flight back to Cairo. He should go to Jerusalem himself and in a dramatic gesture offer peace to the Israelis.

On November 9, in a speech before the Egyptian parliament, Anwar el-Sadat declared that he was ready to travel to the other end of the world if that might prevent the wounding of a single Egyptian soldier or officer. "I am ready to go even to the Israelis' home," he said, "to their Knesset, and talk to them."

The speech surprised Israel. Many Israeli leaders reacted with contempt and sarcasm to Sadat's declaration. They couldn't believe Egypt's president meant what he said. Didn't he declare, a few years before, that he was ready to sacrifice one million Egyptian soldiers in order to regain his lost lands?

Menachem Begin, however, seized the occasion. Addressing a rally at the Tel Aviv Hilton, he invited President Sadat to come to Jerusalem to negotiate a permanent peace between Israel and Egypt. Two days later he dispatched his official invitation to Cairo via the U.S. embassy. And Cairo responded.

On November 19, 1977, Begin stood on the runway of Ben-Gurion airport and watched Sadat's Boeing *Misr 01* land on Israeli soil. As the familiar figure of President Sadat emerged at the cabin door, all of Israel realized that Menachem Begin had achieved the dream of all his predecessors: to host an Arab leader on an official visit to Jerusalem. And he might also achieve the first peace treaty between Israel and an Arab country.

Begin had launched his peace initiative right after winning the national election. He had chosen Dayan as his foreign minister, knowing that the famous hero, even with his tarnished reputation, was the best-qualified Israeli to talk to the Arabs. In August he had asked the president of Rumania to influence Sadat to negotiate with his government. He had also sent Dayan to President Carter with a position paper detailing a peace proposal to Egypt.

Begin was determined to achieve two goals: make peace, and make it with Egypt. Some of his close friends described to me his "burning resolve" to discard, once and for all, the image of demagogue and terrorist that had stuck to him for years. The only way for him to secure his place in history, and achieve the respect and esteem of his nation, was by succeeding where Ben-Gurion and his successors had failed: by bringing peace to the embattled Land of Israel.

Yet Egypt was the only Arab country with which he could make peace. Lebanon was torn by civil strife; Syria wouldn't negotiate with Israel, even if we offered to give back the Golan Heights, which we wouldn't. With Egypt, however, the situation was different: the main obstacle to peace was our occupation of Sinai.

Begin had no special attachment to the arid wastes of the Sinai; the windswept peninsula had never been a part of the historic Eretz Israel. Its main value was as a buffer zone between Israel and Egypt. If he could obtain the demilitarization of the peninsula, the free shipping through the straits of Sharm el-Sheik, and the continuous supply of oil from the Gulf of Suez, Begin was ready to trade Sinai for peace.

Dayan held a similar view. In the past he had fervently preached for the annexation of a large part of the Sinai to Israel. I remember Dayan declaring over and over again: "I prefer Sharm el-Sheik without peace to peace without Sharm el-Sheik." But this brash declaration dated from Dayan's days of limitless confidence, when he was at the apex of his glory. The Yom Kippur War had made him a more humble man. Besides, Dayan was the ultimate pragmatist, a man who was willing to reverse his opinions if the circumstances changed.

Begin and Dayan agreed on another point: they wouldn't give up the West Bank. Begin considered the Land of Israel sacred; unlike Sinai, this was the historic homeland of the Jews, and not negotiable. Dayan, although more pragmatic, stuck fast to his theory of a fluid, functional compromise. He was opposed to a Palestinian state, and rejected any partition of the West Bank between Jordan and Israel.

That's why he was almost relieved to find out that Hussein's attitude hadn't changed and he was still unwilling to discuss a territorial compromise. When Dayan and Hussein met in London on August 22 and 23, their talks were totally fruitless. "If I agree to any partition plan I would be deemed a traitor by the Arab world," Hussein said. To Dayan he seemed gloomy, perhaps because of the recent death of his beloved wife in a helicopter crash.

When Hussein took leave of Dayan, it was the last time he would shake hands with an Israeli leader for more than seven years. The new Israeli government put an end to the secret meetings with the king of Jordan. Begin and Dayan weren't interested in talking with Hussein. It was Sadat they were after.

But in order to seduce Sadat, they would have to tear him away from Hussein and the Palestinians, tempt him with magnificent prizes, make him an offer he couldn't refuse.

They launched their assault as soon as Sadat stepped onto Israeli soil on the Sabbath, November 19, 1977.

* * *

Most Israelis welcomed Sadat with a tremendous explosion of warmth. The newspapers greeted him with banner headlines in Hebrew and Arabic, Egyptian flags were hoisted on government buildings and public institutions, enthusiastic crowds massed wherever he appeared.

We all held our breath when he came out of his plane. He was a tall, swarthy man with a trim mustache, impeccably dressed. The dark spot on his forehead resulted from touching the floor five times a day during his devout prayers. From his first moment among us the president of Egypt behaved with ease and natural authority. With remarkable self-assurance he listened to the national anthems of the two warring countries; then he shook hands with his former enemies, including the Chief of Staff, General Gur, who had unwisely declared a few days before that Sadat's visit was a part of a war ploy against Israel.

Sadat called Golda Meir "the Old Lady" and admitted that he had considered meeting with her while she was prime minister. "Why didn't you come?" she asked reproachfully. "We waited for you in Egypt," he said in jest to General Ariel Sharon, hinting at Sharon's thrust toward Cairo in October 1973. He showered quick-witted greetings on his hosts, smiled, shook hands, and slapped shoulders. But the Israeli leader who won Sadat's affection was Defense Minister Ezer Weizmann.

A former air force general and a daredevil pilot, Weizmann was quick-tempered and impulsive, but immensely likable. Thin and long-legged, sporting an RAF mustache, Weizmann had engineered the formidable air strike that had wiped out Egypt's aviation in the Six-Day War. Before the Yom Kippur War he had claimed that to achieve peace, we had first to conquer the Arab capitals; he had since become a fervent supporter of the "territories for peace" formula.

The youthful, mischievous minister had been badly hurt in a traffic accident a few days before Sadat's arrival. He came to meet Sadat in a wheelchair and stood up leaning heavily on his crutches. When Sadat approached him he raised his crutch like a rifle, jumped to attention, and smartly saluted. Sadat burst out laughing. The next morning he invited "Ezra" Weizmann to his rooms in the Jerusalem King David Hotel; Weizmann became Sadat's closest friend in Israel, and his direct communications line with Begin's government.

Unfortunately, Sadat didn't make any other friends in the Israeli government. General Yigael Yadin, the leader of the Movement for Change, was deputy prime minister in Begin's government, but he turned out to be a paper tiger who had no real say in the negotiations. Moshe Dayan, the smartest man in the government, would steer Menachem Begin into far-reaching concessions, without which no peace agreement could be achieved; still, his relationship with Sadat would remain cold and strained. The two men didn't like each other, although they held each other in high esteem. Sharon didn't trust Sadat, and Sadat didn't trust him. The Labor leaders, exiled to the opposition benches, had no influence on the negotiations.

The main disappointment concerned the relations between Sadat and Begin. Zealous spokesmen described the marvelous chemistry between them that had instantaneously made them fast friends. That wasn't true. There had been no magic between Sadat and Begin. The two men were completely different. Sadat was extroverted, spontaneous, and uninterested in the fine print. Begin was pedantic and attached enormous importance to details; he had a legalistic mind, an annoying habit of mixing Latin and Greek expressions in his statements, a tendency to deliver tedious and condescending lectures.

Sadat behaved like an absolute ruler; Begin was bound by a coalition government and an ebullient Knesset. Sadat naïvely believed that by his dramatic flight to Israel he had already made a tremendous concession; in return he expected Israeli acceptance of a far-reaching territorial compromise on all its borders. Begin had no intention of giving up an inch, except in the Sinai.

Their diverging points of view became clear the following afternoon, when Sadat addressed the Knesset, in an unprecedented ceremony. No theatrical genius could have imagined a sight more dramatic than this archenemy of Israel speaking from the tribune of its parliament, offering peace to its captains. Begin, pale and tense, rose to answer, his face drawn, his balding head held high in defiance. And millions of people throughout the world, watching the scene on their television screens, felt they were witnessing an event of historical magnitude.

Sadat's speech turned out to be a warning that the road to peace was still barred by formidable obstacles. The president of Egypt demanded Israel's withdrawal from all the occupied territories; Begin flatly refused. That same day, however, the two leaders did reach an agreement on two vital points. They decided that no more war would be waged between their nations, and Begin actually promised Sadat to restore all of Sinai to full Egyptian sovereignty in exchange for peace. Begin believed that in spite of this concession, a special status could be achieved for the Israeli settlements and the air force bases in the Sinai.

Begin was soon to find out that the Palestinian problem, and not the Sinai, was the main obstacle to peace. He, therefore, needed a formula for a Palestinian solution that would satisfy Sadat and motivate him to sign a separate peace agreement with Israel.

Although manipulated by Dayan, harassed by Weizmann, besieged by his party's hard-liners, and mocked by the press, Begin hit upon the magic formula. It was called autonomy. In a daring move, departing from his traditional positions, Begin offered the Palestinians free elections and self-rule; the final status of the West Bank and Gaza would be decided five years later.

Less than a month after Sadat's visit to Jerusalem, Menachem Begin unexpectedly flew to Washington to meet with President Jimmy Carter. Both the Israelis and the Egyptians had realized by then that there would be no agreement without the mediation, pressure, and guarantees of the United States. Carter was willing, some say desperate, to help achieve a breakthrough in order to boost his faltering image with the American public. The Sadat peace offensive also helped him to back off gracefully from his dubious initiative, launched earlier, of an international conference on the Middle East with the active participation of the Soviet Union.

Begin came to Washington hoping to convince Carter that his autonomy plan was a major step toward the solution of the Palestinian problem. Therefore, the U.S. president should persuade Sadat to drop his claim for an Israeli withdrawal from the West Bank. Carter, who disliked Begin, had quite a few reservations about his plan; nevertheless, he realized that autonomy was the most he could get from Israel at that time and decided to go along with the plan.

Carter joined the peace process on that cold snowy night of December 16, 1977, when Begin walked into the Oval Office and presented his plan. His closest assistants were also assigned to the task—Vice President Walter Mondale, National Security Adviser Zbigniew Brzezinski, Secretary of State Cyrus Vance. That was the beginning of a Via Dolorosa of summit meetings and aides' meetings and ministers' meetings, of crises and disputes and mutual accusations; of countless drafts and notes and letters, papers, and counter-papers; of endless talks in the palaces of Ismailia, the posh hotels of Cairo, and the medieval fortress of Leeds; of meetings in Washington, Salzburg, and Jerusalem, in the rustic isolation of Camp David and the formal elegance of Blair House; a sixteen-month strained negotiation that finally was to earn Sadat and Begin the Nobel Peace Prize; and achieve peace between Egypt and Israel. On March 26, 1979, with Jimmy Carter as a witness, Sadat and Begin signed a peace treaty on the White House lawn.

The negotiations had been a mixture of chess playing, arm wrestling, and subtle blackmail, with each of the actors playing his own game. Jimmy Carter, who sincerely admired Sadat, didn't spare his criticism of Israel and mostly sided with the Egyptians. Still, his bias turned out to be very helpful, for he won Sadat's trust and succeeded in persuading him to drop his unrealistic demands.

As for Sadat, he was determined to achieve peace and took enormous personal risks toward that goal; during the negotiations he had to fire, or accept the resignation of, two foreign ministers, a prime minister, a defense minister, and many senior aides; Egypt was kicked out of the Arab League and indignantly banished by most Arab countries.

On the Israeli side, the main actor had been Moshe Dayan. By throwing his weight around, manipulating other Israelis, cynically using even the Americans, he steered Begin into abandoning many of his tough conditions. Dayan's contribution to the peace negotiations was crucial. I doubt if peace would ever have been achieved without his involvement. Ezer Weizmann, on the other hand, gradually lost his status in the negotiations; the defense minister's impatience, his disdain for paperwork, and his impulsive outbursts eroded his position on the Israeli team, so much so that even Sadat realized that the irresistible "Ezra" had a lot of charm but no clout.

But of the three statesmen who signed the peace treaty that crisp morning on the White House lawn, the real winner was Menachem Begin. True, he had been forced to leave open the question of the future sovereignty of the West Bank and Gaza, those parts of Eretz Israel that the Likud claimed as Jewish forever and ever; true, he had abandoned the settlements and the air bases in Sinai; and it was only by the votes of the Labor Party that he'd had the Camp David agreements and the peace treaty approved by the Knesset. Some of his closest companions, like Itzhak Shamir and Moshe Arens, openly objected to the treaty; and

Geula Cohen, a hotheaded right-wing Pasionaria, indignantly left the Likud and founded her own extremist faction.

But Begin had achieved his goal: he had signed a separate peace agreement with the strongest Arab country without giving away a single inch of Eretz Israel. He still controlled the Golan Heights. He still ruled over the West Bank, and could continue building new Jewish settlements throughout Judea and Samaria.

He had even kept the Gaza Strip under Israeli control. The strip had been under Egyptian administration from 1948 until Israel had conquered it in 1967. Now Begin refused to hand it back to Egypt, on the grounds that Gaza had never been Egyptian territory, but a part of mandatory Palestine. Not that Gaza was the land of our dreams. Densely populated with refugees, sweltering with hatred, Gaza had always been a springboard for terrorists who operated deep inside Israel. Dayan had called Gaza a wasps' nest; Ben-Gurion had said he prayed a huge wave would rise from the Mediterranean and wipe out the strip with all its inhabitants. Begin knew Gaza meant a lot of trouble, but he didn't want to create a precedent of our withdrawing from any part of Eretz Israel, even if it was a keg of gunpowder.

As for the Palestinian solution, I believe Begin never seriously meant to establish autonomy in the West Bank. True, he committed himself to the autonomy in the peace treaty, but deep in his heart he believed that Sadat didn't care about the West Bank and needed the Palestinian chapter of the treaty only as proof of his loyalty to the traditional Arab positions. Once the autonomy agreements had provided him with his fig leaf, Sadat would not lift a finger for the Palestinians.

The future was to prove Begin right. Today, eleven years after the signature of the peace treaty, Israel still hasn't implemented autonomy in the West Bank, and Egypt still scrupulously adheres to the peace agreement with Israel. But Begin's victory was a short-lived one; had Palestinian autonomy been realized at the beginning of the eighties, the Intifada would not have erupted in the West Bank and Gaza.

A few months after the signing of the peace agreement, Dayan understood that autonomy was stillborn and that Begin wanted it that way. Perhaps the prime minister would agree to establish some sort of autonomy, Dayan reckoned, but only under Israeli sovereignty. Dayan, the only man in the cabinet able to talk to the Palestinians, felt his services were not wanted anymore. His personal relations with Begin had cooled

after the White House ceremony; the Likud openly accused him of maneuvering Begin to dangerous concessions. In October 1979, Dayan
resigned.

Begin hammered another nail into autonomy's coffin by appointing
Dr. Joseph Burg as chairman of the Israeli committee for the autonomy
talks. Dr. Burg, the leader of the National Religious Party, was a Dresden-
born, highly educated man known for his exceptional intelligence, astute
political instincts, and sharp sense of humor.

He was also known for his total ignorance of the Palestinians. He
didn't speak Arabic and had rarely if ever entered an Arab household
or a Palestinian village; most of his utterances on the Palestinian question
were brilliant examples of mental acrobatics and expert juggling with
words. This wise man was mostly concerned with satisfying both the
extremists and the moderates in his own party. With Burg at the head
of the autonomy team one could be sure that this chapter was closed.
His appointment established beyond a doubt that in Begin's eyes autonomy was dead.

A year after Dayan left the government, Ezer Weizmann resigned.
The defense minister had been feeling ill at ease in Begin's government
for some time. He openly mocked Begin, nicknaming him "the defunct"
and accusing him of sabotaging the peace with Egypt. Still, Weizmann
was the number-two man in the Likud; many saw him as the next prime
minister. In one of our conversations I told him he had missed a unique
opportunity to change the course of Israel's history. Had he invested
some patience and political work in his struggle, he might have become
Israel's leader, and perhaps steered his recalcitrant party in the direction
of peace and compromise. But the volatile Weizmann had neither patience nor a real understanding of politics. He resigned, making the worst
mistake in his career, leaving the Likud in the hands of the hard-core
extremists. When asked about Weizmann, Begin shrugged. "Such a
charming, naughty boy," he quipped.

With Dayan and Weizmann out of office, the Likud government lost
its foremost moderate leaders who could have continued the peace process. Their departure had no effect on the power or the popularity of
the Likud. But in the long run it was a tremendous blow for Israel. The
Jewish state was steadfastly moving away from peace, entrenching itself
in annexationist conceptions, insensitive to the fact that the Palestinian
problem had become a cancer that gnawed at it from within.

*   *   *

The peace treaty with Egypt had been Menachem Begin's major contribution to the history of Israel. But after that it would be downhill all the way for the fiery Likud leader. As the dramatic images of the Washington ceremony faded in people's minds, a new mood pervaded the country. Except for the peace agreement, Begin's government had been a dismal failure.

The country's economy was in shambles. When sworn in, Begin's finance minister, Simcha Ehrlich, had declared that he would transform Israel into the Switzerland of the Middle East. He followed up this declaration with a much-publicized liberalization of foreign currency controls, dramatic reductions in taxes, a switch from the pound to the shekel, and various other steps allegedly inspired by Professor Milton Friedman's economic theories.

I guess that the good professor, if asked, would have chosen other disciples to apply his teachings. Three years after Ehrlich's Switzerland speech the economy couldn't have been in worse shape. The 38 percent inflation rate he had inherited from his Labor predecessor had swelled to 133 percent a year. The dollar soared, the shekel lost its value, prices galloped, the foreign debt reached gigantic proportions. Begin's promises for better housing, education, and social reforms hadn't been kept. The verdict of the media was unanimous: the Likud was unable to govern the country.

That also seemed to be the verdict of the nation. As the 1981 elections approached, the polls unanimously predicted a Labor victory. The Movement for Change, which had so dramatically emerged on the Israeli political scene in 1977, had as dramatically collapsed. Ridden with internal quarrels, intrigue, and rivalries, it had broken down a few months after its electoral triumph; most of its voters were on their way "back home" to the good old Labor.

At the end of 1980, Begin sank into a black depression. He realized, he said to his close friends, that he was going to lose the elections. Labor would return for another thirty years. The 1977 Likud victory was short-lived; the party had failed to strike roots in the nation. Begin's government would be remembered as a brief episode in the history of Israel.

And then came the elections for the Histadrut, the general federation of labor, in April 1981.

In Israel, the election of the Histadrut governing bodies is a national event. Most Israelis belong to the Histadrut, mainly because of its social security and public health systems. Most adult Israelis, therefore—about 1.5 million in 1981—take part in the Histadrut vote. Most political parties take part in those elections. For many years, as the elections to the Histadrut preceded the national elections by a few months, they were viewed as a barometric reading of political trends.

It was evident that Labor would win overwhelmingly, as it had in the past; our party was closely identified with the trade unions, and even right-wingers voted en masse for the Labor candidates. Still, the media were curious about the Likud performance.

On April 7 the results started arriving shortly after midnight. Begin was huddled, morose, in a corner of the Likud campaign headquarters. He seemed strangely detached, enveloped again in his notorious black mood.

At 2 A.M. a cheer rippled throughout the vast room. The first results came, and they were astounding. The Likud had got between 25 and 26 percent of the vote! That was, of course, quite small compared to Labor, but it was a tremendous victory all the same. At the last election, in 1977, the Likud had achieved 28 percent. And tonight, after all the disenchantment, the government failures, the pessimistic predictions, the feeling of a forthcoming disaster, the Likud had declined a mere 2 percent, winning 26 percent! That figure could have only one meaning: Begin's party had much deeper roots in the electorate than it suspected. The Likud voters had remained faithful to their leaders in spite of all the blighted hopes.

A friend of mine who is a member of the Likud was sitting close to Begin that night. "You should have seen him, Michael," he later told me. "The man underwent a metamorphosis. First he raised his head, listening, then he asked to see the figures. As people ran and brought him stacks of papers, his entire body seemed to straighten up, like an inflatable doll injected with air. Color filled his cheeks, and he radiated confidence. His eyes lit up. And when he rose, he was our old Begin again.

" 'It's a great victory,' he told us. 'Now, we'll win the Knesset election as well!' "

Chapter 7

The Next Prime Minister of Israel

"Ladies and gentlemen, the next prime minister of Israel!"

The crowd gathered in the ballroom of the Deborah Hotel in Tel Aviv rose to its feet, cheering, shouting, clapping hands. Campaign activists hugged each other. Photographers' cameras clicked, their flashes bathing triumphant faces in soundless explosions of white light. Israeli and foreign reporters elbowed their way toward the entrance, waving microphones and television cameras. From my seat behind the dais I noticed Peter Jennings of ABC News wiping his sweating face. Then Shimon Peres walked in and the cheers turned into a roar.

"Again! Again!" the reporters shouted. They hadn't got the historic moment on tape. Israel Peleg, the Labor spokesman, obediently got up again. "Ladies and gentlemen," he repeated in English, "the next prime minister of Israel!"

Peres made his way across the hall, in a white open-collared shirt, smiling broadly. He stopped over and over again to shake hands and exchange hugs with many leading Alignment figures. (The Alignment was the common ticket of Labor and the small left-wing Mapam Party.) When Peres reached the dais Itzhak Rabin rose to face him. They hesitated a second, then embraced, and Shimon Peres planted a ringing kiss on Rabin's cheek.

The two men had been bitter rivals in 1974, 1977, and a few months before, when they had fought for the party nomination. But now they were both winners. Hanoch Smith, Israel's number-one pollster, had just

85

announced on television that Peres's Alignment had won a decisive victory over the Likud. We were going to form the next government.

The crowd around me burst into song as Peres took his place on the dais. "Has Mr. Begin conceded defeat yet?" a foreign reporter asked. The crowd reacted with laughter and more singing. "You aren't singing, Michael," the correspondent of *Maariv* said to me. I shook my head. I didn't share in the general elation; I still couldn't believe we had won.

It was the night of June 30, 1981. The voting had ended an hour before, and all the leaders of our party had gathered at the Deborah Hotel, our campaign headquarters, to watch the results on a couple of huge television screens. Actually, I wasn't an official of the campaign anymore.

Six weeks before, I had resigned from my position as chairman of the Alignment campaign. That morning I had come to Peres's office carrying two letters in my briefcase. The first was a proposal for drastic changes in the strategy of our campaign and in the structure of our campaign machine. If those changes weren't made right away, I told Peres, we were going to lose the elections.

Peres read the document in my presence, then shook his head. "No, Michael," he said. "I don't agree with you. I think the campaign is doing fine, I'm not going to make any changes."

I had expected that answer. I then handed him the second letter, in which I informed him of my resignation. "I shall not make it public before the election," I promised, "but I'm not going to stay one more day at headquarters. I'll go back to campaigning in the streets of Tel Aviv with my friends from my local branch." Peres refused to accept my resignation, but I was determined to go. I left his office and didn't return to the Deborah before election night.

Now, as the crowd around me was cheering and singing, I kept quiet. Some of my friends and colleagues were already being interviewed, live, on national television, explaining why and how we had won. Then, all of a sudden, Smith's face filled the screen again. He looked embarrassed. "I am afraid there has been a dramatic change," the pollster said. "We are receiving results that contradict my previous findings."

The singing and the cheering died abruptly, as new projections were flashed on the screen. Soon after, it became clear: we had lost again, by one or two seats. Our joy had been premature. The Likud had won the election.

At 3 A.M., Menachem Begin appeared on the screen, in front of cheering Likud members. He had freshened-up and was wearing an elegant suit. He acknowledged his victory and announced he was going to form the next government. Then he sarcastically addressed Shimon Peres, mocking his premature victory announcement. "What about the kiss, Shimon?" he said, turning theatrically to the camera. "The kiss you gave your friend Rabin. Now you have to take back the kiss!"

Our campaign had started immediately after the Histadrut election. We focused our drive on two main issues: the peace initiative, which only Labor could undertake; and the critical illness of the economy, which only Labor could cure. The press predicted a decisive victory for us; I didn't share that forecast. A few weeks before, Menachem Begin's government had shamelessly launched the hugest, most blatant bribery scheme in our history: the buying off of the whole nation.

After the "Switzerland of the Middle East" concept had collapsed, Begin had replaced Finance Minister Simcha Ehrlich with Moshe Dayan's cousin, Yigal Horowitz, who distinguished himself by whining, sighing, wringing his hands, and warning us about the impending catastrophe. But, aside from his dark prophecies and his gloomy tirades, Horowitz achieved nothing and he failed miserably to redress Israel's economy.

Begin then replaced Horowitz with Yoram Aridor, a young, pompous, and pretentious politician who seemed totally devoid of moral scruples. Aridor wasn't concerned by the sorry state of the nation's finances; all he cared about was winning the election.

In the spring of 1981, Aridor began showering the Israelis with money. He canceled inheritance and property taxes; he drastically reduced taxes on color televisions, video recorders, stereos, electrical appliances, and automobiles. By the stroke of a magic wand, everything became cheaper; all of a sudden, luxury products became accessible to many who had never dreamt of acquiring them. The horn of plenty tempted hundreds of thousands of Israelis; people waited in lines outside the stores while special planes unloaded stacks of televisions at Lod airport. Cars and other consumer goods were also shipped over by an unprecedented airlift.

The foreign exchange rate was kept artificially low; for the first time in their lives many low-income Israelis were able to vacation abroad. The banks offered stock that was kept artificially high; everybody who invested was steadily making money. Aridor had practically opened the nation's coffers, throwing around money by handfuls. When he emptied the treasury, he borrowed money abroad. "We are determined to do good for the people," Begin announced magnanimously.

Aridor's measures were smartly calculated; they instilled a feeling of ease and well-being in the Israelis. When the campaign started I would tour the poor neighborhoods and the popular markets, speaking of the economic crisis and the inflation. "Why should we worry about the inflation when our pockets are full?" people would tell me, pulling out thick wads of bills to make their point.

Besides Aridor's cynical policy, the Likud electoral campaign took a nasty turn. Likud speakers accused Labor leaders, Peres in particular, of committing treason and supporting the enemy. Branches of the Labor Party throughout the country were raided and burned; violence erupted at our rallies when Likud supporters tried by force to prevent us from speaking. Our rivals described us as the party of the Ashkenazi establishment, in contrast to the pro-Sephardic Likud. Those slogans triggered a great deal of hatred and social tension.

Still, more than Aridor's cynical acts and the Likud's violent diatribes, it was Peres's mistakes that caused the shift in public opinion in that hectic spring of 1981.

Shimon Peres is a man of contradictions. He is a wise man, but he often refuses to let his wisdom interfere with his decisions. He has been in politics all his life, but still, he is a mediocre politician. He is a shrewd judge of character, yet he surrounds himself only with yes-men. He has a sound and intelligent mind, yet he lets himself be influenced by any third-rate adviser. He knows better than any other party chief what is good for the country, yet he backs away from his positions under pressure, sometimes without even token resistance. He desperately needs the support of his friends, yet he readily sacrifices them for a fleeting chance of winning over a sworn enemy. In his vision he is an incurable optimist, but in his behavior he is a sad, melancholic man.

Peres is a many-faceted man: a genuine intellectual, a gifted writer, a consummate reader. His conversation is brilliant: writers, artists, and statesmen seek out his company. He is the only contemporary Israeli leader who deserves to be defined as a statesman.

Peres's name is linked to some of Israel's greatest achievements. As the youngest director general of the Defense Ministry (he was only twenty-nine when he was appointed by David Ben-Gurion), and later as defense vice minister, he laid the foundations for Israel's aircraft and armament industries; he masterminded the alliance with France and the special relationship with Adenauer's Germany; he equipped our army with French weapons and was one of the architects of the Sinai campaign; in spite of objections from all sides, he led a recalcitrant Israel into the atomic age and obtained France's assistance for the construction of the Dimona nuclear center. He initiated Israel's space and missile projects.

But he did all that in Ben-Gurion's name and under Ben-Gurion's protection. More than any other leader of his age group, Peres was hurt by the founding fathers' syndrome. As long as Ben-Gurion was at the helm, Peres knew exactly what to do, and he did it. But since the moment he was left on his own, he hasn't found the strength to fight for his convictions; instead, he has tried to find solutions or formulas that would satisfy every group in the political spectrum. That system, of course, couldn't work; and Peres, Ben-Gurion's child, also became Ben-Gurion's victim.

Once deprived of the Old Man's patronage, Peres changed and his image underwent a striking metamorphosis. People who admired him and cheered him in the past—especially the North African Jews—turned against him. In spite of his impressive record, his bold vision, and his statesmanlike qualities, Peres's name was tarnished, apparently for good. Some believe that his reputation was destroyed by the systematic campaign of character assassination orchestrated by the Likud. Others claim that Rabin's devastating remarks about Peres, published in his autobiography, shattered his public image.

I think the reasons for Peres's poor rating are deeper. He is haunted by an acute credibility problem. Many doubt his word and distrust his promises. Many of his political allies, including some of his staunchest supporters, have abandoned him, accusing him of disloyalty. When Abba Eban was asked a few years ago why Peres hadn't fulfilled his promise to make him foreign minister, he cracked: "Because he didn't want to set a precedent."

Peres's reputation stems in part from his dubious political practices. I felt the brunt of them myself for the first time in 1977.

After managing Peres's campaign for the Labor nomination, I had been elected by the Tel Aviv party council as a Knesset candidate. I got Peres's warm hug and congratulations on my election. But when he drew up the final list of our candidates, he dropped my name by more than twenty slots down the line and offered my position to one of his former opponents.

I felt betrayed. Israel's electoral system is proportional. Each party presents a list of candidates, and the seats it obtains correspond to the percentage the party has won of the overall vote. Therefore, the position of a candidate on the list is crucial to his election. A high slot means a safe seat; a low slot means the candidate has no chance to be elected.

Peres's last-minute maneuver meant that I was removed from the Labor list and wasn't going to be elected to the Knesset. When I angrily confronted Peres he said to me: "I had to do it, Michael, to rally the party around me."

"But I was elected by the party," I said. "You didn't have the right!"

He looked at me blankly. "What right?" he asked. "Don't you want me to be prime minister?"

Peres's credibility also suffers from his exaggerated efforts to gain popular support. Often, he makes life miserable for his followers by his public statements, which they find very hard to confirm. In his desperate courting of Sephardic Jews, he would declare that the songs of an Oriental pop star and the melodies of a Moroccan band are "the best music he's ever heard." Nobody (the Sephardic Jews less than the others) would believe that this Poland-born, Western-educated Ashkenazi meant what he said.

And nobody would believe Peres's solemn declarations that the Arab films shown on Israeli television each Friday were "the best movies he's ever seen." Such words sound false in the mouth of a man who is a personal friend of Yves Montand and Harry Belafonte, of leading Western writers, philosophers, and actors, and is more impregnated with Western literature, theater, and art than any other living politician in Israel.

Many people dislike Peres even without knowing why. "I don't like the look in his eyes on television," people would say to me. "I don't trust him." He is prey to the wildest accusations. In spite of his modest way of life, people accuse him of owning a splendid penthouse (which he doesn't), holding shares in the huge Tadiran electronics company (he doesn't either); and once, at a political rally, when I asked an opponent why he hated Shimon Peres, he answered calmly, "Because his mother is an Arab." The crowd cheered.

Still, Peres remains the greatest survivor in Israeli politics. Despite opposition from within and incessant strafing from without, he amazingly keeps landing on his feet. For years he has been subject to insults, libel, and criticism; for years he has tasted, over and over again, the bitterness of defeat. Any other politician would have given up long ago, but not Peres. "I am made of steel," he once said to some of us at party head-quarters. "I won't break." He still leads the Labor Party after four con-secutive debacles in the last twelve years. For my part, I believe Peres should have been evicted from power long ago and replaced by a younger generation of Labor leaders. Peres should continue to serve the country and his party, but not at the top slot, as he seems unable to win the nation's support.

In 1977 we attributed our electoral defeat to the mistakes of Rabin's government and Golda's poor legacy. In 1981 we were to find out that Peres, in misreading the political map, had acquired the lion's share of responsibility for our defeat at the polls.

Peres's first mistake was his visit to Morocco. In March 1981 he flew secretly to Rabat and met with King Hassan. His aides leaked the story to the press even before his return to Israel. Peres had hoped the visit would show that he was capable of talking to Arab leaders and bringing peace to our part of the world. The reaction was quite the opposite: many Israelis resented the voyage of a party chief with no official standing to an Arab country and his talking with the king behind the prime minister's back.

The second mistake was crucial. On June 6, 1981, Begin ordered the Israeli air force to raid the nuclear reactor Iraq was building outside Bagdad. All Western experts figured that Iraq intended to develop nu-clear weapons; such weapons in Iraqi hands constituted a mortal danger for Israel.

All the Israeli efforts to thwart the construction of the reactor had failed. France, which supplied the equipment and the experts, rejected our secret interventions. Several attempts to sabotage the reactor's equip-ment, carried out on French soil before its shipment, were attributed by the French press to the Israeli Mossad; but they only delayed by a few months the completion of the reactor.

Finally, Begin sent our air force to Bagdad. Six F-16 jets roared low over the Red Sea port of Eilat, flew over Jordan and Saudi Arabia, sneaked into Iraqi airspace, and dived over the Osiraq nuclear plant. In

a bombing raid that lasted eighty seconds, they destroyed it completely
and returned to base unscathed.

The nation responded enthusiastically to the operation. Rabin made
a statement congratulating the air force for the flawless execution; as for
the political implications, he said, we'd be free to discuss them after the
elections. That was a sensible view, hailed as such by public opinion.
Rabin had made an amazing recovery in the four years since he had
stepped down as prime minister after the bank account scandal. His
comeback resulted, in part, from his cool, nonpartisan attitude toward
divisive issues, like the Bagdad raid.

Peres's reaction, however, was totally different. He called together a
few of his closest aides and published a communiqué harshly condemning
the Bagdad bombing. We soon learned that Begin had hinted to Peres
beforehand that such an operation was being envisaged; Peres had responded by a secret letter warning Begin that the entire world would rise
against Israel, and it would be banned by the international community.
"We shall be left isolated and lonely as a dry tree in the desert," Peres
wrote poetically.

Peres's prediction turned out to be erroneous. The world reacted very
mildly to Israel's operation; many didn't conceal their relief that Iraq's
ruthless leaders were denied the possession of an atomic bomb. An English newspaper revealed that King Hussein of Jordan, sailing in his yacht
in the Red Sea, had spotted the Israeli planes flying over his kingdom,
and in spite of his guess as to where they were heading, he had abstained
from alerting his Arab brethren.

The next several years, and the bloody Iran-Iraq war with its chemical
warfare orgy, were to prove Israel right. In destroying Osiraq, Israel had
probably spared the world a nuclear conflagration with atrocious consequences.

But Peres's condemnation of the raid also had an immediate bearing
upon the electoral campaign in Israel. At many campaign rallies I spoke
my mind, qualifying the Bagdad raid as an act of self-preservation. I
thought and said that Israel had not only the right, but also the duty to
destroy the Iraqi reactor. People would cheer, but then they would add:
"Bar-Zohar, you're all right, but 'your' Peres doesn't think like you. He
wanted the Iraqis to have their damn bomb!"

All the subsequent polls unanimously agreed that Peres's statement caused a large part of the floating vote to shift toward the Likud camp. Not the raid, but the Alignment's reaction to it, tipped the scales in favor of the Likud.

Peres's statement was regarded as a jealous reaction of a frustrated politician. People were convinced that if Ben-Gurion had been in power he would have ordered the raid himself. But Ben-Gurion was dead; so were Golda Meir and Yigal Allon. Moshe Dayan had tried to return to the Labor Party, but the Labor Party didn't want him. He was to be reelected to the Knesset at the head of a tiny party and die of a heart attack soon after his inauguration.

The disappearance of Ben-Gurion, Golda, Allon, and Dayan from the Labor front lines sped up the apparent leftward drift of the party. In Israel, "left" and "right" have little to do with attitudes toward social and economic issues; the terms are used to define a person's or a party's attitude toward the Arab question in general and the Palestinian problem in particular. The more dovish you are, the more leftist you become; the rightists, of course, are the fiercest hawks. The "leftists" are the supporters of far-reaching concessions, a dialogue with the PLO, and a Palestinian state; the "rightists" are the annexionists who believe in Greater Israel and refuse to give up a single inch of land.

Ben-Gurion and his peers hadn't been right-wingers, far from that. But they knew that Israel couldn't ever be governed either from the extreme left or from the extreme right. They navigated the Labor movement so that it would always be identified with the mainstream of the nation and be the rallying force for everybody who didn't identify with right-wing annexionism or left-wing defeatism.

That image of the Labor movement changed under Rabin and Peres, but not because their views were very different from those of their predecessors; actually they keep clinging to the same political platform since 1974. But being weaker, as well as more open-minded, they didn't rule the party with the same iron fist that Ben-Gurion and Golda Meir did; they let *glasnost* spread into our ranks, until nobody was sure anymore what the party really stood for.

Peres and Rabin were unable to impose their authority on Labor leaders, who openly criticized the party's official positions. They didn't even try correcting the wrong impression given by dissenting statements,

fearing to alienate the men who made them. Therefore, "leftist" statements soon began to rain down from Labor headquarters. And the media
loved it.

The press naturally preferred sensational declarations about a Palestinian state, total withdrawal, or talking to Arafat to the trite repetition
of the old party formulas on the Allon plan and territorial compromise.
Every day a new declaration exploded in the front-page headlines. Thus,
the overall image of the Labor Party changed rapidly, and the public saw
it moving away from the center, away from the midstream.

One of the men who contributed to this apparent metamorphosis of
the Labor movement was Knesset member Yossi Sarid. A man of great
moral probity, a bold left-wing activist, and an excellent orator and
writer, young Sarid outshone most of his colleagues within and without
the Knesset. Gaunt, balding, his nearsighted eyes blazing from a sardonic
face, Sarid could unleash a biting tongue and flaunt a merciless wit. A
darling of the press, he kept broadcasting his opinions, which were far
from reflecting the Labor positions.

Many young Labor activists saw in Sarid their natural leader. On the
other hand, quite a few party figures, worried by the popular reactions,
strongly protested against his dangerous game. But neither Peres nor
Rabin dared to refute Sarid or call him to order.

On the contrary: Sarid was appointed one of the party spokesmen,
including director of information in three consecutive election campaigns. His appointment by itself was enough to alienate from Labor a
great number of its more hawkish supporters; and his name by itself was
enough for the Likud to proclaim that the once patriotic Labor Party
had turned into a hothouse of PLO supporters and propagandists.

I was a good friend of Sarid, but I couldn't accept the absurd situation
he had created inside the Labor Party. At a meeting of the party bureau
I asked him to resign from his position as our spokesman. "You can't go
on like that, Yossi," I said to him. "In the morning you give an interview
in your own name, and you explain why we should negotiate with the
PLO. In the afternoon you speak to the same reporters in the name of
the party, and you explain why we shouldn't negotiate with the PLO.
It's preposterous."

Some members of the bureau sided with me, while Sarid's supporters
labeled me a "Bolshevik" for trying to remove him from his job. The
only one who listened throughout the whole debate without batting an

eyelash was Peres. It goes without saying that he refrained from any action, and Sarid remained in his position.

Peres didn't understand that the change in the image of Labor was causing it terrible harm—that we were losing our position as the party of the center, and that by failing to set the record straight we were abandoning power to the Likud. Nothing I said to him on that subject could make him change his mind.

Against that backdrop came his statement about the Iraqi reactor as another prize for the Likud campaign chiefs, who once again could accuse Labor of embracing the Arab view.

The war of words following the destruction of Osiraq marked the turning point of the campaign. Mainly because of Peres's statement, we began the downhill slide.

Another reason for our defeat was our failure to attract Sephardic voters.

One night in mid-May I got a phone call from Shimon Peres. He sounded worried. "Michael," he said, "I am calling a meeting for to-morrow morning with the representatives of the Sephardic Jews in the party. I am inviting a couple of men from each community."

"What's the matter, Shimon?"

"The polls say we are losing the Sephardis," he said. "They are switch-ing to the Likud. Tomorrow then, at headquarters. Seven A.M."

It was a strange meeting. Men and women from most of the Sephardic communities were gathered in the rectangular hall: Moroccans, Tuni-sians, Iraqis, Libyans, Turks, Greeks, Yemenites. Former Health Minister Victor Shemtov and I represented the Bulgarian Jews.

Peres went straight to the heart of the matter. "The Sephardis are deserting us," he said morosely, sipping his black coffee. "We must do something. I'd like to hear your opinions."

I only half listened to the flowery speeches of my friends. There was nothing new in most of them, and what was old was bad. "Labor is the real home of the Sephardis . . . Begin hates Sephardis . . . Socialism means progress for us . . ." Most of the speakers carefully avoided men-tioning the frustration and anger many Oriental Jews felt toward Labor.

I was shaken out of my torpor when Hanania Dahan started to speak. A Moroccan of about fifty-five with thick, curly hair and very fair skin, he was the secretary of our party branch in Bat Yam. "There is something about the Oriental Jews that I must teach you, Shimon," he said. His tone was nonaggressive, matter of fact. "You see, at the place where you Ashkenazis have a heart"—his hand fluttered over his chest—"we have those wonderful musical strings." His fingers descended from his shoulder, suggesting the long strings. "And he who knows how to play those strings can make wonderful music."

He paused. "Begin knows how to play our strings, Shimon. He knows how to make those beautiful melodies."

Peres seemed angry. "Nonsense," he snapped. "The Sephardic Jews are intelligent, and logical . . ."

Hanania smiled. "Of course we are intelligent," he said, "no less intelligent than you. But we are also very emotional, Shimon. We listen to our hearts, to our feelings. You must learn how to play the music."

Shimon Peres brushed him off and turned to the next speaker. I leaned back in my chair. Hanania was right, I thought. We didn't know how to play the music.

We didn't know how to adapt to a changing Israel, different from the one our historical leaders had shaped. Work, hard work had been a symbol and a superior value in Israel's past. The goal of our movement had always been to make the Jewish people a working and productive nation. When Ben-Gurion toured the country he would always include in his schedule a visit to a plant, factory, or farm; he would spot a dirty, sweating worker in crumpled coveralls and have his picture taken with him, to emphasize his respect for the man's way of making a living.

In the Israel of 1981 hard manual labor was not appreciated anymore. People wanted to live an easier, comfortable life; people wanted well-paying jobs. In Labor's Israel, playing the stock market was a shameful activity; in the Likud's new society, the stock exchange was another way of making easy money. We had been taught that pioneering, settlement, industry, science, and education were the guarantees of our future; but all we heard now was publicity about banks, investments, stock, and percentages. New banks were emerging like mushrooms at every street corner. Huge ads, looming over the highways, proclaimed that the banks were "the nation's oxygen."

Modesty in behavior and in dress, as it had been practiced by Labor leaders in the past, had also given way to a flashier life. Instead of Ben-Gurion's open collars, Golda's plain dresses, and Dayan's sandals, we saw Likud ministers strutting like peacocks in tailor-made suits. The newspapers were filled with ads to buy refrigerators "like in America," stereos "like in America," televisions and microwaves "like in America." The Zionist vision was being steadily replaced by the American dream.

The *Yordim*—emigrants who had left Israel in search of an easier life overseas—had been ostracized in the past and labeled deserters, even traitors to the Zionist ideal. People who were leaving the country permanently used to make up cover stories about "studies," "sabbaticals," a sick aunt, or other excuses to hide their shame and embarrassment. Rabin had even nicknamed the *Yordim* "fallout of weaklings."

But by 1981 there was no shame in leaving the country to settle abroad, especially if you were making money in the process. The papers were full of stories about Israelis who had made it in Frankfurt, New York, or Los Angeles. Some of them were coming to visit us, donating to charities, universities, and hospitals, and Israel welcomed them with admiration and warmth. Another pillar of our social and moral edifice had crumbled.

In the past, Israel was a much more uniform society, based on a rather rigid scale of values. The pioneers, farmers, army officers, and kibbutz members were considered to be the elite of the society. This elite was emulated and admired by the younger generation, even by those who had chosen a different way of life. In the new Israeli society that elite had been swept away, and nothing had replaced it. Israel had turned into a nation without an elite. The younger Israelis had nothing to look up to; social and moral values were being replaced by materialistic aspirations and by a phony American dream.

But we were not America. We were still at the dawn of our independence and had to cope with tremendous security problems, the absorption of immigrants, the building of an economy, the establishment of a new society.

Yet many Israelis of the eighties didn't want to know. They were dreaming of a better life while Labor was speaking to them about "a just and equal society"; they wanted more lucrative jobs while we encouraged them to work in factories; they resented the Histadrut's socialist ideology, the Histadrut's maddening bureaucracy, and the Histadrut's ailing health-care system; the "Ashkenazi" kibbutzim; the Arabs; the establishment. And we were identified with all of those. Four years after being ousted from power, we were still viewed as the old, rusty establishment.

In public meetings, young people would yell at us: "You've been ruining the country for thirty years, let the Likud rebuild it now!" Or: "Labor made four wars, Begin made one peace!"

We still had, of course, our traditional electorate. But the people who still adhered to our ideals were getting old and steadily passing away. And the younger generation, the first-time voters, was more and more attracted to the right. As one of my friends put it one day: "Every time I see an ambulance speeding through the streets of Tel Aviv, sirens blaring and lights flashing, I know that either a Labor voter has died or a Likud voter has been born."

On July 20, 1981, the Tenth Knesset was sworn in. Begin, whose Likud bloc had won forty-eight of 120 seats, formed a coalition and became prime minister again. The Alignment had won forty-seven seats. We had recovered fifteen of the nineteen seats we had lost in 1977.

It could have been a great comeback. Had we won only a couple more seats, we would have formed the government and immediately launched a peace initiative. Begin, committed to the idea of a Greater Israel, couldn't offer Hussein and the Palestinians any territorial compromise. We could have. Had we won, the history of the Arab-Israeli conflict might have taken a different turn.

But we had lost, the Likud remained in power, and all hopes for peace evaporated in one single night.

I had been elected in Tel Aviv and became a member of the Knesset.

Peres signed an alliance with Ms. Shulamit Aloni, the leader and only Knesset member of the Movement for Civil Rights, so that our parliamentary group would be equal to that of the Likud.

We were in for four years of opposition.

Chapter 8

After the Battle, a Soldier Cried

My first year at the Knesset started with an outburst of violence on the Lebanese border, in July 1981. It was the classic vicious circle: terrorist raids in our territory across the northern frontier, Israeli retaliation by heavy air strikes on PLO bases throughout Lebanon, then murderous shelling of Galilee by PLO cannon and Katiusha rocket launchers positioned in South Lebanon. The Israeli cannon fired back, but were unable to silence the enemy artillery. The PLO kept their batteries concealed in ravines, orchards, or backyards; the rocket launchers were often moved to new positions aboard their Soviet carriers.

I joined two other Knesset members from the Labor Party, General Motta Gur and Safed Mayor Aharon Nahmias, on a tour of Galilee. It was under heavy fire. We visited the border city of Kiryat Shemona, which looked like a ghost town, with most of the population holed up in shelters. The resort city of Nahariya had also been hit, as were Metula, Hazor, Shelomi, and several kibbutzim and villages in the PLO cannon range. We found out that more than twelve hundred shells had been fired by the PLO on civilian targets in the last few days; our losses were six dead and fifty-nine wounded.

After a few days of sporadic artillery duels, Ambassador Philip Habib, President Ronald Reagan's special envoy to the Middle East, arrived in Israel. A professional diplomat and a talented negotiator, Habib commuted between Jerusalem and Beirut, and finally arranged a cease-fire. The cease-fire came into effect at the end of July, along the entire Lebanese border.

The absurd aspect of that cease-fire was that Lebanon had nothing to do with it. The Lebanese government had long ago lost any power over large portions of its territory, which had become a PLO pirate state. Other parts of the country, including a large section of Beirut, were occupied by the Syrian army. Although Begin cautiously evaded the embarrassing question, it was clear that for the first time in our history we had agreed to a cease-fire with the PLO. That cease-fire already carried the seeds of the tragic Lebanon War, which was to erupt in less than a year.

Two months after the Galilee had calmed down, President Sadat was assassinated in Egypt by religious fanatics. Sadat's death caused concern in Israel, but we soon found out that his successor, Hosni Mubarak, was determined to respect the peace treaty between our countries. He didn't budge when Begin, taking advantage of a world crisis focused on Poland, annexed the Golan plateau in a lightning move. Mubarak kept all his commitments before and after the Sinai Peninsula was handed back to Egypt on April 28, 1982.

That day I was in Cairo, on my first visit to Egypt since the Camp David accords. It was a strange feeling for me, who had taken part in three wars with Egypt, to set foot on Egyptian soil without my uniform and my weapons, and be so warmly welcomed by a friendly nation. After talking with the Egyptians in the streets, markets, and outdoor cafes, I became convinced that, like us, they sincerely wanted peace.

On my first night in Egypt, while all of Cairo was celebrating the return of Sinai, I decided to visit Sadat's grave. After all, he had been the architect of the peace treaty; to him the Egyptians owed the recovery of their lost lands.

Sadat's majestic tomb, built in the form of a pyramid a few hundred yards from the spot where he had been murdered, was guarded by four army officers in parade uniform. As I stood facing them I suddenly realized that I was completely alone. On that night, which in Egypt's history should forever remain the night of Anwar el-Sadat, no Egyptian had deemed it proper to pay him homage, only a member of the Israeli Knesset.

On impulse, I asked my driver to take me to Nasser's tomb. When we reached the tomb of Sadat's predecessor—the man responsible for so many of Egypt's failures, for the futile wars, for the deaths of tens of thousands in the Sinai battlefields—we found the place brightly illuminated, swarming with throngs of people. Nasser was still cherished and beloved by his nation in spite of his tragic errors. Sadat, so deeply admired throughout the world, apparently had never won the affection of his people.

The next day I met with a group of Egyptians who spoke with great warmth of their current president, Hosni Mubarak. "He is a wonderful man," they said to me. "A great leader, an honest man, a brave soldier."

"Like Nasser," one of them said, and the others echoed his words. "Like Nasser!" they repeated.

Six weeks after withdrawing from Sinai, we invaded Lebanon.

In the late evening of June 3, 1982, the Israeli ambassador in London, Shlomo Argov, walked out of the Dorchester Hotel and stepped toward his waiting car. At that moment four Palestinian gunmen converged on him and opened fire. They were armed with miniature Polish-made submachine guns. The ambassador collapsed, hit in the temple, and was rushed to the hospital in critical condition. One of the terrorists was wounded and captured by the British police. The other assassins escaped, but were apprehended a few days later.

I heard about the assassination attempt from a news broadcast the following morning. It was not the first of its kind; two months before, an Israeli diplomat, Yaakov Bar-Simantov, had been assassinated in Paris by Palestinian terrorists. Such despicable acts justified a retaliation, I thought; but I feared the Argov affair would turn into a pretext for Prime Minister Begin to trigger a military operation against the PLO bases in Lebanon. For months many of my colleagues and I had been aware that Begin's government was on the warpath, looking for an excuse to invade Lebanon.

I thought a war would be disastrous. As soon as I heard the news about Argov, I dispatched a telegram to the prime minister. "The murder attempts against Israeli diplomats abroad," I wrote, "call for a proper Israeli response. This response should be entrusted to the Israeli secret services. In the seventies, when Black September launched a bloody terrorist campaign, the organization's leaders were eliminated one by one, until Black September ceased to exist." I urged Begin to send out our secret agents to find and punish the perpetrators. But knowing what he really wanted, I asked him not to bomb or attack terrorist bases in Lebanon. "That's not the proper response," I concluded.

While I was writing my telegram, the Israeli air force was already getting ready for a massive air strike against the PLO in Lebanon. Begin, of course, wasn't at all interested in the "proper response." His advisers had already informed him that Argov's assassins belonged to the Abu Nidal splinter group, which, ironically, was the PLO's vilest enemy inside the Palestinian community. But Begin didn't want to hear about Abu Nidal. What he wanted was to start a war against the PLO in Lebanon.

At an emergency cabinet meeting that morning, he obtained the ministers' approval to bomb several PLO targets in Beirut. He knew, as we all did, that the PLO would inevitably react to the air raids by a massive shelling of Galilee, the northern portion of Israel; the shelling would come from the "Fatahland," that strip in South Lebanon that was completely under Palestinian control. Following the shelling, Begin intended to ask his government to authorize a military operation in Lebanon aimed at destroying the terrorists' artillery. It was the kind of request they couldn't refuse.

This was exactly what happened. The Israelis bombed; the PLO bombarded in return; and on Saturday night, June 5, the government approved the invasion of Lebanon. The next morning Israel was at war.

When Prime Minister Begin addressed the Knesset on June 8, 1982, our army had already thrust deep into Lebanon. The operation, Begin said, was intended to free the inhabitants of Galilee from the PLO threat. Therefore it was named Peace for Galilee.

In his theatrical style which I intensely disliked, he announced: "If a two-legged animal [meaning the PLO terrorists] would raise its hand against our children, that arm would be cut off." Defining the goals of the operation, he stressed that the army would advance only up to forty kilometers [twenty-five miles], which was the maximum range of the PLO artillery. "As soon as we reach the forty-kilometer line, the fighting will stop." Begin also turned to President Assad of Syria, whose army occupied some portions of Lebanon, and asked him not to intervene in the fighting. "No Syrian soldier will be hurt," Begin promised.

At the subsequent vote, the Labor Party supported the government. I raised my hand, along with my friends. True, I had objected to the bombing of Beirut that had triggered the current crisis, but once the shelling of Galilee had started I agreed to an operation of a purely defensive nature and limited goals.

I recalled a former operation in Lebanon that had taken place in March 1978. It had been launched by Menachem Begin after a gory act of terrorism inside Israel. PLO terrorists had landed on a beach not far from Caesarea, and after a spree of random killing, had hijacked a bus and ordered the driver to head toward Tel Aviv. When they ran into an army and police roadblock, the terrorists had savagely assassinated thirty-five of the hostages.

Following that massacre, Begin had ordered an operation in Fatahland. Chief of Staff Motta Gur had carried out a restricted strike, called Operation Litani, after the Lebanese river that had been designed as the limit of our thrust. Our units penetrated into Lebanon and attacked the PLO bases; under the explicit orders of Defense Minister Ezer Weizmann, they refrained from entering the Lebanese cities. I had been called in, shortly after the fighting started, to write an account of the paratroopers' part in Operation Litani. I remember our jeep emerging on the crest of a hill overlooking the white city of Tyre and being stopped by our forward outposts. We drove throughout the area occupied by the army and retreated with it after a few days.

Now, on June 8, 1982, it looked as if Begin was launching an expanded version of Operation Litani. Members of the prime minister's entourage told us that the fighting would last no more than seventy-two hours; Begin wanted to limit our losses to the minimum, they added, and he estimated that in the operation we would incur no more than thirty or forty casualties.

But there were also rumors that Begin had a covert, far more ambitious plan: an army officer reminded me of the secret alliance between Israel and the Lebanese Christians that had been established in 1976. We supplied weapons and assistance to the Phalanges, the Christian military organization. For years the Phalangists had been engaged in bitter fighting against the PLO and some extremist Muslim factions. We even trained Phalangist units in secluded bases in Israel; Israeli senior officers secretly visited the Christian strongholds and met with their leaders. Perhaps the present operation, my friend said, was being coordinated with the Phalanges and had goals other than those outlined by Begin. I should have listened to him.

I should have recalled that the present Begin government was the most unbalanced, reckless government Israel had ever had. It was totally different from the first Begin government established in 1977.

I should have remembered that Operation Litani, four years ago, had been carried out by a government in which tough extremists were balanced by moderate, cautious leaders who also had a real understanding of military matters: Deputy Prime Minister Yadin, Foreign Minister Dayan, and Defense Minister Weizmann. Then Chief of Staff Motta Gur was a coolheaded officer.

Today Dayan, Yadin, Weizmann, and Gur were gone, and there was nobody in the new Likud government to contain the extremists. Begin regarded Arafat and the PLO as the direct successors of Adolf Hitler and the Nazis; he could easily get carried away with the prospect of going to Beirut and "smoking Arafat out of his bunker," which some of his aides flashed before his eyes.

The foreign minister, Itzhak Shamir, was the most hawkish Israeli who ever occupied that position; instead of restraining his bellicose colleagues, as any foreign minister should, he enthusiastically joined them. The new ambassador to Washington, Moshe Arens, in spite of his low-key and soft-spoken attitude, was as hawkish as Shamir. The Chief of Staff, General Raphael Eitan, held even more extremist views than his civilian leaders. He had become notorious for saying that the Arabs behaved like "doped cockroaches stuffed in a bottle."

And the most dangerous of them all was the new defense minister, Ariel (Arik) Sharon.

I had first met Arik Sharon when he was still a handsome young rebel with unruly hair and a brilliant, unorthodox mind. Sharon was a hero. He was one of the most courageous and unconventional soldiers I've ever known. In the early fifties, along with Moshe Dayan, Arik had transformed the Israeli army from a weary, conservative organization into an aggressive, original military machine. He had created the legendary commando unit 101 that carried out daring raids across the border; he later made the entire paratrooper corps into an invincible elite outfit and led it through the reprisal raids and the Sinai campaign.

A born leader and a charismatic fighter, Arik reached the peak of his glory in the Yom Kippur War, when he planned and commanded the crossing of the Suez Canal. I had spent the days before the crossing in Arik's command post at Tassa, in the Sinai, and left him only to join the paratrooper unit that carried out the operation. I knew that without

Arik's perseverance we might never have made it and that this was the turning point of the war. When he joined us after we had established the bridgehead, the troops roared: "Arik, King of Israel!" I know that if ever the army of Israel goes to war again, I'd ask to fight under Sharon.

But only under Sharon in uniform. This excellent soldier is a poor statesman. He doesn't understand international realities and holds the dangerous belief that he can change any political situation with military might. I remember a heated discussion we had on October 24, 1973, the last day of the Yom Kippur War. That day he had given me a lift in his jeep to the Fayid air base, on the African side of the canal. He wanted me to stay, to participate in the next stage of the war, when we, the paratroopers, would strike at Cairo. The plans were ready, he said, his eyes gleaming.

I tried—and failed—to convince him that once the Soviet Union and the United States had reached an agreement the war was over. "No," he stubbornly repeated, "we are going to Cairo. You'll miss that, Michael. Our greatest operation ever. I don't care about the Russians and the Americans. You don't understand."

"Arik," I said. "You're a general and I'm only a sergeant. But it is you who don't understand."

There was, however, something far worse in Sharon's character. He was driven by intense personal ambition and would stop at nothing. With the same doggedness he employed to plan and execute his military operations, he would concoct political intrigues, mislead and deceive both friends and rivals. He is a scheming, untrustworthy politician. In Ben-Gurion's diary, I found the following entry about Sharon: "He is original and intelligent. If he could only cure himself of his defects like gossiping and not speaking the truth, he might be an excellent military leader."

But Sharon hadn't cured himself. Menachem Begin knew that; in spite of heavy pressures in the past, he had refrained from appointing Sharon defense minister. After Weizmann's resignation Begin had assumed the Defense portfolio himself in order to keep Sharon away from it.

But after the 1981 election he gave in. Sharon had been the Likud campaign manager and had brought Begin the greatest victory ever. Sharon was also the most qualified of all the cabinet members for the office of defense minister. Besides, Begin had become much more confident after signing the peace treaty with Egypt. The treaty, he felt, had proved that he understood politics better than Dayan and Weizmann. He also thought he could control Sharon.

This was an egregious error that we were to pay for with blood. And as in Greek tragedy, as soon as the power of peace and war was placed in Sharon's hands, Israel moved toward inevitable disaster.

After Begin's speech at the Knesset, I went home and unearthed my uniform and paratrooper boots. The people of Israel were going to war, I thought, and my place, as a people's representative, was with the troops. I had voted for this operation, therefore I should take part in it. I called my unit's liaison office, but their answer was unequivocal: they had explicit instructions not to recruit any Knesset members. Similar orders, they said, had been relayed to all the roadblocks at the Lebanese border: they were to prevent Knesset members from entering the fighting zone, lest they be harmed or captured.

I decided to get into Lebanon by my own means. The following morning I crossed the border in the jeep of a friend, *Maariv* reporter Yigal Lev. The sentries barely spared a glance for the reservist in the shabby fatigues, sprawled on the back seat. Once inside Lebanon, I left Yigal and hitchhiked toward the front lines. Somewhere near Sidon I got myself an automatic rifle and proceeded north aboard an open jeep. In one village, young girls and old men cheered us, and threw rice and flowers on the jeep. We gathered speed on the open road. Twenty-five miles, Begin had said in the Knesset, but as the jeep sped on the Beirut highway I had the uneasy feeling that we had crossed that limit long ago.

The road wound through a pleasant, opulent suburb. Two young men in freshly pressed Phalangist uniforms came out of a broken shop window topped with a sign reading *Modes Parisiennes*. Their tapered green tunics fit their lean bodies snugly. They waved at the jeep, and one of them proudly hooked his thumbs in his leather belt.

"Look at them, posing like models for safari suits," the driver said spitefully. He was a big, burly Moroccan with a fierce mustache and a slight French accent. "Haven't seen one of the bastards pull a trigger, ever. Their uniforms might get dirty."

A few hundred yards to the north there was a sharp bend in the road between two rows of ugly gray buildings. The jeep screeched to a stop behind a long column of Zelda-type personnel armored carriers, trucks, command cars, and a civilian Peugeot with Israeli rental plates. A military ambulance screamed past us, its left wheels up on the sidewalk.

I jumped out of the jeep and ran along the column. The smell of smoke, burning tires, and gunpowder hit me in a blast; a dark gray mass hovered at the end of the road, trembling in the light breeze. A quick succession of thundering explosions reverberated in the narrow street. I recognized the dry discharges of a Merkava 105mm gun.

The access to the square was blocked by three armored carriers. The crews were in full gear, wearing combat helmets and flak jackets. "What's going on there?" I asked, nodding toward the square.

"The paratroopers are mopping up the place," a young sergeant major informed me from the slanted deck of a Zelda. "Lots of Fatahs still holing up all over."

He took off his helmet and mopped his brow. "You can never tell where the sonofabitches might be hiding. They've been shelling us all night from a hospital." He pointed east. "Hauled their rocket launchers on the roof. Didn't give a damn about the patients. Their own bloody people."

"What did you do?" I asked.

The soldier shrugged. "I don't know, we had to move in the morning. When we left, they were still firing their Katiusha rockets all over the place. I think we should send in the air force, if you ask me."

I turned toward the square.

"Beware of the kids!" the sergeant major's voice thundered behind me, and I paused, puzzled. What did he mean by that? But I was already deep into it all, back amidst the familiar sights and sounds and smells of war. To us Israelis, war is an ever-present reality; once every few years we smell, hear, and see it again. It is like a sudden glimpse into our past, a backward voyage by a time machine. It is a reunion that we both enjoy and abhor; it is like meeting an old and beloved friend, and reaching for him, only to find out that he's dead. War for us is a nostalgic reminder of our reckless youth, of an all-consuming devotion to our country, of deep, sincere comradeship; and a painful confrontation with forgotten horrors, the haunting faces and the bloodied bodies of our dead comrades. And enemies.

The nearest edge of the square was full of troop carriers and tanks. A few soldiers squatted behind a tank, devouring ripe cherries piled high on a crumpled newspaper. Beside them two bearded soldiers in talliths were silently praying, rocking back and forth. A Zelda was burning and spewing a dense column of thick black smoke. Across the square, soldiers were running along the houses, communicating in short, crisp calls. The submachine fire sounded like the patter of children's popguns.

Stray bullets buzzed over my head like angry wasps. I heard a soft voice close behind me and turned around. A Lebanese girl, probably a Christian, watched me from an open window. She was wearing a white silk blouse and coquettishly patted her long black hair. She called out "Bonjour!" with a smile. Her lips were red and moist.

A gust of wind dispersed a patch of fluffy gray smoke and I saw, on the far side of the square, a huge crowd of civilians. Soldiers in combat gear were herding them toward the beach, away from the fighting. From the window behind me came a blast of music. The girl had put on a Pink Floyd record or turned on Radio Monte Carlo from Beirut. The situation was so absurd I could have been in a Fellini movie. The columns of smoke, the soldiers feasting on the red cherries, the civilians fleeing toward the palm-shaded beach, the deadly shooting of the paratroopers across the square, and the carefree laughter of the girl at the window all fused into a bizarre tableau.

I walked between the Zeldas toward the center of the square and emerged into an open space. All of a sudden I was alone, facing a tall yellow building.

"Get back!" somebody yelled at me. "Get back, sucker!" A skinny guy in an oversized uniform leapt toward me and tugged my sleeve. "You're out of your mind, or what?"

I followed the soldier's stare toward the upper floor of the yellow house. As we both dived for cover behind a Zelda, I caught a glimpse of a sturdy machine gun protruding from a heap of sandbags on one of the balconies. A burst of bullets hit the ground not far from where I had been standing.

"Bar-Zohar? Are you Michael Bar-Zohar? The Knesset member?"

I got up on my feet and turned around, dusting off my knees. An armored corps lieutenant stood before me, dressed in stained fireproof coveralls. He was young, with the smooth face of a teenager. He had candid blue eyes and a freckled nose. A typical kibbutz kid.

"I saw you on television once," the officer said. His voice was hoarse, unsteady. "You spoke about the moral values of the Israeli soldier. About waging a clean war, remember? You said we should spare civilians, and protect women and children, didn't you?"

As he spoke, angry spots flared in his cheeks. He reached over and grabbed my arm, pulling me around. "Look!" he said, jerking his head toward the yellow building. "Look at this house!"

"What about it?" I felt the tremor of the youth's fingers on my skin.

"The third, fourth, and sixth floors are full of civilians. Old people, women, lots of children. They're hiding under the beds, behind cupboards." The lieutenant stuck his field glasses into my hand. "See for yourself."

"I believe you," I said.

"The terrorists are on the fifth floor. They have a Gurionov machine gun. Two bazookas, lots of Kalashnikovs." The lieutenant was feverishly rattling off his information.

"What I want to know is . . ." The lieutenant paused, biting his lower lip. "Those bastards up there killed two of my men, wounded five. What I want to know is"—his eyes challenged me with a desperate look—"do I have the moral right to fire back and blast the hell out of them?"

"Why . . ." I started. My throat was suddenly dry.

"I'll tell you why," the lieutenant shouted. "Because when I order my tanks to fire back, we'll kill all those Fatah sonofabitches and at the same time we'll blow to pieces all the old men and the little girls on the other floors, that's why. And the next time you're on television you'll call us murderers and baby killers, that's why. And . . ." He abruptly fell silent and stood staring at me, his nails digging in my arm.

I felt as if a sudden quiet had descended on the large square, and all those boys, the living and the wounded and the dead, the army of Israel, the nation's pride and glory, were waiting for my verdict. Damn this war, I suddenly thought, damn those who brought us to Sidon and to Tyre and to Nabatiyeh. And I knew that the army of Israel would never be the same again, and its arms never pure again.

"You are a soldier, aren't you?" I muttered, defeated, and took a deep breath. "So go tell your men to fire and blow the bloody bastards to pieces."

I pulled my arm free from the lieutenant's grip and trudged away, toward the thick mass of smoke that hovered over the beach. After a minute—or maybe it took longer—I heard the roar of the tank cannon behind my back.

*   *   *

The thundering blasts of the heavy cannon still rang in my ears when I returned to the square later in the day. The sun was about to set. The battle was over and the square was empty, strewn with the sordid refuse of war. Dense smoke hovered over the Ein Hilwe Palestinian camp; the surviving terrorists had gathered for a final stand in the underground bunkers dug under the refugee shacks. A couple of Kfir aircraft were repeatedly diving over the camp, strafing the Fatah stronghold.

As I reached the square, I briefly glanced at the gutted walls of the yellow building, then looked away. Perhaps I was again running away from the young lieutenant and his men; and probably from my own conscience as well. The lieutenant had been right, and I had found no words to relieve his plight. That's how we raised our kids, I thought, generation after generation, turning war into a symbol of valor and morality. Israel fights only defensive wars, we told them, only wars of survival. Israel never harms noncombatants, never shoots at civilians. Our arms are pure, for they are used only for defense.

What kind of defensive war was this one, invading Lebanon with the largest army we ever assembled, to hunt a few thousand badly trained, badly organized terrorists? What kind of survival instinct was driving us northward, away from our border, toward the green hills of Beirut? How could those boys, trained to fight tanks and commandos, avoid harming noncombatants, when the terrorists were entrenched in the very midst of the civilian population, firing at us from hospitals and schools and apartment buildings? And to smoke out one Fatah you risked killing a score of innocent Lebanese or Palestinians. Never before had we carried the war inside the cities, never before had we bombarded apartment houses with cannon fire.

Didn't Begin and Sharon realize they broke our Covenant? The Ten Commandments of the army? Didn't they understand that when our army crossed the frontier between Israel and Lebanon it also crossed the border between a just war and a ruthless military adventure? Our kids were the real casualties of the war. All those candid, patriotic Israeli boys had become the real victims of the Merkava cannon that blasted the yellow house to smithereens.

Now, as I walked through the square, I saw the immobile figure of a soldier sitting on a white stone, his helmet lying on his knees. He was a grizzly reservist in his early forties. His angular face was covered with a caked layer of dust and sweat. His mouth was tightly clamped, and his eyes were red. Tears slowly ran down his cheeks, leaving clear patterns in the bristled skin.

I approached him. "Why do you cry?" I asked.

The man took a long time before answering. He scooped a handful of stones from the ground and aimlessly threw them away, one by one.

"There was this terrorist," he said softly. "He came out of the ruins this morning with a Kalashnikov. He killed my best friend, right beside me."

"Well, that's war," I said. "It happens all the time."

The man wasn't listening. "But I . . . I caught him!" he stammered. "I caught the killer. I held him in my hands!" He stretched his arms forward, his fists clenched.

"And?" I asked.

"It was a thirteen-year-old kid!" he suddenly shouted. "A thirteen-year-old child!" He paused. "I have a thirteen-year-old son. Back in Haifa. David, that's his name. David. And when I held this boy, this killer, in my arms"—he stretched his hands again and they trembled, fingers clawed, as if he held the small prisoner—"I thought I was holding my boy, my David." His lips quivered, and the tears flowed. "I never fought kids before!" he added bitterly.

"What did you do to him?" I asked.

The soldier was shaking his head. "I could have strangled the sonofabitch who made a killer out of that child."

"What did you do to the kid?" I repeated.

The man slowly raised his eyes and stared at me as if he were seeing me for the first time. "What could I do to him? Kill him? Spank him? He's a child. Back home, I never raised a finger against David."

I walked away. Beware of the kids, the sergeant major had warned me when I entered the war.

The soldier's tears haunted me without respite throughout the war. Even after I took off my uniform those tears would surface in my memory whenever I heard about the young terrorists. They were called the "R.P.G. kids" because of the weapon they commonly used, a rocket-propelled grenade.

I remembered the reservist's tears when I saw a couple of R.P.G. kids captured in the ghost city of Damur, where they had kept fighting their lost war long after their mentors had deserted them and fled into the hills; when I found out that the army had captured hundreds of Palestinian kids aged ten to fourteen, trained by the Fatah to use a Kalashnikov or an R.P.G. against the Zionists; when I read reports about the trucks filled with those little prisoners that we sent to the front-line roadblocks, to be delivered to the Syrian army.

"All through the war I kept seeing those kids in my nightmares," a friend of mine, a reserve officer, told me. "While fighting in Beirut and Bahamdun and the Bekaa, I secretly prayed to be spared an encounter with an R.P.G. kid in battle, for I knew I would hesitate just for a second—no more—and then shoot the little bastard dead."

Chapter 9

A Minute of Silence

"Express Tel Aviv–Beirut," some joker had sprayed in black paint on a truck that gave me a ride in Lebanon. I often thought, in the following days and months, of the anonymous author of that graffiti. "You in Jerusalem," he seemed to say, "can declare and vote and state whatever you want, but we, the simple soldiers, know very well where we are going. To Beirut!"

Indeed, one needed very little time with the army in Lebanon to understand that the entire nation, and the whole world, was being deceived. We were not going to Sidon, which was at the limit of the twenty-five miles. We were going to Beirut. Nor were we bound for the southern shores of the artificial Karun Lake. Our real objective was the Beirut-Damascus highway. We were not going to crush the PLO terrorists and go back home. We were off to join forces with the Christian Phalanges in the north. And rather than avoid a confrontation with the Syrian units inside Lebanon, we were determined to provoke them into a bloody showdown.

And if I didn't trust the graffiti, and the rumors, and the confidences whispered by some senior officers, I had only to look around me to learn the truth—when I left Sidon behind and moved north, far beyond the twenty-five-mile limit; when I crossed the Awali River, the lush palm groves and the green fields of Nebi Yunes; when I sneaked along the black, gutted houses in the raped town of Damur, which the terrorists had turned into an awesome fortress; when I joined a paratrooper convoy and climbed, huddled aboard a panting half-track, higher and higher on a sinuous mountain road between steep hills and dark ravines.

Until we saw from the crest of a jagged peak, lying at our feet, shuddering and burning and smoldering under our incessant bombardment, ours for the taking, the white city of Beirut.

"What are we doing here?" The soldier sitting next to me was a skinny Yemenite with a curly head and gleaming white teeth. "I heard the prime minister on the radio. He said we were not going to Beirut."

"So this isn't Beirut," another paratrooper chuckled.

Girls and old men were standing on both sides of the road, offering us flowers and handfuls of cherries.

"It's fun anyway," the Yemenite concluded.

A few days later, when the paratrooper brigade finally entered Beirut, my Yemenite friend turned on his transistor radio. Begin was speaking again. "I assure you," he was saying with great solemnity, "that we have no intention whatsoever of advancing to Beirut."

"Didn't they tell him?" the Yemenite wondered aloud. "Is it a secret?"

But then Begin went off the air, and the voice of a war reporter echoed in the tiny radio. "I am standing in the very center of Beirut. . . ."

The soldiers stared at each other in astonishment.

Astonishment, anger, and frustration were also spreading throughout the Knesset. A few days after my return to Jerusalem, I found out that those feelings were shared by several ministers. We all were being told lies—lies about the war goals, about the movements of our forces, about the change of plan. Our defense minister was deceiving the cabinet, the Knesset, the entire nation.

The government, we learned, was either being fed false information or asked to approve operations and plan changes after the fact. But since Begin stood like a rock by his defense minister, most of the other ministers approved Sharon's requests. Very soon it became clear that Israel was fighting a totally different war from the one it had set out to wage.

We started asking questions. At the Knesset. At army headquarters. We called Defense Ministry officials, senior officers, newspaper editors and reporters we knew, we traveled back to Lebanon to see for ourselves. And one after the other, the pieces of the puzzle started clicking into their slots, and we discovered Sharon's real scheme.

Sharon had concocted a naïve, yet ambitious plan based on raw force. He wanted to deal a mortal blow to the PLO, not only in South Lebanon, but all over the country. He intended to occupy Beirut and expel the

PLO terrorists. The Palestinians would be exiled to Jordan, which would become the Palestinian state; that would ease the international pressure on Israel to evacuate the West Bank and Gaza. In order to have a free hand in Lebanon, Sharon had to force the Syrian army to withdraw; therefore, he had to provoke it into combat and destroy it. Then he would hand the Lebanese presidency to his Christian ally, Phalange leader Bashir Gemayel, who would sign a peace treaty with Israel.

To carry out this plan, Sharon would have to conquer a large portion of Lebanon, including Beirut. The Israeli army would join forces with the Phalanges, whose stronghold was in the Christian enclave in the north. It also would occupy the eastern parts of Lebanon and dislodge the Syrian army, cutting off the Beirut-Damascus highway, to sever the link between Syria and its units in Beirut.

Toward those goals, Sharon had prepared an invasion plan, code-named Pines, that he presented to the government in December 1981. This was the first time an Israeli government was asked to wage a war aimed not at assuring Israel's survival, but at achieving political goals. In spite of Begin's support for the plan, several ministers revolted. Begin backed off and Sharon withdrew his plan.

Pines was shelved, or so Begin's ministers naïvely thought. In June 1982, when the invasion of Lebanon was decided upon, Begin's government was asked to approve of a new operational plan, Small Pines. That plan was limited to the famed twenty-five miles and defined by Begin in a letter to President Reagan. "We have no intention of advancing beyond the forty-kilometer line," Begin pledged.

The truth was, however, that Sharon didn't intend to adhere to Small Pines. He had decided to carry out his original operation, disguising it as a restricted invasion that had been approved by the government. That's how the big deception started. Every day of the war Sharon would appear before the government, ask for some operational modifications in the north or east, describe some new strategic necessities, report Syrian provocations that should be countered. And the gullible ministers would approve, failing to realize that they were actually authorizing, stage by stage, the execution of the full-scale Pines plan.

Gradually, the war grew in scope. In the west, the Israeli army occupied East Beirut, joined Bashir Gemayel's Phalanges, took the Shuff Mountains, and blocked the Beirut-Damascus highway. It besieged the encircled West Beirut, where regular Syrian units and about twenty thousand PLO terrorists under Arafat's command still resisted. In the east, it defeated the Syrian armor. At the same time the air force wiped out the Syrian surface-to-air missiles positioned in the Lebanon valley and shot down scores of Syrian aircraft.

But these victories had a price. Israeli losses grew day after day, soon reaching appalling numbers. This new kind of war, which we had never waged before, also caused many casualties among the civilian population. Many of us couldn't stand the sight of the artillery shellings and air bombings of Beirut. We knew our soldiers were doing their best to closely target the PLO strongholds, but we also knew that civilians were being killed in greater numbers than the terrorists who were protected by their underground bunkers and concrete shelters.

Nor could we agree with the siege of Beirut. In the sweltering summer heat, the army cut off the water, the power, and the food supply. We couldn't bear the thought that the civilian population was starving while the terrorists were living on their emergency supplies.

Out of Beirut, the Israeli units found themselves drawn into ancient blood feuds between Lebanese villages and communities; they had to face a reality of murderous hatred and constantly changing alliances between warring Christian factions, Druze and Palestinians, Shiite Muslims and Sunni Muslims. The Lebanese didn't welcome us with rice and flowers anymore; acts of terrorism against us spread throughout the occupied lands, carried out mostly by fundamentalist Shiites. Young soldiers and officers, fighting in the Shuff Mountains, in the Bekaa, and along the Beirut-Damascus highway, openly confronted their superiors, asking indignantly, "What are we doing here?"

Reserve officers who came to visit me in the Knesset spoke of the deception, illegal orders, and senseless deaths in Lebanon. A paratrooper reserve brigade refused to report for duty; a colonel resigned from his commission to avoid leading his soldiers into Beirut. I tried to remind the soldiers who came to me that they had to obey orders; I feared the disastrous results of a collapse in military discipline. But I couldn't ignore the fact that for the first time in our history, soldiers openly questioned their role in the fighting and criticized the government's decisions.

Speaking in the Knesset, I quoted the unofficial anthem of the Lebanon War. I had heard it while visiting our soldiers in the Shuff Mountains. It was a grim distortion of a children's song:

> *Little airplane, please come down,*
> *Take us to Lebanon.*
> *We'll fight for Sharon,*
> *And in a coffin we'll come home.*

"This is a war of choice," a Likud leader pompously declared, mocking the basic Israeli credo that we should fight only "wars of no choice," meaning of survival. The moral foundations of Israeli society were in jeopardy. The Likud accused the left wing of betrayal; Foreign Minister Shamir reacted to Labor's growing criticism, saying that "because of those people, our soldiers are dying in Lebanon." Deep hatred for the "left-wing traitors" and the "PLO lovers" swelled in the more backward and extremist segments of our society. This hatred was to claim its victim in a few months, when an assassin threw a hand grenade into a crowd of protesters of the Peace Now movement, killing a young man named Emil Gruenzweig.

The national consensus, which had been so natural and obvious in our past wars, was dissolving before my eyes, as was the image of Israel abroad. The foreign press and television harshly condemned Israel's operations. The reports were often exaggerated and viciously distorted. Still, as a nation that had always prided itself on its superior moral standards, we had to expect to be judged more severely than our neighbors.

In the first weeks of the Lebanon War, the U.S. administration played a nefarious role. In spite of angry reports of Sharon's deception, Secretary of State Alexander Haig shielded and protected the Israeli operation, thus providing Sharon with a powerful argument against the growing discontentment in Begin's government.

The American Jewish community was caught in a heartrending dilemma. Used to drawing pride and strength from Israel's feats of arms, American Jews didn't know how to react to the ugly reports coming from Lebanon. Some accused the media of misrepresenting the facts. Others, who blamed Israel publicly, were labeled enemies of the Jewish state. However, the large majority, which had got used to supporting Israel, come what may, tried to justify Menachem Begin's decisions. Friends of Israel all over the world were in a similar quandary.

For several weeks Begin's image was that of a man intoxicated with victory. "Operation Peace for Galilee," he said on June 16, "cured the nation of the Yom Kippur trauma." Four days later he declared: "The PLO in Lebanon doesn't exist anymore." To a delegation of American Jewish leaders he announced: "We will now have forty years of peace," paraphrasing the biblical verse "and the land had rest forty years." To General Ben-Gal, one of the best fighters of the Israeli army, he revealed his plans for Arafat: "We'll get into his bunker and pull him out."

And still, on August 21, 1982, it seemed that Sharon's gamble had succeeded. That day, Arafat and his PLO terrorists entrenched in West Beirut finally laid down their weapons. They were expelled from Beirut and left Lebanon for a new exile in Tunisia. Sharon, overjoyed, watched their departure from the Lebanese capital. The Syrian units encircled by Israeli troops in Beirut also withdrew to their country.

Two days later, virtually under the protection of Israeli cannon, the Lebanese parliament hastily convened and elected young Bashir Gemayel as Lebanon's president. A multinational peacekeeping force made up of U.S. Marines, French legionnaires, and Italian commandos landed in Beirut's harbor.

That was when the army of Israel should have withdrawn from Lebanon. Operation Peace for Galilee had achieved its major goal: the PLO threat in Lebanon no longer existed. But Sharon didn't dream of withdrawing.

On September 14, nine days before his inauguration, Bashir Gemayel was assassinated in Beirut. A powerful bomb exploded in the building where he was speaking, burying him and scores of others under the ruins. Bashir's murder was attributed to the Syrians or his Muslim enemies. Israel had lost its closest ally.

The following morning, the Israeli army advanced into West Beirut, in spite of Sharon's formal commitment not to do so. The same night, the army authorized the Christian Phalanges to enter Sabra and Shatila, two Palestinian refugee camps in West Beirut.

The Phalangists' official mission was to search the camps for suspected PLO guerrillas that Arafat had left behind. But they went in, determined to avenge Gemayel's death on the Palestinians. Their operation quickly became an orgy of killing. Under the cover of night they savagely massacred hundreds of Palestinians, men, women and children. The exact numbers of the dead were never established; estimates vary between eight hundred and twelve hundred.

When news of the massacres spread throughout the world, a tremendous uproar shook Israel. Four hundred thousand Israelis gathered in a gigantic protest rally in Tel Aviv, demanding the establishment of a board of inquiry. It seemed to me that all the anger and the frustration caused by the Lebanon War exploded in that protest. We had had enough.

I was about to set out for a lecture tour of the United States. On hearing about the Sabra and Shatila massacres I had called my hosts and canceled the tour; I was deeply shaken and revolted by the massacres that had occurred under our control. But after the protest, I decided to go after all. The protest made me very proud of being Israeli. Four hundred thousand people, almost 10 percent of Israel's population, had come to express their indignation at atrocities committed not by Israelis, but by others, the Phalangists. We felt that such massacres should never have happened under our control, although we had no part in them. We demanded to find out if we could have prevented the massacres; and if our army, or our government, was directly or indirectly responsible for the Phalangists' acts in Sabra and Shatila. To me, the protest was the proof that we still had our moral values.

I made my feelings known in an interview upon my arrival in New York: "Ten percent of the Israeli population gathered in Tel Aviv, demanding an inquiry. In American terms, ten percent of the nation is twenty-four million people. Did twenty-four million people ever protest in Washington for an inquiry on the My Lai massacre? Or ten million? Or one million? Or even four hundred thousand? Did five million Frenchmen ever protest in Paris against the atrocities of the Algerian War? Or even one million? Or even four hundred thousand? And our protesters demanded justice and punishment for a crime that we hadn't even committed!"

Yielding to popular pressure, Menachem Begin established a board of inquiry headed by Chief Justice Itzhak Kahan. Three months later the board published its conclusions, blaming several Israeli ministers and high-ranking officers, including General Eitan, for their indirect responsibility in the bloody events. Arik Sharon was forced to resign from office, but not from the government.

But it was already too late. Israel was deeply stuck in the Lebanese mire. The twenty-five-mile, seventy-two-hour, thirty-odd-casualties operation had turned out to be the longest and most senseless war in our history. Our dead were approaching the five hundred mark. The Lebanese had elected a new president, Amin Gemayel, the older brother of the murdered Bashir; his attitude toward Israel was cold, even hostile. A long negotiation for an Israeli-Lebanese peace treaty, mediated by the United States, ended in a fiasco.

The different Lebanese communities had merrily returned to their ruthless civil war, using the Israelis as targets or as naïve tools in their devious schemes. Fanatical terrorists, including suicide commandos, kidnapped our soldiers, attacked our patrols daily, and blew booby-trapped cars in the midst of our convoys. They dispatched an explosive-laden car to the Beirut headquarters of the Marines stationed there as part of the international peacekeeping force, killing 241 Americans.

On the first anniversary of the war's outbreak, I presented a motion to the order of the Knesset. When I got on the podium I asked my colleagues to rise and observe a moment of silence in memory of the fallen in Lebanon. The Knesset speaker was surprised by my request, but couldn't refuse it and did as I had asked. In normal conditions I wouldn't have taken such a step without consulting the speaker first, but I wanted to jolt the Knesset out of the torpor that had descended upon it.

Facing my silent audience, I suddenly thought of Menachem Begin's plight. The man who had promised us forty years of peace, and the cure for the Yom Kippur trauma, stood before me gaunt and grim, his head bowed.

This was neither the war he had expected nor the victory Sharon had promised him. I was convinced that if he had only suspected the war might turn out this way, with hundreds of Israeli casualties, he never would have embarked upon this senseless adventure. How did this intelligent man, this shrewd politician, let himself be cheated and manipulated by his defense minister? Was his admiration for Sharon the hero so blinding that he failed to see the danger in Sharon the politician?

A friend of mine, a government minister, told me about the first time Begin had admitted to doubting Sharon. It was at the government meeting on August 7. That day the Israeli air force had bombed Beirut for ten hours straight. One of Begin's ministers, who were by then in open revolt against Sharon, had asked: "Mr. Begin, do you know what our army is doing today in Beirut?"

He had answered: "I know all. There are things I know beforehand, and others that I know afterwards." That had been his first admission that he was being misled. Still, sticking to his gentleman's manners, he never criticized Ariel Sharon in public. And by keeping silent, he sanctioned Sharon's reckless policy.

Begin had recently been struck by a personal loss, the death of his beloved wife, Aliza. Shortly afterwards, his close friend, Minister Simcha Ehrlich, had also died. Ehrlich had been very critical of the Lebanon War and had continually confronted Sharon in spite of the annoyance this caused Begin.

As the moment of silence ended, I spoke of the Lebanon War: I described Sharon's deception, the shattering of our moral values, the rift in the nation, our tarnished image abroad. After harshly criticizing Begin's government, I asked for the prime minister's resignation. Likud members interrupted me with angry shouts. "Wait, Bar-Zohar," somebody called out, "wait till Begin gets back at you!"

Menachem Begin rose to answer. But this was not the Begin of the great days anymore. On the podium stood a pale, distraught, strangely absent man, speaking in a barely audible voice. He admitted that "a tragedy" was taking place in Lebanon and agreed to a full-scale debate in the Knesset.

People looked at him strangely when he returned to his seat. Where was his lashing irony, where was his biting repartee? How could he let me get away with all those accusations without even trying to refute them? He seemed eerily detached from his surroundings, slow to react, his gaze wandering far away. Friends of mine who worked with him told me later that the Lebanon tragedy and his wife's death had broken his spirit completely.

Begin's state worsened in the following weeks. He would sit immobile in his Knesset seat, his head sunk between his shoulders, totally oblivious to what was happening around him; he would talk in monosyllables to his aides when they came to report or ask for instructions. He canceled many of his official obligations. He behaved as if he had taken a final leave from the world of politics.

At the end of June, I faced him again from the podium. Once again I felt Israel had lost its prime minister; I saw before me a broken man unable to face the results of the tragedy he had unleashed. I felt my throat constricting as I turned to him. "Mr. Begin," I said, "lately the nation feels that you no longer function properly as prime minister. I don't say that to hurt you, God knows. You have been afflicted with tragic personal losses this past year, and the Lebanon War is haunting you. Even one who doesn't belong to your party can understand the pain and the weakness that have overwhelmed you. But we cannot deal with personal questions and personal problems, Mr. Begin. The Israeli nation needs a firm and resolved leadership that knows what it wants and can make wise and clear-cut decisions. I cannot prevent myself from asking whether the burden hasn't become heavy for you lately, perhaps even too heavy?"

My words were received in silence.

Ten weeks later Menachem Begin handed his letter of resignation to President Herzog and shut himself into his home, from which he emerges only once a year to visit his wife's grave.

Had Shakespeare been alive, he might have been able to do this tragedy justice. He might have written of a king who had been cheated by his general into sending his sons to a pointless war. When the war had ended in disaster, and his sons' corpses were brought home and laid before him, he had cast away his crown and descended from his throne.

And had imposed on himself a voluntary seclusion in a sealed cave, where his loneliness, his pain, and his repentance might, one day, redeem his tragic error.

Chapter 10

The Day They
Invented Rotation

A man stood before me, small, short-limbed, with gray curly hair, bushy eyebrows, and a moth-eaten mustache. His head seemed too large for his small wiry body. In spite of the heat he was wearing a dark conservative suit. His sharp-lined jaw and low forehead bestowed upon him some of the stubborn look of a royal bulldog.

"Bar-Zohar?" he said. He had a strong Polish accent.

That was my first meeting with Itzhak Shamir, at a Tel Aviv cafe. The year was 1969, and I was writing a biography of Isser Harel, the founder of the Israeli secret services. Harel was very proud of an initiative he had taken in the early fifties: he had personally persuaded many veterans of the former Irgun and Stern underground groups to join the Mossad. This was quite remarkable, for in those days the Irgun and Stern people were labeled terrorists and dissidents, and the establishment treated them as outcasts. When I asked Harel if he had a friend among the Stern veterans who might tell me about their work he mentioned Itzhak Shamir.

I knew very little of Shamir. He had belonged to the most extremist underground organization that had fought against the British, the Stern group. It had a confused ideology, an awkward combination of a Greater Israel cult, Marxist elements, and blind hatred for the British. This hatred was so intense that at the outbreak of World War Two some Stern emissaries had traveled to Beirut and tried to talk Nazi diplomats into a Stern-German alliance against Britain. In 1944, Stern members had assassinated Churchill's personal friend, the British minister Lord Moyne, in Cairo. Four years later, during Israel's Independence War, the Stern had struck again, in Jerusalem, and assassinated Count Bernadotte, the United Nations mediator. Years later, by a strange coincidence, I identified the man who had shot Bernadotte: Yeoshua Cohen, a friend of mine and of David Ben-Gurion, who belonged to Ben-Gurion's kibbutz!*

I didn't know if Shamir, one of the Stern group leaders, had been connected with those operations; I did know, though, that he (*nom de guerre*, Michael) had personally killed at least one suspected traitor and had him buried on a beach south of Tel Aviv.

Our meeting was a disaster. Shamir turned out to be the most close-mouthed person I'd ever met. He answered most of my questions with: "Well . . ." or by staring at me in silence. He barely acknowledged having been a Mossad agent or knowing Isser Harel. He behaved as if he still was in the underground and any word he uttered might betray a fateful secret.

I met Shamir again twelve years later, when he was foreign minister in Menachem Begin's government, after having served as the Knesset speaker. He hadn't changed much. I listened to his speeches at the plenum and to his briefings at the Defense and Foreign Affairs Committee, of which I was a member. His views were extremist; he had voted against the Camp David accords. He was a bad speaker and his vocabulary was limited; the words came out of his mouth hacked and with difficulty, as though he regretted them.

Shamir earned some dubious fame for his speeches at public rallies.

---

*In 1965, while reading Ben-Gurion's private diary, I found the names of those suspected of assassinating Count Bernadotte. They had not been arrested for lack of evidence. To my surprise, I found among them the name of Yeoshua Cohen, one of the founders of Sdeh Boker, Ben-Gurion's kibbutz. Yeoshua had become one of Ben-Gurion's closest friends. I showed the entry to Ben-Gurion, who was stunned. I suggested to Ben-Gurion that he confront Yeoshua. We were at the kibbutz that day, and Ben-Gurion at once called his friend to his study. I waited outside. Yeoshua left, looking deeply upset. I entered Ben-Gurion's room. "Did he confess?" I asked.

"He confessed," Ben-Gurion said.

At a later conversation I had with Yeoshua, he described his role in the assassination and asked me not to reveal it before his death. I respected his wish and released his name only after he died in 1986.

Ben-Gurion never revealed Yeoshua's secret either. Until Ben-Gurion's death in 1973, he and Yeoshua Cohen remained close friends. The former premier and the former Stern member spent many quiet hours together, united by their affection and by the terrible secret that once threatened the very foundations of newborn Israel.

Once, he asked rhetorically why all of Eretz Israel must remain ours, and answered his own question: "Why? I'll tell you why. Because!" Another one of his immortal sayings concerned the hardship of our survival in the Middle East. "The Arabs are the Arabs," he said, "the Jews are the Jews, and the sea is the sea."

Here was a man, I thought, whom nobody would suspect of reading a book or going to the theater. Nobody admired him, as far as I knew, at least until Shirley Maclaine visited Israel in 1989 and told him he was "a legend." He had nothing of the cultured aura, the brio, the Jewish roots, or the eloquence of Menachem Begin.

Still, this was the man whom Begin had chosen as his heir. For a while people had thought Begin would anoint an old friend from his Irgun days, Yaakov Meridor, a businessman whom he had made minister of the economy. But Meridor turned out to be an eccentric. He became the laughingstock of the Knesset after announcing he had discovered an important source of energy that would produce countless megawatts of electricity for nothing. Some joker nicknamed Meridor's invention "electricity powder."

He had us rolling in the aisles with his prophecies during a memorable Knesset session, and Knesset member Yossi Sarid solemnly pledged from the podium to eat his hat when Meridor's invention would light the first electric bulb. Sarid's hat remained intact, of course, and Meridor's amusing political career came to an end.

And then Shamir emerged.

We soon found out that Shamir was poorly qualified for his job. He was unable to cope with Israel's main problems: the Lebanon War, the Palestinian issue, the galloping inflation rate. He was helpless when the stock of the major banks collapsed in the early autumn, triggering an economic catastrophe. Shamir had turned immobility into a religion; under his reign the government sank into a complete torpor.

Watching the uncharismatic, inept Shamir at the helm was too much for Shimon Peres. He thought we shouldn't wait for the elections, scheduled for November 1985. He began feverishly maneuvering in the Knesset to set up a majority for an early election.

I could understand him. He was far better qualified than Shamir to lead the country; I had no doubt of his ability to solve some of our major problems. Still, I felt the nation wasn't ready yet for a change. I met

Peres in Jerusalem, and he pointed out that this was our great chance. We were riding high at the polls, Shamir wasn't Begin, the Lebanon War was a disaster, the economy had collapsed. I tried to dissuade him; my feeling was that the failures of the Likud hadn't yet created a real shift in public opinion. Disappointment in the present government was only starting; we were better off waiting.

Peres brushed me off and went on with his campaign. I didn't hear from him again until I arrived in New York a few days later on official business. As I walked into my hotel room I saw the red light on my phone blinking. A message was waiting for me: call Peres immediately. When I got hold of him, he asked me to return on the next flight. "We've got the majority for an early election!" he announced triumphantly.

"Shimon, are you sure we're doing the right thing?" I asked.

"Positive."

Two days later the Knesset moved to hold general elections on July 23, 1984.

During the entire campaign I had a feeling of *déjà vu*. Peres and the campaign staff were repeating the mistakes of the 1981 campaign. Afraid of being accused of defiling the sacrosanct subject of security, they carefully avoided criticizing the Likud for the tragic Lebanon mishap. On the Palestinian issue as well, they spoke in vague terms of "security borders" instead of describing our peace plan. They counted on our good performance in the opposition, and on the fact that Menachem Begin, immured in his house, had refused to endorse his own party's ticket. Our pollsters, elated, proclaimed the greatest news: we had an advantage of nineteen seats over the Likud!

I clashed with our campaign manager, Motta Gur, over that estimate. I was campaigning in the main streets, the poor neighborhoods, the dormitory towns; I hadn't met anybody who said he would desert the Likud and vote for us. On the contrary: I was told by many people who had voted for Labor or Likud that they were going to switch to one of the small parties.

Four days before the election, Motta Gur came to my district, Tel Aviv. He was rather glum. "I've been fighting with Michael about those polls," he said to the Tel Aviv campaign staff. "Today, for the first time, I have a gut feeling that he might be right."

At the end of election day I didn't even go to the Palace Hotel, where our leadership had assembled to announce its victory. I had no illusions; I was sure it was going to be a long, sad night.

It was. Labor lost three seats, falling from forty-seven to forty-four. The advantage of nineteen seats over the Likud evaporated together with the pollsters, who vanished into thin air and were never seen again. I was not reelected; neither were most of the new Labor Knesset members who had served in the Tenth Knesset. Rabbi Meir Kahane, the leader of the Jewish Defense League from New York, was elected to represent his new racist party.

The Likud won only forty-one seats. These results proved, though, that even without Begin, a large electoral mass in the country felt deep loyalty to the Likud; even Shamir couldn't make them vote for us.

We were the largest party now, but we hadn't won. In spite of our edge over the Likud, we couldn't form the new government, as the religious parties had pledged their support to Itzhak Shamir. The Likud, on the other hand, was also unable to assemble a majority. The deadlock that resulted was broken by the two main losers, Peres and Shamir, who invented a unique formula: a National Unity government, based on a rotation agreement. In the first two years Peres would be prime minister and Shamir minister of foreign affairs; in the last two years of the term they would switch positions. Likud and Labor would have the same number of ministers in the government.

I was opposed to this agreement, as was one third of our Central Committee. We all felt that a government of National Unity would be a government of national paralysis. We differed from the Likud on all the important issues: the future of the West Bank and Gaza, willingness for a territorial compromise with Jordan and the Palestinians, withdrawal from Lebanon, the economic policy needed to curb inflation. We feared that the Likud ministers would simply neutralize their Labor colleagues, and vice versa; and we would be in for four years of deep-freeze.

We were in the minority, though, and not only within our party. The nation warmly welcomed the creation of the National Unity government. One of the most popular songs in Israel is entitled: "The Whole World Is Against Us." The Israelis feel they are completely alone, surrounded by hostile Arabs, misunderstood by an indifferent world, hated by real and imaginary anti-Semites. The only way to confront this hostile world is by uniting our forces and standing together.

Israelis were also fed up with coalition governments always being at the mercy of small parties that blackmailed and pillaged the nation. Israelis were sick and tired of the tail wagging the dog. A large coalition, they thought, would reduce the small parties to their actual size.

Those of us who objected to the National Unity government claimed that in peacetime such an arrangement was the very opposite of democracy. The nation rejected this argument. It rejoiced that the leaders of Israel would now work and act together. Unity was the "in" word as the new government assumed power in the fall of 1984.

Peres's alliance with the Likud provoked a crisis in the Alignment. Knesset member Sarid and the Mapam Party refused to join the government coalition and separated from us; they were replaced, partly, by Ezer Weizmann and his small party, Yachad. Weizmann, the hawkish Likud leader, had become a dove, split from his party, and drifted toward us. In 1977 he had been the Likud campaign manager and had brought Peres down. Now he was Peres's greatest supporter.

In the unity government Sharon was minister of trade and industry, and Itzhak Modai minister of finance. Chaim Bar-Lev became minister of police, Motta Gur minister of health, and Itzhak Rabin minister of defense. Former President Itzhak Navon, who had run on the Labor ticket, became deputy prime minister and minister of education.

Shimon Peres was named Israel's eighth prime minister.

Chapter 11

Life Insurance for the King

Reviving the peace effort became Shimon Peres's main objective when he assumed power in September 1984. The sixty-one-year-old prime minister was determined to once again set in motion the rusty wheels of the peace process that had ground to a halt with the invasion of Lebanon two and a half years before.

Israel, Peres believed, could cope with any military threat. He saw the only real danger to the existence of the Jewish state in the demographic explosion in the occupied territories. There were 1.5 million Palestinians in the West Bank and Gaza, and the Palestinian population was increasing at a rate that would soon challenge the Jewish majority in Israel.

Itzhak Rabin shared that view, and Peres's aides recalled a phrase of Rabin, on the eve of the July 1984 election: "If we win and fail to achieve a breakthrough with Jordan, we don't deserve winning."

Yet, it seemed that there were more urgent matters on the government agenda than the search for peace. The nation was in deep trouble. Tensions and hatreds between Sephardis and Ashkenazis, stirred and fueled by extremist political leaders, tore us apart; the economy was crumbling under an inflation rate of 445 percent; the entire banking system was in a shambles after the crash of its artificially inflated stock; the Israeli army was stuck deep in the Lebanese mire; the fragile peace with Egypt seemed on the verge of collapse; and Israel's image abroad had been tarnished by the war in Lebanon and the Phalangist massacres at Sabra and Shatila.

Peres got off to a slow start. He didn't achieve any tangible results in his first months in office, and the press labeled him a lame duck. But in utmost secrecy, the lame duck was engaged in one of the most ambitious operations of his career.

The details of this operation were, and still are, secret. When it was launched I was not in the Knesset and didn't work with Peres. I learned about the peace initiative much later. By interviewing people in Israel and in the United States who were involved in this endeavor, I pieced together the story that follows.

Peres, I found out, had sent out his first feelers in the spring of 1984, long before the election. From his bare office in the Labor Party building in Tel Aviv he had sent some tentative messages to King Hussein, offering to renew their relationship "as in the good old times," when he had served as defense minister in Itzhak Rabin's government. The messages were discreetly delivered by the U.S. State Department and the British Foreign Office. But the entire peace offensive rested mostly with a curious group of young men, who called themselves "The Hundred-Day Team," but were better known to the public as the Peres boys.

This group was created and headed by Peres's longtime assistant, Dr. Yossi Beilin, a baby-faced, bespectacled young man perpetually wearing a timid expression and a gold-buttoned blazer, who is a political scientist and a former spokesman of the Labor Party. He combined three qualities that made him indispensable to Peres: a sparkling intelligence, an orderly mind, and a devotion to his boss so overwhelming that Rabin was to nickname him "Peres's poodle."

Convinced that Peres was going to win the July 1984 election, Beilin quietly recruited a group of scholars and economists who came to be called the Hundred-Day Team. Their purpose was to set up the goals of the new government, plan the measures to be taken in different fields, and define each minister's tasks. Long before Peres became prime minister, his boys had everything ready for him—position papers, reform projects, even detailed briefs for discussion with each candidate for a ministerial portfolio.

At the beginning, the suspicious Peres was reluctant to talk freely to the young intellectuals, some of whom he had never met before. He feared they might be seeking to gain political clout or media exposure. But weeks, then months passed, and results started coming in without anything being leaked to the press. Gradually Peres peeled off his protective shield and revealed his intimate thoughts to the group about what had to be done.

"I want to bring Israel to a crossroads," Peres said to his boys. "I want her to choose between her present course and the road leading to the Jordanian option. If the Jordanian option exists, if Hussein wants to go along with us, we should take that road. If not, I want Israel to face the mirror and ask herself what we should do with one and a half million Palestinians."

Peres didn't conceal his private conviction that the Jordanian option still existed because Hussein's basic interests hadn't changed. For the king the question was who would give the orders to whom: Jordan to the Palestinians or the Palestinians to Jordan. As one of Peres's aides said: "The king is determined that the spooks controlling the West Bank be his own and not Arafat's."

It was of utmost importance, Peres said to his men, to lure Hussein to the negotiating table using any means necessary. But he had no intention of entrusting his foreign minister, Itzhak Shamir, with that task. He knew Shamir objected to any initiative that could lead to a territorial compromise; Peres had no doubt that the Likud leader would sabotage the process. Besides, Peres, a suspicious, insecure man, often bypasses established channels and procedures, using members of his inner circle to carry out his most delicate business.

In September 1984, as soon as he settled into the prime minister's seat, he chose two of his boys for the operation: Yossi Beilin, whom he appointed government secretary, and Dr. Nemrod Novik, his foreign policy adviser. Beilin was given overall responsibility for the negotiations. He also was unofficially put in charge of improving the living conditions in the West Bank and Gaza. Novik was assigned the great powers, mainly the Americans and the Russians.

Novik was a member of the Strategic Research Center at Tel Aviv University. A graduate of the University of Pennsylvania, he had worked in Philadelphia at the Foreign Policy Research Institute under Alexander Haig, before the former Supreme Allied Commander had been appointed secretary of state. Haig had taken a group of Novik's American friends with him to Foggy Bottom, and they were now holding key positions at the Departments of State and Treasury, the White House, and the CIA.

This old-boy network was to become very useful to Peres's young adviser as he plunged, together with Beilin, in the murky labyrinths of secret diplomacy.

Still, Beilin was Peres's closest assistant in the forthcoming negotiations. As secrecy was vital, not even a typist was allowed to see most of the letters, messages, and minutes concerning the contacts. Beilin would spend many nights writing memos and position papers, and personally photocopying documents. He was in sole possession of the only existing files on the peace initiative.

Another member of Peres's team was the director of the prime minister's office, Reserve General Abraham Tamir. He and Beilin had prepared several position papers for Peres, including a study on the unpopular international conference. In the future peace initiative, Tamir was assigned the negotiations with the Arabs, mostly the Egyptians. Tamir had been chief of the planning department in the army. He was a former assistant of Sharon and a close confidant of Weizmann—an unusual, rather puzzling combination. Tamir was never part of Peres's inner circle, though, and was excluded from the more delicate stages of the negotiations.

Peres knew well that no serious talks with Jordan could begin before Israel pulled out of Lebanon, so he immediately started preparing for Israel's retreat. The pullout from Lebanon was also a condition for the improvement of relations with Egypt. Egypt had a major place on Peres's chessboard: it could play a crucial part in bringing Israel and Jordan together.

But Egypt's President Mubarak wouldn't even talk to Peres before another condition was fulfilled: the settlement of the Taba issue. Taba was a tiny piece of beach on the Israel-Egypt border which both sides claimed.

Peres tried unsuccessfully to convey to Mubarak his sense of urgency. Mubarak remained adamant: no meeting before the Taba matter was resolved. A long, frustrating negotiation ensued that would result, eighteen months later, in an agreement on international arbitration. Only then would Mubarak agree to receive Peres in Cairo. Israel and Jordan were to pay dearly for those eighteen months, wasted because of Mubarak's stubbornness.

•   •   •

Peres didn't wait for Mubarak to start his approach to Hussein in October 1984. The first stage in Peres's secret peace initiative lasted from October 1984 to September 1985. From the very start, Peres realized he had to overcome a formidable obstacle to the negotiation: Hussein's firm position that talks with Israel could be held only in the framework of an international peace conference.

In the secret meetings of Peres and Hussein in the Middle East or in Europe, and in the undercover missions of Peres's emissaries to Amman, the Jordanian leaders were unyielding: no talks without an international conference, including the five permanent members of the U.N. Security Council.

The same attitude was reported by high officials of the State Department and the British Foreign Office, who served as goodwill intermediaries between Peres and Hussein.

Peres categorically refused, realizing that an international conference, by definition, would want to impose its resolution on the belligerents. No responsible Israeli leader would willingly walk into such a conference room and let the five powers decide on his country's boundaries and how to guarantee his country's security. When speaking about the conference, he didn't mince words. "The idea of an international conference has been rejected by everybody in Israel," he said in the Knesset in December 1984. "Its real aim is to deprive Israel of the possibility of negotiating on equal terms." In June 1985 he added: "At such a conference Israel would be isolated; she would be invited to supply territorial food to the conference's guests. This is a plan of subduing Israel and not of negotiating with Israel."

To find a way out he offered Hussein any other formula he could think of: direct negotiations; simultaneous bilateral talks with several Arab states; negotiations by proxy; a regional peace conference with Egypt and Saudi Arabia; a meeting in Cairo chaired by U.S. representatives; talks at Camp David, at Williamsburg, Virginia, in San Francisco, the symbolic cradle of the United Nations.

No, Hussein said, international conference and nothing else.

He also said why. First, he didn't trust the Americans. They were far too pro-Israeli. He couldn't rely on the Soviets either, as they were the patrons of Syria and the PLO. Only at an international conference, he said, would the conflicting interests of the great powers neutralize one another.

Didn't he trust anybody? the Israelis asked.

Margaret Thatcher, Hussein replied.

His second argument was that he couldn't exceed the bounds of the Arab consensus. That could cost him Arab support. In plain language, he was afraid to lose Saudi subsidies.

Hussein's third argument was apparently the main one. He knew, he candidly admitted, that if he went to a negotiation with Israel he would not get all his territories back. He would have to give up some portions of land that were considered Arab. That would provoke a tremendous outcry against him among the Palestinians and the more extremist Arab countries. His life, his family, his regime, his country would be in mortal danger. The Hashemite Kingdom would need life insurance. Somebody had to be there to restrain Arafat, Assad, and Qaddafi. And this "somebody" was Moscow.

The Soviet Union, he went on, was the only power able to hold in check the extremists in Tunis, Damascus, and Tripoli. It supplied them with arms, funds, and diplomatic support, and could force them to accept a compromise. In order to do so, it must be part of the peace process. If the Soviets were kept out of the negotiations they would be utterly hostile and could unleash the Syrians, Palestinians, and Libyans on Jordan.

Even those among Peres's aides who were skeptical about Hussein's first two arguments had to admit that the third one rang true. Israeli emissaries who discreetly met the king's closest aides were struck by the importance the Jordanians attached to personal security.

The Jordanian leaders still remembered the days before September 1970 when the PLO controlled the streets of their capital. They couldn't get out of the royal palace without an armored car or drop into a restaurant without the protection of armed bodyguards. Even their homes weren't safe.

That state of anarchy and physical danger had ended in September 1970 when the king's army had crushed the PLO. The king and his men were determined never to return to the days that preceded Black September.

The Israelis tried to reason with them, hinting that if an agreement between Israel and Jordan were reached, Israel's power would be a formidable deterrent for the Syrians and the PLO. The Jordanians didn't wish to entrust their security to Israel. "Anyway," they would say, "we don't want, ever again, to feel in danger even in the privacy of our own homes."

And the talks stalled.

Still, the Israelis and the Americans didn't lose hope. At that time the king was interested in modernizing the Jordanian army and tried to purchase weapons in the United States. He didn't want to buy Soviet weapons, as he knew that they were invariably accompanied by "advisers" and implied a risky political cost. Lacking the necessary funds, he couldn't buy European weapons. But a deal with the United States which included a package of loans and grants would solve his problem. Hussein regarded the arms deal with Washington as a test case of American and Israeli goodwill.

The State Department decided to use Hussein's demand as leverage for steering him into the negotiation path. Our Congress would approve of your demand, U.S. diplomats said to Hussein, if you would proclaim the end of belligerence with Israel.

After a long hesitation Hussein decided to visit the United States, speak at the U.N. General Assembly, then meet with President Reagan at the White House. There, on the White House lawn, he was supposed to utter the magic formula. State Department officials assured him that a declaration by His Majesty on the end of belligerence would sound like an "open sesame" in Washington. The American treasure trove of weapons and funds would be at his disposal.

In September 1985, Hussein arrived in the United States. Before flying to Washington, the king spent a weekend in New England with Ambassador Richard Murphy, the assistant secretary of state for Near Eastern and South Asian affairs. They went over several drafts of the proposed statement. The king even checked some of the language with Arafat. Then, on the last day of September 1985, the king made a promising speech at the U.N. Assembly; it was a good preliminary step to his statement at the White House.

But when he stood with Ronald Reagan on the White House lawn, Hussein—as he had so many times in the past—backed off. Instead of saying that the conflict with Israel would be solved only "by nonbelligerent means," he said "in a nonbelligerent environment."

The Americans and the Israelis were deeply disappointed. "The man was asked to give a commitment," Peres said in Jerusalem, "and instead he gives us a weather forecast."

The United States refused to supply the king with arms, and he went back home, disappointed. "The Zionists are in control in Washington," he said angrily to a U.S. envoy, "and the U.S. Congress is a branch of the Knesset." After so many years in power Hussein had failed to understand the American system and the importance of saying the right thing at the right moment.

Still, Peres wouldn't give up. As the summer of 1985 ended, he realized that Hussein would never budge. The U.S. initiative to launch a negotiation from Washington had backfired. There would be no direct negotiation without an international conference.

Therefore, he decided to square the circle, and, in the words of one of his aides, "castrate" the conference.

Let's remove from the conference all the elements that worry us, Peres said to his confidants. Let's keep only the international umbrella Hussein needs.

Some of his men disagreed. They believed Hussein was bluffing and using the international conference only as a means to sabotage the entire peace process. "This man is stalling you, Shimon," one of them said. "He has been making a living out of saying no."

But Peres persisted. He didn't doubt Hussein's sincerity. The king wants an agreement, he said. And if he can't go along with us without a conference, let's give him one.

And he gave it to him, in October 1985, from the podium of the U.N. General Assembly.

During the summer Peres's boys had worked overtime, preparing the prime minister's first trip to the General Assembly in New York. His speech had been written and rewritten, with every word and expression carefully weighed.

The speech had a secret goal: to launch, for the first time, several terms connected with the international conference; and test the response of international and Israeli public opinion. Peres wouldn't go as far as saying the magic words "international conference"; that would be giving away a negotiating asset. But he would agree to an international opening and an international "support" of the negotiations.

On October 21, Peres addressed the General Assembly. He offered Jordan direct negotiations, then added: "If deemed necessary, those negotiations may be initiated with the support of an international forum, as agreed upon by the negotiating states. . . . The permanent members of the Security Council may be invited to support the initiation of these negotiations. . . . This forum, while not being a substitute for direct negotiations, can offer support for them."

International reactions were excellent. In Israel, right-wing political leaders protested angrily. Still, no political storm erupted, not even when Peres made the same speech, translated into Hebrew, in the Knesset in Jerusalem. Despite some furious interjections from the floor, the government coalition voted to enter the prime minister's address in the Knesset record.

Peres was satisfied; he had survived the baptism by fire, in his own home. But he misinterpreted the Likud's moderation. He sincerely believed the Likud was ready to swallow his peace initiative. He didn't understand that Itzhak Shamir and his men were violently opposed to the initiative, but they feared that if they provoked any confrontation inside the government Peres would refuse to vacate the prime minister's office in October 1986. As their foremost goal was to assure that Peres would respect the rotation agreement, they let him go ahead with his plan.

Encouraged by his success at home, Peres sped up the contacts with Hussein, entering into the second and most fruitful stage in the negotiation, which lasted from October 1985 to January 1986.

Richard Murphy, George Shultz's special envoy, served as a permanent liaison between Peres and Hussein. He continuously hopped between Jerusalem and Amman when both leaders were in their capitals. When Peres left for a visit in London and Hussein visited Holland, Murphy continued his shuttle diplomacy. In January 1986, Murphy met with the king in London, completing a strenuous and dramatic diplomatic effort.

The result was a secret draft agreement that was never published. In the history of the peace negotiation, it was labeled "the first London agreement." It contained ten points that defined the mechanism of the future negotiation. Its first paragraph was a grand personal triumph for Shimon Peres. The paragraph said, in so many words, that both sides agreed to convene a pro forma international conference. The formula got the full, though secret approval of King Hussein.

This was a major breakthrough. Hussein had accepted Peres's "castrated conference" concept and proved that he sincerely wanted to go ahead with the negotiation.

But the success was only partial. Israelis and Jordanians still disagreed on three major points.

The first point concerned the Soviet Union. Because of the Israeli objection, the Americans suggested an international conference without the participation of the Soviet Union.

Peres had formulated two conditions to Soviet participation in the conference: free Jewish emigration from the USSR to Israel, and normalization of diplomatic relations between the two countries. The Soviet Union had broken relations with Israel two decades before, during the Six-Day War of 1967.

"Hussein said to us: 'Just a moment,' " one of Peres's aides recalled later. " 'You Israelis don't expect me to tell the Russians "Sorry, but you're excluded from the peace process because you refuse to allow Jewish emigration and won't restore diplomatic relations with Israel." That's Israel's problem, not mine. If the Russians disqualify themselves from participating, I'll go to a conference even without them.

" 'But if you, the Israelis, reject them, you are the ones who undermine the peace process.' "

After long discussions the State Department accepted the Jordanian point of view. But it would take more than a year before the Soviets would move, and that year would be critical.

The second point of disagreement concerned the PLO. At that time Hussein and Arafat were enjoying one of their sporadic honeymoons, and the king was very keen on securing the participation of the PLO in the peace process. In February 1985 he had signed an agreement with Arafat establishing a common front; the king had traveled all over Europe and China at the head of a seven-member delegation, seeking support for an international conference. The journey had been successful, except for an unpleasant episode in Moscow, where the Soviets had bluntly rejected the idea.

Still, Hussein was hopeful because of a solemn commitment he had obtained from Yasser Arafat. The PLO chief had promised him to publicly accept Resolutions 242 and 338 of the Security Council (the so-called territories for peace resolutions) and give up terrorism. Arafat had agreed to those major concessions in exchange for an invitation to the international conference.

Hussein wouldn't dream of a peace negotiation without the Palestinians. He needed them "up front," he said to the Americans; the king was also convinced that a full agreement with Arafat about their respective roles in the future was imminent, and the PLO chief would submit to Hussein's authority. Therefore, he declared, if Arafat fulfilled his promises from last February, he would qualify for a seat at the conference.

That was also the attitude of the United States. When he came to meet Hussein in January, in London, Richard Murphy brought him written guarantees from Washington, saying that if the PLO renounced terrorism, recognized Israel, and accepted the Security Council resolutions, it would qualify for participation in the peace conference. Hussein had obtained Arafat's promise to accept the U.S. conditions, and the road seemed paved to PLO participation in the conference, at least from the American point of view.

No, said Peres. He knew about the letter Murphy had brought to Hussein, but didn't agree to it, at least officially. Arafat hadn't budged from his old positions, Peres asserted. He still refused to renounce terrorism and recognize Israel; therefore he wasn't a partner. Besides, Peres was enchanted with his "Jordanian option." He didn't need Arafat.

Still, some of Peres's aides hinted to the Jordanians that his "no" might mean "yes, if." In other words, if Arafat fulfilled his promises then Hussein should raise the subject again. Peres's boys claimed that if the PLO repudiated terrorism and recognized Israel it wouldn't be the PLO anymore and could become a partner for negotiations.

But they sincerely doubted that this would happen. They knew that a few months before, in a closed session in Bagdad, the PLO leadership had secretly decided to reject the Security Council resolutions. Arafat's promises to Hussein were nothing but a bluff. Besides, the Israelis were very skeptical about Arafat's willingness to give Hussein a superior status in a future settlement. The next few weeks were to prove they were right.

The third point of disagreement between Peres and Hussein was the most serious one. This was the "Referral Clause" formulated in paragraph 7 of the draft agreement, a clause without which Hussein wouldn't budge.

Paragraph 7 set out the structure and the terms of reference of the international conference. The plenary opening session, according to that paragraph, was to be only formal and ceremonial. Afterwards the con-

ference would split into bilateral committees—Israel-Jordan, Israel-Leb-
anon, Israel-Syria, with no third party participating.

But at this point Hussein introduced the Referral Clause. In case of
a deadlock in the bilateral negotiations, he said, we would refer the issue
to the plenum of the international conference.

No way, the Israelis retorted. If Hussein's clause were accepted, then
it wouldn't be a pro forma conference anymore. A referral to the plenum
meant their worst nightmares coming true: the conference would decide
on all the major issues and impose a solution upon Israel.

Once again, the talks reached a stalemate. The first London document
was stillborn.

In spite of the setback, the negotiations continued, evolving around two
formulas that U.S. diplomats had nicknamed "the name game" and "the
hang back." As both sides believed that a negotiation might finally start,
they wanted to clear away as many obstacles as they could. The first
hindrance concerned the Palestinian delegation. Who could qualify for
participation in the Palestinian-Jordanian team?

Israel objected to PLO official members, claiming that all of them
belonged to a terrorist organization. The United States maintained that
the Fatah and other terrorist groups were only one branch of the PLO;
a member of the PLO National Council wasn't necessarily a terrorist,
they said. Hussein had been helpful in that respect: he had obtained
Arafat's consent that the Palestinian delegates wouldn't be senior PLO
leaders or members of terrorist organizations.

In order to cut short the endless debate, the Israelis suggested "the
name game" to the Americans. "Forget about categories," they said.
"Don't tell us why this guy or that guy qualifies. Just give us a list of
names, and if we find some among them who are acceptable to us we'll
tell you."

And so they did. A joint U.S.-Egyptian effort produced six names.
The Israelis agreed to two well-known Palestinians: Fayez Abu Rahme
and Hanna Siniora.

The third one was Sheik Sayah, the chairman of the Palestinian
National Council, the PLO parliament. "He is a senile old man," a Peres
aide told me afterwards, "but we were stupid enough to say no."

The fourth was Nabil Shaat, a brilliant man, one of the most promising younger PLO leaders. The Israeli Shin Beth punched him up on their computers and found out that he had been a prisoner of Israel in South Lebanon because of semi-military activity. He was refused.

The last two names were of PLO hard-liners, both involved in terrorism and therefore unacceptable.

During the discussions Richard Murphy decided to come to Jerusalem and meet several Palestinians, hoping to find a few more candidates for a joint Palestinian-Jordanian delegation. But at the last moment Secretary Shultz canceled the Murphy meeting, fearing that the process itself would only strengthen the PLO and its influence over the delegation.

Similarly, with the help of Hussein, the Americans were playing "the hang back" game with Arafat. That game consisted of two formulas: "hang back" and "the foot in the door."

The U.S. diplomats, like the Israelis, were aware of the PLO secret decision not to accept the Security Council resolutions. They wanted to give Arafat some more time, so he would have the opportunity to join the talks later. Their message to Arafat was "We understand that perhaps you aren't ready to accept our conditions right away. So just hang back, and let some Palestinians with whom both Jordan and Israel can live start the process. In return, we guarantee you that at a later stage you'll get your foot in the door."

The Americans hinted that if Arafat wanted to join the negotiations a few months after they started, the United States would help him. What counted was that he didn't thwart the process.

The Israelis weren't supposed to know about the Americans' secret game. Actually, Peres and his boys were thoroughly informed about the foot in the door; they knew perfectly well which door it was and whose foot was in it.

But all those games ended abruptly in February 1986, when the idyll between Hussein and Arafat turned into bitter confrontation.

On February 19, King Hussein spoke for three and a half hours on Jordanian television. In a surprisingly frank and sincere speech, he denounced Arafat's behavior and openly accused him of aborting the peace settlement.

Arafat had failed to keep his promise, the king said. Jordan had obtained the support of the United States for an international conference and for the PLO's participation. It was a tremendous victory for the Arab nation and the Palestinian cause.

And then Arafat had abruptly backed off. In a meeting in Amman on February 7, Arafat had suddenly put forward a new condition for fulfilling his promises: first, he said, the United States must recognize the Palestinians' right of self-determination. Without that recognition he wouldn't agree to any negotiation.

That was a mortal blow to the entire initiative. That meant the Americans had to agree in advance to Palestinian independence, which, of course, they couldn't do.

The king indirectly accused Arafat of being unreliable and unstable; he directly accused him of destroying the chances for peace. He couldn't work with him anymore, he said.

"My fate," he concluded, his voice choking, "me, son of the Hashemite clan descending from Muhammad, is to live in an Arab state overlooking the land of Palestine. My fate is to see what happens in the occupied land and outside it, and my heart is full of anguish.

"God be my witness."

In the next few days the king became much more outspoken against Arafat. "The Palestinian people must decide who represents them," he declared on American television, hinting that Arafat must be replaced. The palace leaked reports about a stormy scene between Arafat and the Jordanian prime minister, Zaid al-Rifai, in which Rifai had shouted at Arafat: "By your actions you only serve the Likud in Israel, so go ahead and join them!"

The PLO spokesmen, on their side, blamed the United States for refusing to recognize Palestinian rights to self-determination. But Ambassador Wat T. Cluverius IV, Shultz's senior adviser for Middle East peace, and other reliable sources revealed in reports from Amman some additional and much deeper reasons for the split between Hussein and Arafat.

During the early February discussions at the royal palace, Arafat and Hussein had tried to reach an agreement about the future association of the Palestinians and Jordan after the Israeli withdrawal. They had agreed that Jordan and the West Bank, including Gaza, should form a confederation. Arafat had presented five conditions to the establishment of such a confederation.

The first three conditions were that the Palestinians would have their own flag, parliament, and currency. Hussein had agreed.

But the fourth condition was that the Palestinians would have their own army. No, Hussein had said.

The fifth condition was that the chief executive of the confederation would be alternately a Palestinian and a Jordanian. The rotation would start after the end of King Hussein's "era."

This triggered all the alarm bells of survival in Hussein's mind. He understood that this clause would motivate the Palestinians to end his "era" by getting rid of him as soon as possible. Hussein rejected this condition as well, and the talks with Arafat broke down.

The world media were eager to announce the total collapse of the chances for peace. They were mistaken. They didn't pay heed to the king's declaration to the New York *Times*: "This is the end of a chapter, but not the end of the book."

And while world opinion was mourning the death of the peace process, people on both sides of the Jordan were busy resuscitating it.

Far from killing the chances for a settlement, the rift between Hussein and Arafat removed one of the three major obstacles to Israeli acceptance of the London document. Peres was a staunch supporter of the Jordanian option: a solution based on cooperation with King Hussein and a pro-Jordanian Palestinian delegation. The king's speech seemed to steer the negotiation toward the Jordanian option. Now that the PLO was out of the way, the Soviet reluctance and the Referral Clause remained the last issues to be resolved.

The approach of spring found Peres and his team deeply engaged in an effort to improve the quality of life of the Palestinians in the occupied territories. Peres acted with the active support of Itzhak Rabin and the Defense Ministry coordinator of the West Bank and Gaza, Shmuel Goren. Peres's representative in that endeavor was Dr. Beilin. They prepared a large-scale plan for electing new mayors, establishing an Arab bank, and starting several joint projects in the fields of agriculture, irrigation, and industry. They lifted all restrictions on money transfers across the Jordan River bridges, encouraged direct agricultural exports from the Gaza Strip to Egypt, and inaugurated direct telephone dialing from the West Bank to the outside world.

They weren't acting out of altruism, and some of Peres's boys actually regarded the entire project as a gimmick; but they had yielded to the unrelenting pressure of George Shultz.

The bettering of Palestinian conditions had turned into a veritable obsession of the U.S. secretary of state, who regarded the project as a noble humanitarian accomplishment. His enthusiasm was shared by the Egyptians, who called the endeavor "confidence-building measures." The Egyptians had joined the peace negotiations after the partial resolution of the Taba issue.

Strangely enough, the only one who didn't draw any confidence from the new measures was Hussein. He watched the Israeli project with growing suspicion, fearing that it was intended to improve the image of the occupation in the world media. At the beginning he even refused to cooperate, failing to grasp that if well handled, the new project might renew his weakening influence in the West Bank. He didn't realize that the Arab bank could become a formidable instrument in his hands to further his interests and those of his supporters in the occupied lands.

At that time Hussein still didn't realize how deep a change had taken place in the West Bank, and how little influence he had left. The social and political structures Jordan had left behind in June 1967, while hastily retreating before the Israeli army, had long ago crumbled. Hussein's traditional supporters had lost their say in the new Palestinian society; most of the West Bank and Gaza population had been born or had grown up under Israeli occupation. The king was unaware that they were indifferent or even deeply hostile to him.

"He still believed that his supporters had just run aground temporarily," one of his Israeli contacts recalled. "He thought he would only have to whistle and they'd jump to attention."

Hussein painfully awoke from his illusions barely a fortnight after his anti-Arafat speech, when Zafer el-Masri, the mayor of Nablus, was assassinated.

Masri, a youthful, warmhearted Palestinian, was the youngest son of one of the wealthiest and most influential families in the Middle East. The family controlled huge economic interests all over the Arab world, Europe, and the United States. Zafer's uncle, Hikmet el-Masri, was a member of the Jordanian parliament and its former speaker; Zafer's first cousin,

Taher el-Masri, a resident of Amman, was Hussein's foreign minister. Zafer himself was at home at Hussein's palace.

In December 1985, Zafer had been appointed mayor of Nablus. The young tycoon had served as deputy mayor in the past, but had turned his back on politics. "I love the good life and the business world too much!" he confided to his friend, Israeli General Benyamin (Fuad) Ben-Eliezer. But under the pressure of his family, city inhabitants, and Israeli authorities, he had agreed to assume the leadership of the largest city in the West Bank.

His appointment had been supported by Hussein and Arafat, who were still good friends. In spite of Zafer's close ties to Hussein, the PLO regarded him as a proud Palestinian nationalist.

But after Hussein's anti-Arafat speech, things changed dramatically. PLO leaders were expelled from Jordan; their offices were closed; carefully staged rallies throughout the country hailed the king's new policy toward Arafat, while Jordanian television showed phony "delegations" from the West Bank hurrying to Amman, to pledge loyalty to the king. In this atmosphere, the Palestinian terrorist organizations had to prove very quickly where the real loyalties of the people of the West Bank lay.

On March 2, on his way to the city hall, Zafer el-Masri was attacked by two men who fired three bullets into his back. One of the bullets pierced the mayor's heart. A few hours later, George Habash's Popular Front, one of the more extremist factions of the PLO, assumed responsibility for the murder. Arafat himself condemned the assassination and praised Masri. But the message to the palace in Amman was clear: the Palestinians wouldn't tolerate any of Hussein's supporters in an important position.

The next day, as more than twenty thousand people came to take part in Masri's funeral, his family was to find out that the PLO had another surprise in store for Hussein. Hundreds of youths, waving PLO flags and chanting national slogans, wrenched the coffin from the astounded family, draped it in a big PLO flag, and carried it to the cemetery. They turned the funeral into one of the largest pro-PLO demonstrations in the West Bank. The crowd yelled slogans, praising Masri as a PLO hero and a martyr of the revolution; they angrily waved their fists at the mention of Hussein's name. "You're a pig, Hussein," they screamed, "we'll put you in chains!"

Hussein helplessly watched the hostile procession on his television screen. One of his closest supporters, and certainly the most gifted and popular one, had been assassinated; his funeral had turned into a display of force for the PLO.

The men who had taken Zafer el-Masri's life had also stolen his death.

Now Hussein started to realize how shaky his position was in the West Bank and hurriedly tried to improve the situation. It was a pathetic effort, doomed from the start. Desperately striving to convince the reticent Palestinians that he was the only one able to bring them salvation, the king launched a grandiose 1.5-billion-dollar development project in the West Bank over the next five years.

That was nothing but a mirage. Actually, Hussein didn't have the money to finance his project. He relied on U.S. support, but he hadn't even consulted the Americans yet. Even when the Israelis stormed Capitol Hill, trying to help Hussein, the sum allocated by Congress was only eighteen million dollars. The Hussein plan failed miserably, and its failure only increased the bitterness of the Palestinians against him. Hussein's move had been too ambitious; its effect—if any—was too little, too late.

It was becoming too late for Peres, too, although he was slow to realize it.

Chapter 12

The Fatal Mistake
of Shimon Peres

April 10, 1986 was a turning point in Israel's history and in Shimon
Peres's career. That night, in the packed Mann Auditorium in Tel Aviv,
basking in the admiration of three thousand enthusiastic supporters,
cheered by a jubilant crowd, exuding power and self-confidence, Shimon
Peres easily won his battle against me and my handful of supporters—
and lost his bid for future success.

Had we succeeded, Peres would have remained prime minister, won
an early election, rescued Israel's ailing economy, and perhaps brought
peace to the embattled, blood-soaked Land of Israel. But Shimon Peres
has never been a farsighted politician. A shrewd manipulator, yes; a
survivor, certainly; a visionary, definitely. They are great qualities, but
sadly inadequate. Since that night, when he overwhelmingly won the
battle against me, it has been downhill for him and for our party.

I had been in open opposition to Peres for a long time. Still, as 1985
drew to a close, I realized he was doing very well as prime minister. At
the beginning of his term he was sharply criticized by the media for being
unable to achieve the goals he had set for his government: retreat from
Lebanon, economic recovery, peace with Jordan and the Palestinians.
It seemed that the government of National Unity was a government of
national paralysis; that the bitter Shamir and the disruptive Sharon would
block any initiative of Peres and the Labor Party. But Peres had braced
himself and slowly, patiently, had maneuvered his impossible government
in the right direction.

He had turned out to be a fine prime minister. His first success was the withdrawal from Lebanon. That grim, unnecessary war had cost us 660 lives, thousands of wounded, hundreds of millions of dollars; it had shattered the national consensus on that most sensitive and vital issue, security. It had brought destruction and death to Lebanon, and fathered a new breed of terrorists: the Hizballah.

Hizballah means "God's party." A fundamentalist Shiite group, extremist in its religious beliefs, fanatically devoted to the Iranian ayatollahs, the Hizballah inaugurated a new kind of war—that of suicidal terrorism. To die in the name of God, killing your enemy, would grant you eternal bliss in Allah's heavenly paradise. That became the credo of so many young Shiites who became members of the Hizballah.

And after a few weeks of training they would suddenly materialize beside our troops, their eyes glassy, their mind numb, as if drugged, their mouth mumbling verses from the Holy Koran. These modern kamikazes would rush to their death, blowing themselves up with hand grenades in the midst of a crowd of Jewish infidels, emptying their guns in a trance at a column of marching soldiers; driving their explosive-laden cars into a U.S. Marines compound or into the middle of an Israeli convoy. Quite often they would kidnap innocent Westerners and hold them hostage, or submit them to cruel torture that would end in assassination.

Peres managed to overcome the stubborn reluctance of his Likud bedfellows and mobilize a majority in the government supporting an immediate pullout from Lebanon. He did this by subtly manipulating some of his Likud colleagues, convincing Development Minister Gideon Pat, enticing the vain but sensible Vice Premier David Levy, and securing the abstention of Finance Minister Itzhak Modai. On January 14, 1985, the pullout from Lebanon was finally voted by the government; it started a week later and was completed in June.

Only a security zone of 360 square miles, slightly larger than the one Israel had established before the Lebanon War, remained under Israeli control. A local military force, the South Lebanese army, was created and placed under the command of a pro-Israeli officer, General Lakhad.

Peres's second achievement was the smothering of inflation. It had become a living nightmare, spiraling up daily to break new records. I couldn't walk into a supermarket without bumping into harried salespersons stamping new price stickers on every item on sale. By the end of 1984 the inflation rate had reached a peak of 445 percent a year.

Peres and his handpicked team conceived an overall plan, including drastic cuts in wages, a 30 percent devaluation of the shekel, a rigid control of prices, and the introduction of the new shekel, worth one thousand old shekels. Peres worked out the details with infinite patience, gradually rallying around the plan the skeptical leaders of his own party, the management of private enterprises, and the reluctant trade unions without whose cooperation no wage cut was possible. Then, in order to break the automatic stalemate in the government, he convinced a couple of Likud ministers to cross party lines and vote for his plan.

David Levy had been the key Likud minister Peres had seduced a few months before, to tip the balance on the Lebanon withdrawal. But the operation couldn't be repeated, as Levy strongly objected to any measures that could hurt the low-income classes. Instead, Peres targeted the finance minister, Itzhak Modai.

Modai is a brilliant but unpredictable man, armed with an incisive mind but greatly impeded by abrupt mood changes. He was, however, vain enough to believe Peres's assurance that the bold economic plan was in great part his own. I recall meeting, in Eilat, a leading member of Peres's team who was preparing the reform. When I asked him if the finance minister had indeed developed the main lines of the plan, my friend almost choked on his beer. "Modai doesn't understand and doesn't even know what it's all about," he scoffed. "He isn't even invited to the important meetings. But we work hard on making him believe he's a founding father of the plan."

It was worth it. When the reform was brought to a vote, in July 1985, Modai, Shamir, and Korfu were the only Likud ministers who raised their hands in its favor. The plan was a tremendous success. In a few months the inflation rate shrank from 450 percent to 19 percent and stayed there. It was the first time ever that a galloping inflation rate had been crushed without imposing a severe strain on democratic institutions. It is no wonder that Peres's economic reform is being taught today at universities around the world. And there is no doubt in my mind that nobody but Peres could have carried out that reform.

During his term of office Peres also managed to improve the tarnished image of Israel. We had become utterly unpopular abroad after the Lebanon War and the countless refusals of Begin and Shamir to undertake a peace initiative with Jordan and the Palestinians. Peres, speaking moderately, asserting his willingness to make peace, openly proposing a territorial compromise in the West Bank and Gaza, stood out as strikingly different from his predecessors. The leaders of the Western world saw a new Israel emerge, a wise, reasonable Israel intensely striving for peace.

I knew Peres wouldn't be able to make peace as long as he was immobilized by the National Unity government. At the Labor Bureau meetings I continually warned him that there was only one way to start a real peace process: dissolve the government and call a new election. That became my personal goal.

I launched my initiative in March 1985 when I published an article entitled "Elections Now" in the party newspaper. I described the dark prospects for the economy and the peace process, which would become reality when we handed power to the Likud, in October 1986. I wrote that as soon as the pullout from Lebanon was completed, we should dismantle the National Unity government.

"Many of my friends ask me: Didn't we sign a rotation agreement with the Likud? What about our commitment? What about our credibility? My answer is that our supreme commitment is to the people and the State of Israel, and it should prevail over any other agreement. As to our credibility, we went into a partnership with the Likud, but on one condition: that this partnership would function properly. It is already certain that those two horses, Likud and Labor, can't pull the same carriage. Therefore, we should put an end to the partnership and call a new election."

My article was warmly received by many in the Labor Party, and my next step was to circulate a petition among the Central Committee members. According to our party rules, any motion supported by 10 percent of the members (roughly one thousand at that time) was automatically inscribed on the committee's agenda. I proudly brought the 101 signatures I had collected to our secretary-general, Uzi Baram. He was pleased by my initiative. He openly told me he supported it, and he would let me officially present the proposal at the forthcoming party convention.

But long before the scheduled debate on my proposal, several crises shook the government, each of them providing Peres with an excellent reason to dismantle the Labor-Likud coalition.

In August 1985, Sharon violently attacked Peres, using harsh, brutal language. Peres threatened to fire him; Shamir countered that Peres had no right to do so. It was obvious that if Peres carried out his threat the government would fall apart. But at the last moment Peres backed off, and the crisis faded away.

In November, the foul-mouthed Sharon once again insulted the prime minister. Again, Peres threatened to fire him. The end of the government seemed a matter of hours. At a meeting of the Labor Party Central Committee, party activists enthusiastically cheered a determined Shimon Peres; many came to shake my hand. "You won, Michael!" they said. "We are leaving the government." But Peres, unable to go all the way, backed off once again, after Sharon reluctantly scribbled a note of apology.

In January 1986, there was a third crisis. The cabinet met to decide whether the question of the small Taba enclave, which had been poisoning our relations with Egypt, should be submitted to international arbitration. The Likud was vehemently opposed to Peres's proposals; Peres said Shamir and his colleagues were sabotaging the peace process. Peres threatened to resign if the Likud rejected the arbitration.

In the early evening of January 12, the cabinet convened. The meeting ran through the whole night, for twelve long hours. The Likud ministers attacked Peres, some of them bluntly insulting him. The debate was interrupted several times. Any other politician would have thrown in the towel and gone straight to the president's residence to submit his letter of resignation. But Peres had seemingly infinite patience. Finally, in the early morning, an agreement was reached and the cabinet accepted the arbitration.

When all the ministers left for a few hours of sleep, Nemrod Novik walked into Peres's office. Peres looked at him bleary-eyed. Novik didn't say a word, but Peres understood: his assistant felt he had missed the chance to resign and call a new election. The prime minister looked back at Novik and said: "I still have time, Nemrod."

Thus, the government swayed and limped and staggered from one crisis to another, but remained in power until the Labor Party convention in April 1986.

Shimon Peres was at the peak of his career. The party seemed to be stronger and more confident than ever before. The Likud convention, held a few weeks before, had turned into a violent confrontation between rival factions. It had been cut short when hotheaded delegates had jumped on the dais and overturned the chairman's desk. Fistfights had broken out in the convention hall.

In sharp contrast, the Labor convention was characterized by order, unity, and optimism. Recent polls showed that Peres's popularity had soared to unprecedented peaks; the return of Labor to the country's hegemony seemed to be within reach.

On the day the convention opened, another government crisis made the headlines. Once again a Likud minister had launched an ugly attack on Shimon Peres. This time it was Modai who had offended the prime minister. Peres announced he wouldn't take it anymore. The newspapers predicted the collapse of the government.

Against this backdrop the convention was asked to vote on my motion to break up the government and call for a new election.

The day of the vote, I was invited to lunch at the French ambassador's residence, a magnificent white house perched on top of a hill in Jaffa, commanding a breathtaking view of the Mediterranean. The lunch was given in honor of the Socialist leader Pierre Maurois, the former prime minister of France, who was visiting Israel as an honorary guest of our convention.

Only a few of us were at the ambassador's table: a couple of diplomats and Maurois on the French side; Peres, Bar-Lev, Motta Gur, and I on the Israeli side. A few aides were whispering at the far end of the table. Maurois, a big, jovial man, joked with Peres and me about the possibility of breaking the rotation agreement and calling for an early election in the fall. He was well informed about our internal struggles.

When the lunch was over Peres approached me and said, "Michael, let's go somewhere and talk."

I assumed that he would rather like it to be a discreet conversation. So I said to him, "Why don't we just take your car and drive around town? We can talk freely without being interrupted."

"Good," the prime minister said.

When we were comfortably seated in the back of his car, with the bodyguard in the front seat and the Shin Beth car opening the way, he turned to me and said, "Michael, why don't you remove your motion from the agenda tonight?"

I said, "Shimon, in six months you're going to hand the keys of this country to Shamir. That's going to be a catastrophe for the nation, for the party, and for you. We shouldn't allow this to happen. I have a feeling that the majority of the delegates will vote with me if you don't interfere. So don't."

He leaned toward me. "Do you really believe that I am going to give the premiership to Shamir?"

I stared back at him. "What do you mean?"

"Do you think I am out of my mind?" he said. "I'll give them the power? Don't you worry. I'll take care that the government collapses before the rotation date. David Levy will attack Shamir from one side, and Sharon from the other. They are at each other's throats anyway. I'll take such initiatives that will force the Likud out of the government. They won't be able to go along with my policy, they'll have to leave the government."

"Are you serious?" I asked.

"I know what I am doing, believe me."

I replied, "Shimon, you are not an 'untiring underminer' [as Rabin had bitterly named him in his memoirs], but you're an untiring optimist. Good God, what are you talking about? Do you really believe that they'll leave the government of their own free will? For almost two years now your Likud partners have been biting the bullet and enduring the worst humiliations, with only one goal in mind: reach October 20 when you'll transfer your powers to them. They'll crawl on their bellies, they'll swallow all the insults you'll feed them, just to reach the rotation date."

"Don't you trust me?" he said. He looked very confident. It was a prematurely hot day and the air conditioner blew a pleasant chill into the car.

"No," I answered. "Shimon, if you don't want the Likud to return to power, don't fight me tonight. Just go up on the podium and say that you'll accept the convention's verdict. Don't take sides. They'll understand."

He shook his head. "No, we don't need this. I'll oppose your motion."

As of that moment, I knew that the battle was lost. Although he didn't dare to admit it, Shimon Peres was too worried about his credibility to risk breaking the rotation agreement. I didn't want to remind him that he had instructed one of his aides to call me almost daily and encourage me in my initiative. Now he had decided it was too risky for him, so he backed off.

I didn't tell anybody about our conversation, but the news spread quickly among the delegates. An hour later I met Motta Gur on the convention floor. The previous Friday, after listening to me for hours, he had declared he would support my motion wholeheartedly. He had made a brave and articulate appearance on national television and explained why he would vote with me.

But that was last Friday. "I'm going to vote against you," he now said with somewhat puzzling cheerfulness. I shrugged and walked away. Uzi Baram, our secretary-general, turned to me with a somewhat embarrassed smile. "I'll vote against your motion," he informed me.

Voting was not enough. The well-oiled machinery of the party, drunk with false confidence, had decided to turn the vote into a show of strength and rally around Peres. For that reason they brought a well-known singer, Sarale Sharon, and a large kibbutz choir to open the evening session. It was a memorable evening. Sarale Sharon swept the audience with her popular songs; in a few minutes she had three thousand people singing along with her, clapping their hands, thumping their feet; many party leaders, including Knesset members and a couple of ministers, merrily danced on the stage.

I watched the festivities from my seat in a corner. What are they singing about? I asked myself. What's the big celebration? Where are we all going to be in six months? Don't they realize?

The sing-along achieved its goal. It left the convention delegates in an ebullient mood, with a feeling of elation, power, and self-confidence. A delegate from Acre read a poem she had composed in honor of the great statesman and leader Shimon Peres. Everybody cheered. In that atmosphere, my fellow-delegates must have regarded me as a killjoy who comes to spoil everybody's fun with his dark prophecies.

When the debate on my motion finally started, Peres's men didn't even have the decency to let me present it properly to the convention. I was not allowed to open the debate; they summoned Itzhak Navon to do so and explain why we shouldn't call new elections now. I was allowed to speak for seven minutes. "You have no more rights than any other participant in the debate," the chairman, Nissim Zvili, who had been appointed by Peres and was a firm supporter of him, told me. I was very tense. I had to cut short my speech and hear Peres, Baram, and the entire party establishment denounce my proposal. When the vote was finally taken, I got a mere nine votes out of three thousand.

On October 20 the rotation took place and Shamir became prime minister. Shortly afterwards I came to see Peres on another matter in his office at the Foreign Ministry. I reminded him of our talk in his car and his assessment that there would be no rotation. "So I made a mistake," he said curtly.

Chapter 13

The London Letter

Shimon Peres had barely seven months left in office. That was the time to act. The PLO was out of the game. The king was genuinely alarmed, therefore willing to listen. The Egyptians, at last, were involved. The Americans and the British were helpful. Gorbachev was boldly reshaping the Soviet Union and its foreign policy.

And still nothing happened. Peres believed he had time; he was still convinced that he could outsmart the Likud leaders by finding a way to avoid the rotation. Hussein completely misread the Likud's silence: he mistook it for tacit consent to Peres's peace initiative. There was no reason to believe, he said coldly to an American journalist, that the Likud would oppose the peace process.

Thus the peace initiative moved smoothly, irreversibly, toward dismal failure.

A feeble effort to rekindle the process slightly rippled the lethargy of Peres's final months in office. It was his sudden official visit to Morocco, as a guest of King Hassan.

The visit by itself was very significant. I knew that Rabin had secretly visited Morocco as prime minister, as had Dayan as foreign minister and Peres, a couple of times, as head of the opposition. But those had never been official visits covered by the world media. This time, in the final days of July 1986, Peres flew officially to Morocco, an Arab country, and was the formal guest of its king.

Everybody expected this visit to be the opening to some dramatic move, like a summit between Peres and Hussein and perhaps another Arab leader. It didn't make sense that Morocco's King Hassan would have taken such a bold initiative just for the pleasure of showing Peres the legendary Arab hospitality. But when nothing happened, and Peres returned empty-handed to Israel, the general feeling was that another project of his had misfired.

Indeed, Peres's visit could have produced a dramatic breakthrough in the peace process. It was originally intended to turn into a summit meeting with the participation of Hussein and Mubarak. But it had been very poorly and amateurishly prepared. After arriving in Morocco and settling in the magnificent royal guesthouse at Ifran in the Atlas Mountains, Peres was asked to make a statement including a few key formulas such as "international conference" and "national rights for the Palestinians." Peres refused, and both Mubarak and Hussein decided to stay home. Shimon Peres returned to Jerusalem on July 23.

On October 20 he handed the prime minister's office to Itzhak Shamir. The handshake of the former and future prime ministers sealed the death warrant for the peace process. But on that crisp October day nobody realized it.

Ironically, Peres was the last to understand that a tremendous change had taken place. True, he wasn't prime minister anymore, but in practice very little seemed to have changed. He was vice premier and foreign minister, which allowed him to continue his diplomatic initiatives. He kept doing what he wanted without asking Shamir for permission and reporting to him only what he wanted to.

He had transferred all his team from the prime minister's office to the Foreign Ministry. After some foolish quarrels with Shamir and an ill-advised attempt to amend the law in order to create a deputy minister slot for his confidant, Yossi Beilin, he had finally appointed him "political director general of the Foreign Ministry," beside General Abraham Tamir, who was now only "director general of the Foreign Ministry." This division of duties would become a source of friction and scandal, but for the time being Shimon Peres didn't care.

He regarded Shamir with contempt. Shamir wasn't popular; he was openly criticized within his own party. His record as foreign minister over the past two years showed him to have been quiet on Peres's initiatives. People remembered him from his former term as a mediocre premier who hadn't been able to cope with Begin's legacy and had lost the elections. Even after assuming the premiership, he had remained close-mouthed, awkward, suspicious, and lacking in originality and grace.

But Peres, on the other hand, didn't understand what my friends and

I saw clearly: Shamir was the boss now while he, Peres, was out of the game. Peres's economic recovery plan had been cut short, and he had lost his power to push through his peace initiative.

He didn't feel that way. The Labor Party continued to follow him blindly, convinced he knew what he was doing. He was still riding on the waves of popularity in Israeli public opinion; people still remembered that he was the one who had pulled the army out of Lebanon and put an end to the inflation; world leaders still saw him as the one Israeli who counted.

Margaret Thatcher still received him warmly, Helmut Kohl toasted him at the Bonn Chancery, François Mitterrand made a show of their personal friendship and fed him sumptuous dinners at the Elysée Palace. The Americans continued cooperating with him on the peace process.

And the Soviets, after such a long and exasperating process, were finally sending out feelers in his direction.

At the beginning of November 1986, a few weeks after the rotation, Peres's adviser, Nemrod Novik, was invited to the Soviet embassy in Washington. He was ushered into a private office for a secret two-and-a-half-hour conversation with a young Soviet diplomat named Rogov. The Soviet was a frank, confident man—an astounding contrast to the stuffed robots of Brezhnev's era who sat stone-faced through diplomatic meetings, repeating their trite formulas. The Soviet Union wouldn't be caught again with its pants down as at Camp David, Rogov said with a smile. It would launch its own initiatives.

Novik asked about diplomatic relations. Breaking relations with Israel had been a mistake, the Russian admitted. They must be restored—in the right context, of course.

And what about Jewish emigration? Novik asked.

Rogov was ready for that question. Novik left the embassy with the promise that in March 1987 Jews would be allowed to emigrate to Israel at the rate of five hundred a month. (The emigration actually started in May.)

This was not the only piece of amazing news Novik was to enter in his report. The two diplomats had also discussed the peace process and the international conference. The USSR would agree to the concept of an international conference, breaking down into bilateral committees, the Soviet diplomat said. But he was adamant on one point: No separate

agreement between two parties was possible. One of the bilateral committees couldn't reach an agreement if the others failed.

Novik understood that the Soviets were trying to protect the Syrians,
and that Hussein had given them his word of honor that there would
be no Jordanian-Israeli agreement without a Syrian-Israeli agreement.
"The walls of the bilateral committees should be somewhat transparent,"
Novik's Soviet host said. "Third parties shouldn't be worried." While
writing his report, Novik had only one thought in mind: nobody in the
Foreign Ministry would believe him.

Nobody did.

But the Soviets didn't stop at that. They wanted to make public the
new look in their Mideast policy. And for that they used, against his
will, their old ally, Syria's President Hafez al-Assad.

For years the Soviet Union had been funding, arming, and diplomat-
ically protecting Syria. By their mutual defense treaty the USSR was
committed to rush to Assad's help if Syria was threatened by a foreign
attack. This made the Soviet leaders very jumpy each spring, when Assad
would start rattling his tanks and missiles and threaten Israel with a new
war. They feared that the Syrian president might drag them, against
their will, into a confrontation with Israel and perhaps even the United
States.

The young *perestroika* diplomats had had enough of this strange arrangement with Assad. In an article published in Moscow, a young Soviet
diplomat named Zotov openly suggested that the time was right to modify
the Soviet Union's relationship with Syria. It was not for Syria to define
Soviet policy in the Middle East, he wrote in substance; the USSR should
clarify for Damascus who was the boss and who was the client.

The occasion to do so arose in March 1987, when Assad was invited
to visit Moscow. Before his visit the Kremlin decided to starve him
deliberately. Assad was desperate to achieve three objectives: alleviate
the burden of his debt, negotiate a new aid package, and get MiG-29
fighter jets.

Prior to Assad's trip, the Soviets had openly abused him. They eluded
any discussions on his debt and on future aid. They offered MiG-29's to
Zimbabwe and Jordan, and sold them to India and Iraq. But Assad
couldn't even get a couple of aircraft for his air shows on Independence
Day.

At the state dinner in Moscow, facing the television cameras, Foreign

Minister Eduard Shevardnadze toasted President Assad, and vociferously declared that the lack of diplomatic relations between the Soviet Union and Israel was not normal. The Arab-Israeli conflict, he insisted, should be solved only by diplomatic means.

Assad listened in astounded silence.

Simultaneously, the Soviets gave the Syrian president all that he wanted. They eliminated 25 percent of Syria's debt, granted him a loan of three billion dollars over the next three years, and signed a contract for the delivery of MiG-29's to the Syrian air force.

The message couldn't have been clearer: if you want something we'll give it to you, the Soviets were saying to Assad, but keep quiet, and don't interfere with our policy.

The message was well understood in Damascus, and in Amman as well. Zaid al-Rifai, Hussein's prime minister, had close ties to Damascus. Like Assad, he was an enemy of the PLO. Rifai still has a scar left by a Palestinian bullet.

Rifai visited Assad shortly after his return from Moscow and reported to Hussein that the Soviets were changing their policy in the Middle East. Israel, too, spotted the first effects of the new Soviet outlook: in March 1987 the Soviets stopped jamming the broadcasts of Israeli radio to Jews in the Soviet Union.

The Soviets were starting to play ball, removing one of the last two obstacles to the negotiation. Gorbachev was at last initiating *perestroika* in Soviet foreign policy. But the Soviet leader didn't understand that he was too late. A year before, his concessions might have been crucial; at least they would have won him a seat at the international conference. Today they were worthless.

The first to awaken was Hussein. Closely monitoring any utterance of Israel's ministers, he noticed the change of tone in the public declarations of Sharon and Shamir. It slowly dawned on him that he had been wrong all along. The Likud was not going to pursue Peres's initiative.

The Likud leaders, Hussein realized, weren't interested in peace talks, in territorial compromise, in any settlement that implied a pullout from the West Bank. They wanted no international conference. They had kept quiet in the last two years because they hadn't been in power. Now they were initiating a tough line in Israel's policy. To secure Israel's control over all of the occupied lands, they might even resort to mass expulsions of Palestinians; and the influx of bitter, frustrated pro-PLO refugees into Hussein's kingdom could jeopardize his throne.

He had no time to waste; he would have to move while Peres still had some influence over Israeli public opinion. When a message from Peres reached him requesting a meeting, he agreed promptly. The meeting was to take place in London on April 11. Hussein's official reason for his trip was, as so many times in the past, a visit to his doctor. This time he had trouble with his ear.

Before leaving for London, Hussein made a last effort to gain U.S. support for the Referral Clause. He sent Zaid al-Rifai to Washington. But the reception awaiting Rifai was cool and reserved. The Americans already felt that Peres was having troubles with his partners at home; they didn't want to complicate his life even more with the Referral Clause.

Rifai didn't understand that his own king was softening and that his mission to Washington actually was Hussein's last battle in the Referral war. After his talks in Washington had misfired, Rifai vented his disappointment in several interviews and press briefings, accusing the United States of misunderstanding Middle Eastern realities and aborting the chances for peace. Then, after having dispensed his message of gloom and doom, Zaid packed his suitcase and flew to London to meet his king.

Hussein traveled to London via Cairo, where he conferred with Hosni Mubarak. "Forget about the Referral," the Egyptian president frankly advised him. "Peres's situation is bad enough as it is."

The king was to hear similar advice from Margaret Thatcher in London. "Peres cannot accept your conditions," she said in his good ear. "Don't you see what the Likud is doing to him?"

On Saturday, April 11, Peres and Hussein met as usual at the doctor's clinic. Peres was accompanied by Dr. Yossi Beilin. Peres claimed later that he didn't have high hopes at that time and didn't expect the king to say anything new. He believed Hussein was deeply entrenched in his positions about the international conference; Zaid's mission to Washington only proved the king was sticking to his guns.

The main reason for his visit, as Peres presented it to Shamir before leaving, was to discuss with the king a project that was dear to him: the digging of a canal between the Red Sea and the Dead Sea, which would bring substantial benefits to both Jordan and Israel, solve Jordan's energy problems, enable both countries to move their ports inland, and free miles of beaches for tourism. Peres had already discussed the two-seas canal with Thatcher and Mitterrand, and they had promised to provide 1.5 billion dollars for the financing of the project.

But as Hussein made his opening remarks, Peres suddenly realized that the king wasn't interested in the canal at all. Something much more dramatic was happening: Hussein seemed ready to give up the Referral Clause.

"Why don't we try," Peres said carefully, "to define our points of agreement and put them on paper?"

"Good idea," the king responded. "I have to keep an appointment in town [Hussein was to meet with the Soviet ambassador that day], but I'll be back soon. Perhaps you'll prepare a draft, and we can go over it later."

The king was back after a couple of hours. With his prime minister, he closely perused the document Peres and his team had prepared. They suggested several changes, and the agreement was redrafted a few times. Zaid al-Rifai added, in his own hand, some of the corrections in the final version. The meeting continued late into the afternoon. After seven hours the king of Jordan and the foreign minister of Israel shook hands. They had reached a historical agreement. The document was entitled *A Three-Part Understanding Between Jordan and Israel*.

Its Chapter A defined the procedure of the calling of the conference. "The Secretary-General of the United Nations would issue invitations to the five permanent members of the Security Council and the parties involved in the Arab-Israeli conflict," in order to negotiate a peaceful settlement. The chapter mentioned U.N. Resolutions 242 and 338, and defined the aims of the conference: bring a comprehensive peace to the area, security to its states, and respond to "the legitimate rights of the Palestinian people." The last formula had been adopted from the Camp David agreements.

Chapter B invited the parties to form "bilateral committees to negotiate mutual issues."

Chapter C, by far the most important, defined the procedure of negotiations agreed to by Jordan and Israel. The international conference, it said, wouldn't impose any solution or veto any agreement the parties would reach; the bilateral committees would conduct direct negotiations; the Palestinians' representatives would be included in the Jordanian-Palestinian delegation.

A special clause specified which Palestinians would qualify for the delegation: "Participation in the Conference would be based on the Parties' acceptance of Resolutions 242 and 338 and the renunciation of violence and terrorism."

In the next paragraph, C (VI), King Hussein actually betrayed Syria. The paragraph said "Each committee will negotiate independently." That clause was in blatant contradiction to Hussein's commitment to the Soviets and the Syrians not to negotiate a separate peace. It was an important breakthrough because it allowed Israel, Jordan, and the Palestinians to reach an agreement even if Israel and Syria remained at war.

But the major breakthrough was in paragraph C (VII). Instead of the notorious "referral" of problematic issues to the plenum of the conference, the paragraph now simply said "Other issues will be decided by mutual agreement between Jordan and Israel." That meant that any intervention of the conference in the negotiation was formally excluded.

The document concluded: "The above understanding is subject to approval of the respective Governments of Israel and Jordan. The text of this paper will be shown and suggested to the U.S.A."

That conclusion was aimed at protecting King Hussein. Peres and Hussein agreed that the Israelis would deliver the document to the Americans; the United States would then officially offer it to the Jordanian and Israeli governments as an American document. That way no one could accuse King Hussein of secret collusion with the Israelis.

For the same reason it was decided that Chapters A and B would eventually become public, but Chapter C would remain secret.

That night Peres flew back to Israel, convinced he had cleared the road for peace.

Now that he was so close to achieving his goal, Peres should have moved with utter caution, as he had done on the Lebanese withdrawal and the inflation issues two years before. He should have prepared the ground meticulously by secretly gaining the support of at least one Likud cabinet member and personally convincing U.S. leaders to back his initiative.

He did neither of these. So excited was he by his achievement that he assumed the London document alone would do his job for him. He went on the offensive without any preparation.

The next morning Peres placed the London document on Shamir's desk. The prime minister, frowning, perused the agreement between

Hussein and his foreign minister. Peres described the meeting with Hussein and Rifai, and outlined the next stage agreed on by the two parties. "Shamir was stunned," one of Peres's aides recalled. "Until that morning he had thought nothing would come out of Peres's initiative. Now, all of a sudden, he found out this was a serious matter."

"When we came to him before to report," another one of Peres's men told me, "he would listen in silence, or sigh and say, 'What can come out of that? There's no fire, why's Shimon in such a hurry?' But he never expressed any objections."

On the morning of April 12, Shamir didn't voice any objections either, although his angry face betrayed his thoughts. An embarrassing moment ensued when he picked up the London document to have it photocopied, but Peres refused. "That's the only copy," he said, "and the handwriting in the margins is Zaid al-Rifai's. I have to protect him."

Shamir seethed with anger. "He felt hurt and humiliated," one of his aides told me afterwards. Peres's boys had the right to read and handle the document, but he, the prime minister of Israel, was even denied the right to keep it in his files.

After the meeting Peres showed the document to Itzhak Rabin. The defense minister was deeply impressed and enthusiastically voiced his support.

While Peres was in Jerusalem, Yossi Beilin was meeting with U.S. Ambassador Thomas Pickering in Tel Aviv. Pickering immediately grasped the tremendous significance of the London document; he urged Beilin to fly at once to Helsinki to intercept George Shultz. The U.S. secretary of state was on his way to Moscow to confer with Soviet leaders.

Beilin looked at his watch. It was 10 A.M.; the next flight was leaving in an hour. He rushed to the airport. He didn't have a ticket, but the airline chief of station agreed to let him board the flight and settle the account later. As the aircraft climbed to cruising altitude over the Mediterranean, Beilin leaned back in his seat. He thought, We've done it. We are going to put an end to the conflict. I'll bring the document to Shultz, he'll show it to Gorbachev, the great powers will support us, and we'll have peace. He briefly thought of the internal Israeli scene. The Likud couldn't reject such a document. It meant peace!

In Helsinki, Beilin met with Ambassador Charles Hill, a close aide of the secretary, and handed him a copy of the document. Shultz read it the same night and realized the overwhelming importance of the agreement. He nevertheless decided not to reveal the document's existence to the Soviets, and during his talks in Moscow didn't even hint that Israel and Jordan had reached an agreement.

Back in Washington, Shultz proceeded according to the Israeli demand. A few days later U.S. Ambassador Thomas Pickering walked into Itzhak Shamir's office. He was visibly moved and made a dramatic opening statement. An Israeli high official described the meeting to me. "I come to you not only as the American ambassador to your country," Pickering said to Shamir, "but also as a special envoy of the secretary of state. The secretary believes that a historic breakthrough has been achieved."

Secretary Shultz, the ambassador went on, wanted to come to the region and bring the parties together. In the secretary's agenda, the schedule for the month of June was very busy, but he didn't believe the trip could be postponed till July or August, for in the meantime the hostile parties might take steps against the agreement.

The ambassador didn't realize that he was talking to the "hostile parties" at that very moment.

Therefore, Pickering concluded, Secretary Shultz would like to come at the first date in May convenient to Shamir.

Saying so, he solemnly handed over the agreement to the prime minister. The same day a copy of the document was delivered to Shimon Peres.

Peres glanced at the document and couldn't believe his eyes. The U.S. State Department had made a colossal mistake. Under the heading "Secret/Most Sensitive" was written: "Accord between the Government of Jordan, which has confirmed it to the United States, and the Foreign Minister of Israel, ad referendum to the Government of Israel. Parts 'A' and 'B,' which when they become public upon agreement of the parties, will be treated as U.S. proposals to which Jordan and Israel have agreed. Part 'C' is to be treated, in great confidentiality, as commitments to the U.S. from the Government of Jordan to be transmitted to the Government of Israel."

Then came the text of the agreement, and below it "11/4/87—London."

London!

The dateline and the words "will be treated as U.S. proposals" disclosed the most crucial secret of the document—that it wasn't an American suggestion, but an Israeli-Jordanian agreement signed in London.

Shamir didn't hesitate to photocopy the document and distribute it to all his colleagues as proof of Peres's plotting with Hussein behind his back; Likud Minister Modai, who had a grudge against Peres, made a public appearance. "They wanted to cheat us," he thundered. "They said it was an American document, but it says 'London'! An American document? Nonsense!"

Another mistake was the inclusion of Part C in the official U.S. document. It had been agreed between the parties, on Hussein's insistence, that this ultra-secret chapter would be presented orally, but not put on paper. For Hussein's enemies, there was the proof that he had betrayed the Syrians and the Palestinians.

In Amman, indeed, King Hussein was astounded to find out that the Americans had made such a blunder and exposed the collusion.

Still, in spite of the State Department mishap, all the parties were willing to go ahead with the plan.

All the parties except Shamir.

Shamir staunchly opposed the idea of an international conference; he also deeply feared that the Jordanian-Palestinian delegation would include PLO members. And finally, he didn't even consider giving back any part of the historical Land of Israel in exchange for peace.

In a last-minute effort to thwart the project, the prime minister of Israel dispatched Minister Moshe Arens to Washington. His mission was to dissuade Shultz from coming.

Arens has never been a subtle politician, and on quite a few occasions he had shocked with his straightforwardness. Meeting with Shultz now, he openly said that a visit by the secretary at this time would interfere in the internal affairs of the State of Israel. The convening of an international conference was a very controversial subject in Israel, he pointed out. "We'll have to fight it at home," he said. "You'll always be welcome, but the prime minister feels it's not the appropriate moment."

It was now Shultz's turn to make his own mistake. He bowed to Shamir's refusal. "He's the prime minister of Israel," he said to his aides.

"I cannot force myself upon him. If the prime minister doesn't want me to come, I shall not come."

American diplomats, Peres, Hussein, and their aides pulled out their hair in despair. Shultz's role was crucial in the forthcoming negotiation. "If it had been Henry Kissinger," a U.S. diplomat mournfully remarked, "he would have brushed aside Arens's arguments and said 'Sorry, but I'm coming in the name of the president.'"

But Shultz wasn't Kissinger. An affable man, very elegant and moderate in his pronouncements, he held the leaders of America's allies in high esteem. He had also never been enthusiastic about the idea of an international conference. The prospect of Soviet participation made him rather lukewarm to that aspect of the London agreement. True, he had been ready to come to the Middle East, but Arens had little difficulty in dissuading him now.

Shultz backed down, and by doing so, condemned the London agreement to a dusty death in some forgotten archive.

From that moment on, nothing could help: neither the frantic letters and telegrams from Washington to Shamir trying to quell his fears about PLO participation in the conference, nor the marathon talks between Ambassador Pickering and the prime minister; nor Peres's aides' psychological warfare by leaking the London document to the press and briefing leading Israeli and foreign journalists; neither Peres and Rabin's threat to quit the government and provoke early elections if the cabinet didn't approve the London document; nor even Hussein's bold declarations to the Boston *Globe* that it wouldn't be realistic to expect an Israeli withdrawal from all the territories occupied in 1967; and that Jerusalem shouldn't be a divided city again.

The peace initiative was dead. On May 13, 1987, the Israeli cabinet discussed the London document but refrained from approving it.

In late 1987 and during 1988, Secretary Shultz was to halfheartedly attempt to relaunch the peace offensive by visiting the Middle East several times. In the Jerusalem Hilton, where he always stayed, a huge peace dove made of cardboard and fabric was placed in the lobby with a long string hanging down from her tail. Whenever Shultz arrived, he would pull the string and the dove would flap her wings. But as the months passed, Shultz's face grew more glum and resigned, and even the dove didn't seem to spread her wings with the same eagerness.

Then one night, Shultz was bluntly told by Shamir and Arens that, in their view, U.N. Resolution 242's "territories for peace" didn't apply to the West Bank and Gaza. He had never heard that before, in so many words. Disillusioned, the secretary of state left Jerusalem and the Hilton white dove, never to return.

I must stress that I was very skeptical about the London document. Today, three years later, I still am. I think Peres was very naïve to believe that the Soviets, the Chinese, the Syrians, the Egyptians, and even the French and the British would have accepted an international conference that was devoid of any decision-making power.

The Soviet Union would be committing political suicide in the Middle East if it were to abandon its support of the PLO and the Syrians, the cornerstones of its policy; and let Israel, Jordan, and an impotent Palestinian delegation decide the future of the Arab-Israeli conflict.

Hussein himself was to demand, a few months later, that a "reporting" clause be added so that the bilateral committees would have to report regularly to the plenum of the conference. Even this "reporting," under hostile questioning and admonishments, could transform the conference into an international tribunal automatically ruling against Israel.

In all the Labor Party deliberations about the peace initiative I warned Peres that the international conference according to his concept was a beautiful dream, but would never come into being. That was also the feeling of the Israeli public. I fought against including the call for an international conference in the Labor Party platform before the 1988 elections. "In the best case," I said to the Labor Party Central Committee, "the international conference can be presented as a necessary evil. The Israelis don't want the Russians and the Chinese to decide for them. If we have to go to that conference, let's at least tell the truth: that we don't want it, that we don't need it, that it's risky—but that it's better than a stalemate. But let's not embellish it and present it as the new gospel."

I was outvoted, and my warnings were not heard. Today we know that by making the international conference the main Labor slogan in the 1988 elections we lost many of our potential voters.

Still, I believe that back in the spring of 1987 the adoption of the London document might have inspired the Palestinians with hope. It might have spread the feeling that there was a chance for a peaceful

solution. And mainly, it might have led to a far-reaching interim agreement between Israel and Jordan that would have cooled passions and
instilled a feeling of peace in our region.

The failure of the London initiative deepened the frustration and
despair of the Palestinian people, and contributed to the building pressure
in the West Bank and Gaza that would soon explode in the rocks and
firebombs of the Intifada.

Chapter 14

The Gathering Storm

At 9:50 P.M. on the night of November 25, 1987, a hang glider silently landed in a Galilee field, close to the city of Kiryat Shemona. The glider came from Lebanon. It was equipped with an auxiliary engine, but the flier had turned it off shortly before crossing the Israeli border.

Milud Ben Alnajakh, the young man who flew the tiny aircraft, was a member of the General Command of Ahmed Jibril's extremist Popular Front for the Liberation of Palestine. A squat, curly-haired Palestinian dressed in crumpled coveralls, he was an expert flier and a crack shot. For more than a year he had been training intensively in a mountain camp of Jibril's organization. Tonight, finally, the moment had come. He knew that a second glider had been sent simultaneously to the northeastern part of Israel, on a similar mission.

Milud undid the harness and swiftly moved toward the highway that gleamed dully in the moonlight, barely 150 yards to the south. He was carrying a Kalashnikov assault rifle, a bag full of hand grenades, and a pistol equipped with a bulky silencer.

As he reached the highway he saw the lights of an approaching car. An army pickup truck was coming toward him from the east. He waited for the pickup to come close, then stepped on the road and fired a short burst into the windshield. The vehicle swayed wildly and skidded into the ditch beside the road. The Palestinian didn't bother to find out what had happened to the passengers, but crossed the highway and ran toward a military base, another two hundred yards to the south.

The base was a temporary tent camp of a Nahal company. The Nahal is a unique army corps made up of volunteers who divide their service between military training and pioneer work in kibbutzim; they are well trained, highly motivated, and have the reputation of being excellent soldiers.

That night, though, they didn't live up to their reputation. On approaching the illuminated camp entrance, Milud threw a hand grenade and fired a few bursts toward the sentry's booth. The sentry, a young man from Safed, panicked and ran away. The terrorist darted into the unprotected base, throwing grenades and firing.

A group of soldiers were standing outside the "club tent," unhurriedly preparing to set out on patrol; only minutes before, they had been alerted by headquarters, as fragmentary reports about a penetration of low-flying gliders had arrived from the Lebanese border.

Milud fired at the soldiers, killing four of them and wounding several others. On hearing the shots, the company commander, Captain Yaakov Weier, jumped into his car and sped toward the terrorist, lights blazing. He attempted to run over Milud, but his enemy was quicker. Milud fired a single shot toward the approaching vehicle, and the officer slumped over the steering wheel, hit in the forehead.

The camp quartermaster, a young sergeant major, emerged from between the tents. The terrorist fired at him, hitting him in the crotch; but the wounded NCO kept running toward the Palestinian, firing his submachine gun. A bullet hit Milud in the head, and he collapsed. He was dead before his body hit the ground.

In a few minutes, Army Headquarters, Northern Command, had taken over, and hell broke loose all over the northern part of the country. The terrorist's death wasn't the end but rather the beginning of an intensive manhunt throughout Galilee. A curfew was imposed on the cities and villages, and roadblocks were set up on the highways, as the army combed the countryside looking for other gliders and terrorists.

In the confusion, a patrol opened fire at a suspect shadow in a field, slightly wounding a foreign volunteer working at a nearby kibbutz. Other units sped toward the border, checking reports that a second glider had been spotted; they were assisted by several combat helicopters.

The operation lasted all night. The army units patrolled in the light of hundreds of flares, which cast an eerie orange incandescence on the land, as they swayed under their tiny parachutes. Hundreds of reservists, organized in special emergency teams, roamed the fields of Galilee.

Early the following morning, the wreck of the second glider was spotted close to the Lebanese border; it had crashed during the landing. The terrorist who flew it, though, was nowhere to be seen. A commando unit accompanied by a couple of scouts was dispatched to the region. They followed the second terrorist's trail and killed him in a short fire-fight. He was carrying papers in the name of Khaled Muhammad Abed.

The state of emergency was called off, but from Israel's viewpoint the results of the incident were grim. Milud Ben Alnajakh had killed six soldiers: the four soldiers in the camp and the company commander in his car, as well as the driver of the pickup truck, a young lieutenant. A female soldier, riding in the truck, had been slightly wounded.

The incident had a disastrous effect on morale. For the first time in Israel's twenty-two-year-old conflict with the PLO, a terrorist had attacked a military base, single-handedly killing six officers and soldiers. The sentry had fled. This was not like any other act of terrorism. The Palestinian's victims this time were not defenseless women or children, but soldiers, some of them fully armed. And he'd had the upper hand.

His remarkable achievement shattered another myth about the supremacy of our army; it was interpreted by many Jews and Arabs as a symbolic exchange of roles. This time the Jews had been cowardly and inept, while the Palestinian had carried out his mission with courage and unusual skill.

In a satirical article I published in the *Davar* daily, I reversed the role of that night's protagonists, as if it had been a Jewish commando fighter who had penetrated an Arab army camp. I described an imaginary dialogue between two Arabs about the superhuman skills of this Jewish devil who had managed to fly into their territory and kill six Arab soldiers.

"These Jews are devils, not humans," Hassan said to Ahmed. "Just one of them was enough to blow our security. He flew in, he landed, he killed, no problem, like he was walking into his house in Tel Aviv.

"And did you hear how the sentry split? He was shitting in his pants. Now everybody says: 'Those Arabs, they're all yellow. One Jew in a glider, and they scatter like mice.' "

"Each one of those Jews is a Rambo, believe me," Ahmed said. "We were lucky we had a crazy quartermaster; if not for him that Jewish superman would have wiped out the entire camp."

"You know, Ahmed, sometimes I wonder. Maybe we Arabs could screw the Jews just once, the way they are screwing us."

"Forget about it, you jackass, with the Jews we have no chance."

Although my article was intended as satire, I didn't feel like laughing. I knew that any Israeli soldier would have been awarded a medal for such a feat of arms.

The Arab world awarded the Palestinian terrorist much more than a medal. Overnight Milud Ben Alnajakh became a hero in Damascus and Beirut, Gaza and the West Bank. Here was the proof that the Israelis were highly vulnerable and could be beaten on their own turf. Here was the proof that the Palestinians could win.

The gliders' raid was the last link in a chain of apparently unrelated events that inexorably led to the Palestinian uprising.

The night of the gliders had given the Palestinians the feeling that they could defeat the Jews in spite of their military inferiority. It was the second time they were experiencing this intoxicating feeling. The first had been the notorious "Jibril exchange" in May 1985.

It was another case of fallout from the Lebanese War. Quite a few soldiers had been reported missing in action in Lebanon. Israel is extremely sensitive to casualties and dedicated to bringing its prisoners of war back home. No other nation has paid such a tremendous political and military price for the release of its POWs and hostages.

In early 1985 it was established that three Israeli MIAs were being held by the terrorist organization of Ahmed Jibril. Israeli emissaries, secretly dispatched to Europe, and using the good offices of foreign statesmen, negotiated a deal with Jibril: our three soldiers would be released in exchange for 1,140 terrorists held in Israeli jails. Among those released was the Japanese assassin Kozo Okamoto, who had massacred, with three other Japanese, twenty-seven Israeli and foreign passengers at Lod airport thirteen years before. The deal also included some of the most brutal murderers in the history of the Israeli-Arab conflict. Even worse, about half of the released terrorists were to be allowed to stay, absolutely free, in the West Bank and Gaza. The deal was approved by our government.

I heard about the exchange while dining at a friend's house with the former president of France, Valéry Giscard d'Estaing. The news was brought to us by Ben-Porat, a leading Israeli journalist. On hearing about the exchange, Giscard was stunned. "You must be out of your minds," he said.

That was my feeling, too. I knew how important it was for us to bring our boys back home, but to exchange three soldiers for 1,140 terrorists? And to allow hundreds of terrorists to stay among us, absolutely free? This was the proof that terrorism paid: that the worst assassins could get away with it; and that Israel, obsessed with the idea of bringing its soldiers back home, was sacrificing its limited deterrent power while exposing its Achilles heel.

That night I wrote an open letter to the Israeli government which I published in one of Israel's leading papers. "If I were a young Palestinian in Hebron or Nablus," I wrote, "I would have marched in the streets in triumph, sung nationalistic songs, and chanted slogans on the forthcoming liberation of Palestine. I would have visited the homes of the liberated prisoners and asked to join their organization. I would become like them; I would plant a bomb in a crowded market or assassinate a hitchhiking soldier by the highway. Afterwards I would spend a year or two in prison and return home as a hero."

That was, indeed, exactly what happened when Jibril's terrorists were liberated. We watched them leave our prisons in new jogging outfits, waving their hands and making the victory sign at the television cameras. For the first time since 1967 huge Palestinian crowds filled the streets, forming spontaneous triumphant processions, where they chanted slogans and waved PLO flags. They even ignored several harried Jewish settlers who drove to their cities and angrily opened fire in the streets, damaging cars and property. The Palestinians didn't seem to care; they had won!

"I think that was the night when the uprising actually started," a high-ranking Defense official told me years later, "although the actual outburst came only in 1987."

The year 1987 also became the Year of the Promise for the Arabs. There was a nebulous prophecy that the liberation of Palestine was near, for July 4, 1987, was the 800th anniversary of the Hattin Battle.

On July 4, 1187, the destiny of Palestine for many generations had been sealed at Hattin, close to Tiberias. On that scorching summer day, eighteen thousand Muslim warriors had fought against the fifteen thousand knights of Guy de Lusignan, King of Jerusalem. The Muslim warlord, the legendary Saladin, had dealt a mortal blow to the Crusaders' Kingdom in the Holy Land. He had slaughtered the Crusaders' army, but had valiantly spared their king; three months later he conquered the city of Jerusalem.

In the minds of contemporary Arabs, the State of Israel is a new version of the Crusaders' Kingdom. Countless statesmen, writers, and preachers have predicted a similar fate for Israel at the hands of a new Saladin.

In the posh reception hall at President Assad's palace in Damascus hangs a large painting representing Saladin's historic victory. The Syrian president considers himself to be Saladin's successor. In a proclamation to his army on the 800th anniversary of the Hattin Battle, Assad compared the Zionists to the Crusaders and predicted the Arabs' final triumph.

Ministers, Arab princes, and Muslim sheiks, in palaces, chanceries, and mosques all over the Middle East, have echoed these words. As the entire Arab world celebrated Saladin's historic victory, the Palestinians perceived a symbolic omen in the figure of 800. The end of the Jewish Crusaders was approaching.

In this part of the world, where imagination and reality are so closely intertwined—where religious beliefs, fantastic prophecies, and dark superstitions can turn anything into a mystical symbol—hundreds of thousands of Palestinians saw in the Hattin victory a palpable source of strength and conviction that the day of reckoning was coming. "The Jews are the new crusaders," I heard a young Arab girl say to a radio correspondent. "And eight hundred years after the Crusaders, we'll throw the Jews into the sea."

The Hattin anniversary, the Jibril exchange, and the night of the gliders had infused new hope into the hearts of the Palestinians. But much more powerful and motivating was the despair that the times had brought upon the wretched inhabitants of the occupied territories.

The Israeli settlements, launched on a grand scale since 1977, kept sprouting up in the West Bank and even in the Gaza Strip. The cautious policy of the Labor governments, the confinement of the settlers to rigorously outlined areas, was gone. The Begin and Shamir governments encouraged unrestricted settlement throughout the biblical Land of Palestine. The Likud had managed to impose the continuation of the settlement policy even on the National Unity government.

The image of the common settler had also changed: The settler of the eighties was no longer a friendly kibbutz or moshav member, keen on respecting the rights of the Arabs, settling in the empty areas, far from their densely populated regions. Today he was mostly an Orthodox Jew, wearing skullcap and beard, carrying a submachine gun, often aggressive, convinced of his divine rights to the entire Land of Israel. The national confrontation was therefore magnified by a religious clash between Jew and Muslim.

A few years earlier, in 1984, the nation had been amazed to learn that a Jewish underground had been exposed and dismantled by the security services. The underground members, mostly religious settlers from the West Bank, had carried out several acts of terrorism and murder against Palestinian radical leaders, West Bank mayors, and innocent civilians. They had been tried and condemned to long terms of imprisonment. But for some fanatical settlers, the Jewish terrorists remained patriots and heroes.

The sight of new Israeli settlements thriving in their midst infuriated many Palestinians; it was their land and their water that the Israelis were taking. The feeling that nobody abroad cared turned the fury into despair. Once in a while the United States condemned the settlement policy, produced another quickly forgotten peace plan, and sent emissaries to the region. But this didn't change the fact that the Reagan administration was more pro-Israeli than ever, and there was no hope that it might change its policy. Europe behaved differently, lending a more sympathetic ear to the Palestinians' outcry; but Europe was completely impotent in the Middle East.

The collapse of the Peres-Hussein peace initiative added to the Palestinians' desperation; the assassination of the charismatic mayor of Nablus, Zafer el-Masri, put an end to the frail hopes that an authentic Palestinian leadership could ever emerge under the Israeli occupation; and the Amman summit conference, held at the outset of 1987, brought the Palestinian bitterness to the boiling point.

In November 1987 a summit meeting of Arab heads of state took place in Amman. It was a tremendous success. King Hussein was a perfect host, and the Arab leaders discussed many topical issues, concentrating mainly on the Gulf war between Iran and Iraq. The only subject that was swept under the carpet by common accord was the Palestinian issue. Nobody seemed to care about that embarrassing, insoluble problem.

Yasser Arafat, who came to the summit, went through an ordeal of humiliations; he returned to Tunis embittered and disappointed. And the Palestinians, who had looked forward to the Amman summit with high expectations, felt once again abandoned by their own brothers.

But the worst, deepest feelings of bitterness and despair emerged from the humiliation that was inflicted upon the Palestinians as individuals.

The bloodiest act of terrorism in the history of the Intifada was to be the suicidal deed of a young Palestinian from Gaza, Abd el Hadi Suleiman Ranem. On July 7, 1989, Abd el Hadi boarded a Jerusalem-bound bus at Tel Aviv central station. As the bus approached Jerusalem, Abd el Hadi jumped on the driver, grabbed the steering wheel, and forced the bus down a 495-foot ravine. The vehicle overturned several times and caught fire. Sixteen people perished. The terrorist, who miraculously survived, said he had been planning his action for months, but not for a nationalistic purpose. When he had hurled himself on the driver, Abd el Hadi was yelling his best friend's name. The Israelis had imprisoned him, he said later, and beaten him. By his gory deed, Abd el Hadi had tried to avenge his friend's humiliation.

This craving to avenge the humiliations inflicted by us has motivated thousands of Arabs to rise up against Israel.

I had the opportunity to talk to several Palestinians, mostly from the Gaza Strip, who had been active in the first wave of stone-throwing and street fighting of the uprising. "Why did you do it?" I asked.

Only two or three said they had done it for the cause of freedom or for the sake of Palestinian independence. Most of them had a personal account to settle with us. "I was beaten in a Tel Aviv street because I spoke to a Jewish girl," one replied. "I was kicked and punched by border police outside the restaurant where I work," his friend said. "They caught me late one night, and I had no permit to stay." Others told me about humiliations at the Erez roadblock between Gaza and Ashkelon, about soldiers stopping their cars at random and ordering them to erase PLO graffiti from the walls or remove a PLO flag from a telephone pole; about members of their families being arrested, beaten, searched, taken out of their homes in the middle of the night and questioned for many hours.

Some had seen their furniture smashed when soldiers carried out a search in their homes; others had relatives whose houses had been blown up by the army because of terrorist activity. Each seemed to carry in his heart a simmering hatred, an obsessive thirst for revenge waiting to explode.

Beneath the personal bitterness there was a much deeper collective frustration. The population of Gaza and the West Bank is young; 80 percent are below the age of thirty-five. That means most of the Palestinians have been born or raised under Israeli occupation. The feelings of oppression, injustice, and desperation have crystallized over twenty years. Since the birth or early childhood of most Palestinians, the Israeli soldier has told them what to do, allowed them to go to school or closed the school gates, authorized them to go to work or imposed a curfew upon their cities, let them sleep in their bed or pulled them out for a midnight search, ignored them while patrolling a busy street or flung them against a wall for a humiliating search.

Nevertheless, I know that if I compare the Israeli occupation to any other foreign occupation in our century, the Israelis will top the list as the most fair and the most humane, leaving all the others far behind. No other foreign power has ever given an occupied hostile population such freedoms of speech, press, movement, and legal representation; no other foreign power has involved its own citizens, media, voluntary organizations, political parties, state institutions, parliament, even the Supreme Court, in the defense of the occupied nation's rights. But this fact is disregarded by world public opinion, which rarely looks in its own mirrors; it is disregarded by an outside world that rightly demands much more from a Jewish state. And the comparison is utterly irrelevant in the Middle Eastern reality, especially at a time when most nations in our region have gained their full independence.

True, the Palestinian elders remembered that King Hussein had been much more ruthless before 1967: How many times had the king broken up their protests and mass meetings by firing into the crowds and sending his tanks into their streets? How many people had been killed, abused, or imprisoned by the Hashemite regime with cynical disregard for their human rights? But oppression by one's own kin is not the same as an occupation, even an enlightened one, by a foreign, loathed nation.

The Palestinians, on the other hand, were not the same either. In the past, all their revolts against the British, all their attempts to unite against the Jews, all their outbursts against King Hussein, had failed because of their internal disputes. The conflicting interests of the leading clans, the antagonism between the ruling elite and the lower classes, always brought failure to their initiatives. But that reality was long past. Palestinian society had undergone a tremendous change since Israeli tanks came to a stop along the Jordan River in June 1967.

I well remember the backward, conservative society I discovered in the West Bank and Gaza while touring those regions with Moshe Dayan. Its elite consisted of several wealthy and influential families who produced members of the Jordanian parliament, ministers of the Jordanian government, high-ranking civil servants, mayors, lawyers, physicians, engineers, and businessmen. Those people spoke excellent English, lived in spacious houses, owned summer residences out of town, and sent their sons to English or American universities.

Religious leaders also enjoyed a prominent status. In the smaller townships or villages, the local chieftains and the Muslim clergy held absolute authority.

The Palestinians in the cities and villages were mere subjects; they had no say in the shaping of their lives. On the bottom step of the social ladder crouched the refugees. Crammed in their miserable camps, kept in poverty, filth, and ignorance, they were the pariahs of that rigidly tiered structure.

Twenty years of Israeli rule erased that picture and produced a new society. The members of the ruling class, desperately hanging on to Hussein's coattails, gradually lost their influence. Political power wasn't in their hands anymore; they no longer controlled jobs, funds, subsidies, development projects, legislation, building permits, and import-export licenses. For all of those, the Palestinians now had to turn to their new rulers, the Israelis.

The Israelis also became the largest employer ever: They offered more than 110,000 jobs inside Israel to the Palestinians. The jobs—in construction, agriculture, industry, and various services—pumped millions of dollars into the West Bank and Gaza. The standard of living of a large part of the Palestinian community, especially the refugees, rose dramatically. For the first time in their lives they bought refrigerators, electric appliances, television sets, and secondhand cars. Many Palestinians built houses they couldn't afford before. For the first time in their lives, some of them walked into an airport, bought tickets, and visited the outside world.

The rise in their standard of living and the collapse of the wealth and power of the elite produced a much more uniform society. Class differences became blurred; in many cases they disappeared. The middle class that had always contained and controlled the outbursts of militant youngsters had lost its hegemony. "What made the Intifada possible," observed Dr. Mishal of Tel Aviv University, "was the alliance between the middle class and the radical youth, or in other words, between the potbellies and the Rolling Stones generation."

In a strange way, the Israeli occupation also contributed to the bridging of social gaps. Rich and poor, aristocrats and refugees, suffered equally from the military rule. The curfews, the night searches, the sudden commandeering of cars for military purposes hurt everybody. In some respects, the upper-class families suffered even more than the lower classes, for the Israeli occupation didn't offer their children positions suiting their education and social status. Rashad A-Shawa, the mayor of Gaza and a member of a leading family, revealed on his deathbed what bothered him most in the Israeli occupation. "I fear," he said, "that my son may become a dishwasher in a Tel Aviv restaurant."

A-Shawa's fears were well founded. Since the early eighties most of the Arab world was suffering from an acute economic crisis. The Arab states could no longer offer lucrative positions to thousands of university-educated Palestinians who used to fan out all over the Middle East and send their earnings to the West Bank. The college graduates were thus left with only one way of making a living: the manual jobs Israel offered. They had to forget about their diplomas and join their compatriots who built houses, collected garbage, washed dishes, or swept the streets of Israel's cities. This humiliation, even if we weren't responsible for it, generated more bitterness and hatred toward Israel among the young elite.

Education also played a major role in the social metamorphosis. When we conquered the West Bank, we found there only one college of dubious standards that wasn't even allowed to grant academic degrees to its handful of students. Twenty years later the number of universities and colleges throughout the West Bank had soared to twenty, with twenty-five thousand students; many of them were children of illiterate fellaheen and poverty-stricken refugees.

Besides serving as a melting pot, the universities molded a new intellectual elite, fiercely nationalistic, highly radical. They wanted freedom; they wanted independence; and most of all, they wanted to beat us with our own weapons. They had grown up in our midst; they knew us well; they were, in more than one way, a product of our society.

Ironically, this new intellectual elite was about to be joined in its revolt against us by a ruthless ally from the opposite end of the social and political scope: the Islamic fundamentalists. The winds of religious fanaticism that had swept the world of Islam had also reached our region. In the West Bank, but mostly in the Gaza Strip, thousands were rallying around the most extremist ideas of Islam, returning to strict observance of its rules, sinking back to the hatreds and passions of the darkest ages of their faith. They dreamt of feats of arms, of fighting the infidels, of dying for Allah. They absorbed, with ecstasy and abandon, the diatribes of their leaders who preached a jihad, a holy war, for the total liberation of Palestine from the Jews.

All the signs were there for us to see: the Palestinians were ripe for a revolt against Israel. In his remarkable book *The Yellow Wind*, author David Grossman vividly describes the time bomb, loaded with hatred and bitterness, that ticked thunderously in Judea and Samaria. But Israel didn't notice the bad omens. Smug and complacent from so many years of quiet, Israel once again ignored the warnings of the few who perceived the gathering storm.

One of those few was my friend Fuad Ben-Eliezer.

Born in Iraq, Ben-Eliezer emigrated to Israel as a child and grew up in kibbutz Merhavia. His teacher gave him a Hebrew first name, Benyamin, to replace his Arabic one, Fuad. But the stubborn kid stuck to Fuad; in later years he was to become the only general in the Israeli army with an Arab name.

Because of his stubborn attachment to his roots, Fuad once almost caused Golda Meir to have a heart attack. In 1972, while still a colonel, he was in Singapore assisting the local authorities in setting up a staff college. On December 28 news reached Singapore that Palestinian terrorists, members of Black September, had taken over the Israeli embassy in Bangkok and captured several hostages. Fuad was ordered to fly to Bangkok immediately. On his arrival he was driven to the command post that Israeli officers had set up in the building facing the embassy. A direct phone line connected the command post with the prime minister's office in Jerusalem.

At the most dramatic moment of the crisis, Fuad heard the phone ring and he picked up the receiver. "Yes," he said.

"Who's that?" he heard a deep voice.

"Fuad," he answered.

"What?" He recognized the voice. It was Golda Meir's.

"Fuad," he repeated.

He heard a gasp, then Golda's panicked voice: "My God," she moaned. "The terrorists! They have taken over the command post as well!"

The crisis was finally resolved without bloodshed, as the terrorists surrendered to the Thais and were flown out of the country. Sometime later Golda met Fuad. He became one of the first Israeli officers to be sent to Lebanon, where he negotiated with the Phalangists and trained their forces, although he expressed unequivocal reservations about their reliability. In 1978 he was appointed military governor of the West Bank; in 1982, government coordinator of the area, becoming one of the top specialists on Palestinian issues. Unfortunately, after he was discharged from the army and turned to politics, nobody heeded his warnings.

In 1984, Fuad was the first to perceive the connection between the Lebanon War and the West Bank. "After its defeat in Lebanon," he wrote, "the PLO will now increase its activity in the West Bank. The stone-throwing has become the main tactic of the PLO because it feels the Israeli army doesn't have an appropriate response to this activity. The kids who throw stones are getting the special status of 'freedom fighters,' exactly like the R.P.G. kids in Lebanon. The stone-throwing is becoming a means for stimulating the Palestinians in the West Bank. . . . It's a very effective means to bring the issue of the occupied territories to the attention of the media, in Israel and all over the world."

This was absolutely true. The importance of the Palestinians in the West Bank increased dramatically after the PLO debacle in Lebanon. They suddenly became the single Arab group to still resist the Israelis. The clashes between the Israeli army and West Bank inhabitants, mostly youngsters, grew considerably. Activities labeled by the army as "disturbances"—protests, strikes, stone-throwing, hoisting of PLO flags—increased from five hundred a year before the Lebanon War to five thousand in the mid-eighties. The steep increase in the West Bank unrest resulted directly from the loss of the PLO Lebanese stronghold.

Fuad Ben-Eliezer was elected to the Knesset in 1984 on the slate of the small Yachad Party that later merged with Labor. He continued to broadcast his warnings in interviews, articles, and Knesset speeches. "The new form of terrorism," he said in 1985, "is a spontaneous, sporadic activity carried out by a young generation that has been born mostly after the Six-Day War. . . . They might soon become the decisive element in the Palestinian population and lead it toward civil disobedience." In a Knesset speech he stressed that the young Palestinians were influenced by the PLO, although they were not acting on its orders. He urged his colleagues to act immediately, while the young rebels were a small minority; if the passive majority joined them, it would be too late.

Fuad had a ready solution: the establishment of autonomy in the West Bank and Gaza. The idea was not new; it had been described and agreed upon in the Camp David accords; Moshe Dayan had been one of its staunchest supporters. But most of the political establishment in the mid-eighties regarded it as a mere formula, not as an operative plan. The Likud had mothballed autonomy long ago; Labor, under Shimon Peres, was pursuing the Jordanian option. Most Labor leaders, although favorable to Palestinian autonomy as an interim stage, claimed that it couldn't be achieved without Jordan's cooperation.

Fuad was among the very few who called for a unilateral Israeli decision to establish autonomy, no matter what Jordan or Egypt might say. As signs of the forthcoming conflagration multiplied, he repeated his warnings that only by leaving the Palestinians alone and letting them take care of their own affairs might a disaster be prevented.

Nobody took him seriously. Nobody cared about unilateral autonomy. At the Labor Party convention of March 1986, Gad Yaacobi and I, together with a group of friends, presented a draft resolution for unilateral autonomy. It was watered down by several committees, then unanimously accepted by three thousand bored delegates who didn't even bother to discuss it; it was dead before it was even approved. I must admit that we didn't fight very hard to have the decision implemented.

Only in 1988, after the Intifada had violently erupted, did a few politicians admit Fuad had been right. "Fuad was the only one who wasn't surprised by the Intifada," Knesset member Dan Meridor sadly admitted. "For more than two years he warned us, at the Foreign Affairs and Security Committee, about what was going to happen. . . . Anyone who reads Fuad's remarks in the committee minutes may think he's reading today's papers."

Moshe Dayan, in the last years of his life, had also understood the urgency of establishing unilateral autonomy in the West Bank. Like Dayan, Fuad had failed to get anyone to listen.

When the Intifada finally erupted, I recalled a speech Dayan had delivered in September 1977: "An important component of our strength in a negotiation is the fact that we can carry on living as we are living today even without a settlement. [But] if we don't act wisely, we may find ourselves in a different situation: they [the Palestinians] will start protesting, and we'll start shooting at them, and all that will be photographed and published. Then we won't be able to say, in a negotiation with the Arabs, that we have an alternative, and we can carry on living as before."

Unwittingly, ten years earlier, Dayan had predicted the Intifada.

Chapter 15

Days of Stones
and Blood

You who pass between the fleeting words
Take your names and go.
Take your hours from our time and go.
Steal whatever you wish
From the blue of the sea and the sands of remembrance.
Take with you the pictures you want
To understand what you never will:
How a stone of our land builds the roof of the world . . .

From you the sword, from us our blood;
From you the steel and the fire, from us our flesh;
From you another tank, and from us the stone;
From you the gas grenade, and from us the rain . . .
So take your portion of our blood, and go.

. . . Take the past, if you want, to the flea markets
And give back the skeleton, if you want, to the Phoenix,
  On a tray of clay—
. . . Bury your illusions in a deserted hole and go.
Return the time hand to the rules of the golden calf
  or to the age of the gun's music.
For we have what you haven't got:
A homeland covered with the blood of her people.

. . . Time has come for you to go.
Dwell wherever you wish but not among us;
Die wherever you wish but do not die among us.
Ours is the past . . . the present and the future
So go . . .
Out of our land, out of our sea,
Out of our wheat, of our salt, out of our wound,
Out of everything.
Out of the memories of the remembrance
You who pass between the fleeting words. *

When this poem, by the Palestinian writer Mahmud Darwish, appeared in a Kuwaiti magazine in January 1988, it ignited a controversy throughout Israel. Darwish's message to the Israelis was clear: go, leave our land, leave our country, take your living and your dead and go away. Israel's intellectual world was in turmoil: Darwish, known by many as the PLO's leading poet, was the darling of the Israeli left, widely publicized in Israel for his moderate opinions. A few years before, he had initiated a dialogue between Palestinians and Israelis.

Darwish's poem was quoted angrily in the Knesset; editorials analyzed it as a painful blow to the Israeli peace camp. Many of our liberals couldn't believe Darwish had written a poem that was a declaration of war rather than a message of tolerance and compromise. They claimed the translation had twisted the meaning of the poem; finally, the *Maariv* literary supplement ran four different translations on the same page. The proof was overwhelming: Darwish, indeed, had turned from a gentle friend, a courted partner, into an all-out enemy.

Darwish's passionate poem was written in the first days of the Intifada. Much more explicit was the poem of his colleague, Nizar Kabani, that later appeared in *October* magazine, in Cairo. My friend Semadar Peri, one of the foremost Israeli experts on the Arab world, brought me her Hebrew translation of Kabani's poem. Kabani had entitled it "Doctorate in the Chemistry of Stones."

He throws a stone or two,
Crushes the Israeli viper,

*English translation by Michael Bar-Zohar

Chews the cannon fodder,
Returns to us with no limbs.

And right away
Land appears behind the clouds,
A homeland is born in a look.
Haifa appears, and Jaffa.
Gaza emerges from the sea breakers
And Jerusalem illuminated by a tower, between the lips.

. . . And right away
The olive trees swell
And the milk flows between the breasts.
He paints a field in Tiberias,
Saws wheat spikes,
Paints a house on Mount Carmel.
A woman grinds coffee at its door
And two jugs . . .

And right away
Rises the perfume of lemons
And a homeland is born between the pupils.

. . . A child falls, and right away
Thousands of children are born.
A full moon in Gaza
And right away
A crescent rises over Beisan,
Throws the homeland into a prison cell
And a homeland is born in a glance.

. . . He throws a stone,
Carves the contour of Palestine
Like a song.
He throws another stone—
Acre rises from the sea, a bottle of perfume.
He throws a third stone—
Ramallah emerges, scarred from a night of torture.

He throws a tenth stone
And the Lord's face is revealed.
The dawn breaks.

He throws the stone of the revolution,
Throws
And throws
Till he'll uproot the Star of David
And will cast it into the depth of the sea. *

And so the Intifada suddenly emerged in the eyes of many Israelis not only as a revolt against our occupation, but also as a candid disclosure of the real goals, the real dreams of the Palestinians: total destruction of the Jewish state, recovery of the entire land of Palestine, including all the territory of the State of Israel. That was the ancient and the new banner, the old dream and the new, revived hope. "Forward, forward, to our Galilee!" an Intifada song called. "To our Galilee, to our plain, to Jerusalem! We said to the Zionist: 'Get out! Get out! Before the stone destroys your house.' "

But the Intifada didn't start with songs and poems. It broke out with a hail of stones and firebombs on the morning of December 9, 1987. The powder keg had been there for a long time; the Erez incident, at the gates of Gaza, had only provided the spark. The spontaneous protests that spread throughout the West Bank and Gaza were a surprise to everybody: to the Israelis, the Arab states, the PLO, even the Palestinians themselves. Tens of thousands—crowds the likes of which had never been seen before—invaded the streets; the simmering brew of frustration, hatred, and despair broke all the dams erected during twenty years of occupation.

The meager Israeli army forces in the occupied territories, about two thousand troops, were almost submerged by the huge throngs that faced them. Palestinians—many of them teenagers or younger—raised PLO flags, burned tires, brandished clubs, kitchen knives and axes, built roadblocks on the highways, and stoned Israeli cars, which were easily distinguishable by their license plates. Small army units, surrounded by

* English translation by Michael Bar-Zohar

Palestinian crowds, opened fire, wounding, sometimes killing their assailants. Many of the casualties were teenagers, even children.

The Army General Staff reluctantly pumped more units into the West Bank. The Chief of Staff, General Dan Shomron, had dreamt for years of making the Israeli Defense Force a "small, mischievous, highly effective" army equipped with sophisticated weapons. Now he suddenly had to cut short most of his plans, stop the routine training of the elite forces, and shelve many of his development projects. Instead of modernizing the army, he had to rush thousands of soldiers into the West Bank to confront women and teenagers; forget about sophisticated arms or "Star Wars" strategy, and concentrate on rubber bullets, plastic slugs, gas grenades, and gravel-throwing catapults. The Intifada was drawing the most sophisticated army in the world back to the Stone Age.

All throughout the West Bank and Gaza, the army imposed curfews, arrested suspects, and pursued the protesters in the crooked streets of the city Casbahs or the dark mazes of the refugee camps. As the riots continued, day after bloody day, we stopped paying heed to the assurances of government and army spokesmen that the disturbances were nearing their end. The Intifada was turning into a roaring vortex, drawing into its depths our energy, our resources, and our sons. It also threatened to swallow up many of our moral values.

Glorious front-line units—the tough Givati brigade, the legendary paratroopers, the border guards—spread over the cities and villages of the West Bank. They were sent not to fight enemy armies, but to chase civilians along city streets, break into people's houses, carry out searches, and arrest and interrogate suspects; in doing so, soldiers often damaged private property and furniture, or hurt civilian suspects, especially after one of their comrades had been wounded by a stone or burned by a firebomb. The soldiers hated their new duties and said it openly to their commanders; it was not why they had volunteered for the elite units.

When Prime Minister Shamir met with some of these young men on a hill above Nablus, a reserve paratrooper said to him: "We grew up on universal values, moral values. But when we are sent to restore order in the Casbah we have to use violence and brutality toward innocent people. I am knowingly breaking the military law in order to make innocent people fear me. When I wake up in the morning I ask myself, Why do I have to go down and beat up somebody? I have to slap a man's face and beat him up . . . just to make him fear me. I feel humiliated in front of this man. For these are not my values, these are not values of honor. He gets stronger and I get weaker."

"Here, in this place," another paratrooper said, "a nation is being born, while on our side, unity is fading away."

Soon after returning from his U.S. visit, Defense Minister Rabin had issued a controversial order to beat up the stone-throwers; for the first time in Israel's history soldiers were issued wooden and plastic sticks.

From the fury of the first protests, local Palestinian leaders emerged; they quickly established contact with each other, laying the groundwork for organized action. Local resistance committees were formed, and a secret hierarchy was established, soon topped with a United National Command (UNC), grouping together the PLO, the Communists, and the various splinter groups. PLO sympathizers had an absolute majority in the UNC. Some of the Islamic fundamentalists formed the Islamic Jihad, but most of them joined another organization, the Hamas. The Hamas was the main resistance force in the Gaza Strip; the United National Command predominated in the West Bank.

The two underground organizations established a shaky modus vivendi and coordinated most of their actions in spite of their differences. The UNC was more moderate than the Hamas, which regarded all of Palestine, including the State of Israel, as a holy Islamic land; the Hamas sheiks preached a holy war till the ultimate victory over the Zionists. But the Hamas and the UNC didn't quarrel about their philosophy. They had learned their lessons from previous revolts, which had failed because of internal rivalry; this time they were determined not to repeat that fatal mistake.

Soon, local committees were mushrooming all over the occupied lands, organized by the UNC and the Hamas. An effective means of communication was established: the tracts. The leaders of the uprising published their instructions in hastily printed tracts that were photocopied and distributed all over the West Bank and Gaza; for a while the Jerusalem committee tranquilly used the photocopying machine of Israel's Supreme Court. The tracts' contents were read over the phone to the Arab countries, and Radio Monte Carlo, operating from Beirut, broadcast them to the West Bank population.

The tracts became the bible of the Intifada. They carried detailed instructions affecting every aspect of Palestinian life. They ordered general or partial strikes and fixed their duration; they forbade or allowed the Palestinians to buy Israeli products; they regulated the campaign of civil disobedience, publishing interdictions to pay taxes, apply for permits with the military governors, or cooperate with the Israeli authorities. The tracts ordered Palestinian civil servants, policemen, and clerks to resign from their jobs. Most of them complied, some refused; but several cruel assassinations soon convinced them that the UNC meant business, and bloody business at that.

The PLO leadership in Tunis, confounded at first, hesitated for a while and finally jumped on the bandwagon. After a few declarations intended to create the impression that the PLO was the instigator and the leader of the uprising, Yasser Arafat staged a spectacular media event: he decided to dispatch a ship packed with Palestinian leaders to Israel. The ship, purchased in Cyprus, was christened *The Return Ship*. It was unarmed, as were its passengers, who were condemned terrorists or radical leaders formerly expelled from the West Bank. The projected voyage was inspired by the 1947 sailing of the *Exodus*, the famous Hagana ship that had challenged the British blockade on Jewish immigration to Palestine.

The Israeli government was confused. It couldn't sink the ship; nor could it capture it on the high seas and throw its passengers in jail, for either of these moves would have served the PLO purposes perfectly. It had difficulty explaining abroad the difference between the *Exodus*, which had carried thousands of death camp survivors to the only haven they had in the world, and *The Return Ship*, conceived as a publicity gimmick that would ostracize the Israelis as the new oppressors.

But the main embarrassment stemmed from the internal reaction in Israel. I should remind the reader that the Jews have refined masochism and self-hatred to the degree of art. Some of us are keen on embracing our vilest enemies' positions, even if it might amount to political, even physical suicide. As soon as news of the projected voyage reached Israel, a group of writers, poets, and actors announced that they were going to rent a boat and meet *The Return Ship* in the open seas, to welcome the Palestinians on their return home. It was obvious that these Israelis of goodwill were stupidly volunteering to participate in a PLO propaganda scam.

My friend, the poet Chaim Gouri, published an open letter to A. B. Yeoshua, a world-famous Israeli writer who had signed the intellectuals' petition. "Abraham, don't go there!" Gouri pleaded. "Don't be a part of that swindle, of that media trick. You're offering those who 'return' a thousandfold of what they have been offering us since the war against us began out of a total denial of the Jewish people's right to exist and live in Eretz Israel. You signed the appeal to welcome them without asking them to change even one word in their charter [that makes the destruction of Israel their main goal]. . . . Were you to call for a conciliation between the sons of Shem, for a negotiation that would put an end to the bloody feud, be it by direct talks or any other technique, with any Arab factor involved in the conflict, including the PLO, you would find me at your side. I believe, too, that one people should not dominate another. . . . But what you are doing now isn't a mature and balanced political act. It's a fraud that will only add fat to the fire. Abraham, don't go there!"

The controversy soon spread and engulfed the entire country. It is hard to tell how it would have ended. Fortunately, on the eve of the ship's departure, somebody—foreign sources claim it was the Israeli Mossad—conveniently blew a hole in the flank of the ship, which immobilized it without sinking it. The PLO project was called off, and Abraham stayed at home.

But the Intifada went on; and we couldn't escape it, couldn't ignore its existence, couldn't blow a hole in its flank. Its ugly sights and ugly facts haunted us, as did the ugly Israeli who emerged out of its spiraling violence. Daily in our papers, nightly on our television screens, we saw the clashes between Palestinians and Israeli soldiers; we saw youngsters throwing stones, dropping rocks from roofs, burning the Israeli flag; we saw Palestinian children hunted, beaten, lying on the ground, their hands tied behind their backs; we saw them dead. We saw parades of men dressed in black, their faces hooded, waving the Palestinian flag; we read about one hundred, then two hundred and three hundred dead; tens of thousands imprisoned, scores expelled. We saw the houses of convicted terrorists blown up as their families watched with dark eyes welling up with tears; we saw Palestinian women, emerging from the shadows of their courtyards and their traditions, advancing toward the Israeli soldiers, screaming in anger. We saw closed universities, closed schools, closed stores, closed workshops, closed cities, abandoned fields, unshaven prisoners, blood-spattered wounded, sprawled dead. We ground our teeth at the latest joke from the Ketziot detention camp: "The Arab is a man's best friend."

We read about shocking excesses. There was the night at Hawara, that small village in the West Bank, where a company of soldiers had rounded up twelve wanted men known to be active in the Intifada; they had been taken to an orchard where the soldiers, using their heavy sticks, systematically broke their arms and legs, and left them lying in the dark. One of the victims was able to return to the village and spread the news, as his legs had been spared.

We read about the four soldiers of the Givati brigade who had brutally beaten an Arab prisoner in the Gaza Strip; the man had died soon after. We learned about an attempt to bury some Arab prisoners alive; about others dead from beatings; about revolting acts of cruelty and abuse; about killings of youngsters, sometimes of young girls, by wild-eyed West Bank settlers who claimed they had been acting in self-defense. And we kept asking ourselves in agony: Could this be true? Could our sons, our Jewish boys, be doing this?

The Intifada had yielded its crop of ugly Israelis. I didn't find any comfort in the fact that ugly Palestinians were also making their appearance, like evil genies emerging from the Intifada bottle. These were the Palestinians who kidnapped and savagely assassinated hitchhiking soldiers, children who wandered out of their settlement, a friendly settler who exchanged jokes with them and took their smiling pictures before they stabbed him in the back; the Palestinians who expertly threw their firebombs into the open windows of cars and buses, to make sure the passengers would burn to death, or lured patrolling soldiers into the depths of the Nablus Casbah, to shatter their skulls with a block of granite. Some had come from Gaza or Nablus to Tel Aviv, Jerusalem, or Gan-Yavne, pulled knives from their shirts, and cold-bloodedly murdered people at random, mostly elderly, defenseless Jews. Others had hanged, burned, beheaded, and stabbed more than one hundred fellow Arabs whom they suspected of cooperating with the Israelis. The dead bodies were savagely mutilated afterward. A group of Palestinian avengers raped and tortured an Arab girl, but after failing to assassinate her hunted her down in her hospital room to complete their grisly task.

These acts were revolting, but we weren't responsible for the Palestinians' morality and values. I knew that our worst problem in the Middle East was having to face people who had a different mentality, a different culture—people who lived in a different age, were often motivated by dark religious fanaticism, attached a lesser value to human life, and never tried to understand the other side. I knew there was an unbridgeable gap between us and them in our attitudes to justice, morality, and human and national rights. But I feared that we might become like them; it was so easy, and at times, so tempting. And if we wanted to, we could find justification in our Scriptures: An eye for an eye, a tooth for a tooth.

I had to judge our deeds by our own criteria and disregard the behavior of our enemies. I knew that the Intifada leaders placed women in the front lines of the protests on purpose, and cynically dispatched children and teenagers with homemade slings to throw stones at our soldiers. They knew that we would hesitate for long, sometimes fatal moments before we fired; they also knew that if and when we did fire, we would provide the Intifada propaganda with appalling facts and photographs that would shock the world when published. In the UNC tracts, the children were called the front-line fighters and the cubs of the revolution. In an Intifada song, a child addresses his mother:

> *Dear mother, I am the revolution's cub.*
> *Don't say that I am too small*
> *Because I grew up into an erupting volcano*
> *That cruelly spurts its lava.*

A disturbing study, completed in late 1989, revealed that many Palestinian children had become obsessed by a death wish, a desire to die in order to become *Shahed*, martyrs of the revolution. They would take the wildest risks during street protests, in spite of their parents' warnings.

Nevertheless, I couldn't accept the official statements of army spokesmen that our soldiers had strict orders to shoot only at the stone-throwers' feet; or that rubber bullets and plastic bullets don't kill. I was haunted by Knesset member Tzahar, who threw at Itzhak Rabin: "Mr. Defense Minister, do you sleep well at night?" And by the questions Yossi Sarid asked from the Knesset podium in the name of the dead Intifada children: "Why do they say they shot us in the feet when we weren't hit in the feet, but in our heads and chests? Why do they say that rubber bullets don't kill? Our heads are full of rubber bullets that don't kill. And why do they say that plastic bullets don't kill, and we are lying dead, riddled with plastic bullets?"

Still, I knew that all the ugly facts reached us only because they were reported by a free press; and all those who had committed excesses—

the officers from Hawara, the soldiers from Givati, the trigger-happy settlers, and those who had opened fire against the rules or used force against the rules, privates or generals—had been brought to trial, judged, and punished.

I also knew how easy it was for a civilian to criticize. I often traveled in the West Bank and Gaza, met with the inhabitants, and watched our soldiers in action. I understood what an Israeli soldier, a kid of barely eighteen, must feel when attacked by stones and firebombs; when Palestinian youths surrounded him, burning the Israeli flag in front of him, cursing his mother, mocking his lack of response; or standing behind a low stone wall that reached up to their thighs and taunting him, reminding him he couldn't hurt them, for he was allowed to fire only at their feet. I could understand how, in one out of a hundred cases, a young soldier might lose his self-control and press the trigger. But I also knew that I had to protect him, to show him a way out of his agonizing quandary; that if I wanted to preserve his sanity and his values, I had to take him out of there, and as soon as possible.

Even without the Intifada, the twenty-year occupation had inflicted tremendous moral disarray upon our society. In spite of the cruel realities of the Middle East we couldn't get used to ruling another people. Our past as an oppressed nation, our values, made it almost impossible for us to behave as masters and trample the Palestinians' rights. Scores of organizations—Peace Now, peace centers, peace leagues, civil rights organizations, volunteer lawyers, women's groups, political lobbies, writers' leagues, left-wing associations—acted vigorously to protect the Palestinians, and furnish them with legal, financial, and moral support. Israeli writers and poets poignantly described the Palestinians' plight and sympathized with their national aspirations, often comparing their struggle to ours; some twisted minds went much too far in their exaltation, making the nauseating comparison of the Israeli army with the Nazis.

Political leaders of left-wing parties relentlessly preached direct negotiations between Israel and the PLO. In spite of the law forbidding encounters with PLO leaders, left-wing Israelis kept flying to Tunis to meet Arafat and his cronies; yet, Israeli justice reacted with extreme leniency and let most offenders walk away free.

This hectic activity was tremendously amplified as the Intifada spread over the occupied territories. Some reacted with hysteria, like my friend

Yaakov Sharett, the son of Israel's second prime minister. He saw in the Intifada the beginning of Israel's end; he advised me to collect my things and emigrate, and published a book entitled *Israel Is No More*. Others predicted an imminent war, the end of the peace with Egypt, or an international *diktat* imposed on Israel.

The Intifada tarnished our image abroad. The outside world condemned us in harsh terms, but its accusations paled in comparison to our own. Any act of violence committed by our army, any unexplained death, any report of beating or other abuse, triggered an immediate reaction in the press, public opinion, and the Knesset. Pop singer See Heiman expressed the feelings of her generation in a song entitled "Shooting and Crying." The Supreme Court prevented the destruction of any terrorist's house or the expulsion of any radical Palestinian until due judicial process was exhausted. I must stress, though, that the right-wing parties and the West Bank settlers very rarely, if ever, protested against any abuse of Palestinian rights.

But I must also stress that our understanding and frequent support of the Palestinians was unilateral. Nothing like a Peace Now movement had emerged in the Arab world; not one Arab voice was ever raised in defense of the right of the Jews to their land; not one Palestinian writer, poet, or political leader ever condemned acts of terrorism perpetrated against the Israelis. The bloodiest massacres were received by the Palestinians with ecstatic joy as long as the victims were Jewish.

Amos Oz, our most famous writer, revolted against that shameful attitude. Oz, who held unequivocal dovish views, advocating negotiations with the PLO and the establishment of an independent Palestinian state, didn't mince his words in criticizing the Palestinian struggle. "The national Palestinian movement," he wrote, "is in my view one of the most obtuse, evil and fanatical of this century. Sometimes I fail to understand how so many good men from the moderate camp in our country can throw themselves so rapturously into the arms of Palestinian Kahanists [Oz alludes to the racist, fanatical Rabbi Kahane] and plan an enthusiastic welcome to a ship full of Palestinian Kahanists, while they rightly condemn Jewish Kahanism. . . . The Palestinian national movement has drowned all of us, Jews and Arabs, in sixty-five years of blood and mud. I pray we are not getting infected by it this very day." Some liberal Israelis never forgave Amos Oz for daring to condemn the PLO and its good, peace-loving leaders.

Reviewing a single weekend of Israeli press coverage, another eminent writer, Aharon Meged, counted forty-three articles dealing with the Intifada, out of which thirty-six supported the Palestinians and were full of terrible accusations against Israel. "The Palestinians were presented," Meged wrote, "as the innocent victims of abuse by the army, the police, the courts, the central and local government. . . . The Palestinians' testimonies were accepted at face value. . . . There was no mention whatever of their violence against soldiers and civilians, including attacks intended to kill.

"I find no parallel in human history," Meged went on, "where the media in the rear express an almost unanimous support and identification with an enemy fighting its own nation, as they do here and now.

"Those who speak from morning till night in the name of morality, must remember this: if the Intifada lasts so long, it is only because of the existence of moral criteria in Israel. If not, the Intifada would have been 'crushed' in a single blow, as demanded by the right wing; the same way the Jordanians crushed the terrorists in Black September, the Syrians the Haleb rebels, the Russians the Georgians, and the Chinese the students in the squares of Beijing."

A few months after the Intifada broke out, Professor Fouad Ajami came to Israel. A brilliant scholar and academic, Ajami, a Lebanese, visited several Arab countries in the Middle East before coming to Tel Aviv. "I studied the newspapers and the television news in those countries," Ajami told me. "They report on the Intifada with banner headlines. On television, however, and in the photographs they print in the newspapers, they don't show kids throwing stones or women protesting against your army. They don't want to give their nations any wrong ideas about what people can do when they can't bear it anymore.

"You know," Ajami went on, "those children who throw stones at you—they are not Arab children. They are not our children. You have made them into what they are. They have grown in your open society. They know the importance of free media, they know what are their rights in a democratic regime; their actions stem from their environment, from your society that has made them.

"We don't want them," Ajami concluded. "Nobody in the Arab world wants them. They are not ours. They are your children!"

*   *   *

And because they were our children, they won the Intifada.

The Intifada was won by the Palestinians in its very first days, although it took Israel more than a year to realize it. The army and the government, indeed, failed to understand the real goals of the Intifada. They were not the liberation of the West Bank and Gaza. The Intifada leaders knew they couldn't dislodge us from their land; protests and stone-throwing, assassinations and firebombs could wear us down, but they could never defeat the most formidable military force in the Middle East. The "conquest" by the Intifada youths of some city streets and mountainous villages, and their later "retreat" from our soldiers, were both ridiculous. The stone war was not what the Intifada was about.

The Intifada strategy was to conquer the television screens, the radio waves, and the front pages of the newspapers all over the world. And in this respect the Intifada fully succeeded.

The Intifada leaders—our children, as Ajami called them—knew the tremendous importance of the media in an open society. They wanted to bring their plight, their suffering, their cry for freedom to the attention of the public, in Israel and all over the world. They wanted nations and governments to understand: they wanted to be free.

They succeeded beyond their wildest expectations. For more than two years now, the events of the West Bank and Gaza have occupied a prominent place on any television newscast and in any newspaper. I remember the first photograph I saw in an American magazine, in the first week of the Intifada. It showed an Israeli soldier, in uniform and helmet, holding his M-16 rifle, and in front of him, a huge crowd of Palestinian women and youngsters, shaking their fists, brandishing heavy clubs and throwing stones. A tire was burning in the background, spewing fire and thick black smoke.

And I knew: the lonely soldier, even if he doesn't use his weapon, even if he is stoned to death, would always be the oppressor. The thousands protesting, burning tires, throwing rocks would always be the oppressed. That's the way of the world, and frankly, this is as it should be.

When I saw that picture I knew that we had lost. No matter how many months it would last, and how many casualties it would cost to both sides, the die was cast.

The Palestinians were the winners of the Intifada.

Chapter 16

God for President

The Year of the Intifada, 1988, was also election year in Israel. I spent almost ten months waging several successive campaigns. After the 1984 elections I had decided to put an end to the anti-democratic system of the Labor Party by which a handful of politicians appointed the Knesset candidates and graded them on the party slate. It was time for us to freely elect our representatives. The Likud was already electing its Knesset members by secret ballot of its two thousand-strong Central Committee. The result was that they had a young, promising team, while our list was old and uninspiring.

I launched my reform project in the fall of 1984; after a long struggle, in which I gained the support of our secretary-general, Uzi Baram, the reform was unanimously adopted by the party convention in 1986. That had been my consolation prize after I had failed to convince the party to hold early elections.

According to the new system, half of the party candidates were to be elected in their districts and the other half by the twelve-hundred-member Central Committee. In a subsequent vote, the Central Committee would grade the candidates on the list.

In April 1988 the Labor Party started electing its representatives. I was elected to the top slot in my district, Tel Aviv; two months later, on June 16, our Central Committee elected me to a "safe" position on our list, and the way for my comeback to the Knesset was open.

But first, we had to win the general elections.

The Labor Central Committee unanimously elected Peres as our candidate for premier, cheering and applauding. I didn't participate in the rejoicing. I knew we had a very slight chance of winning an election with Peres, in spite of his being far better than Shamir. People simply didn't like him. The only time his popularity had soared was during his term as prime minister, but that was history.

Our campaign was launched soon afterwards. I was well aware of the proverb about old dogs and new tricks; therefore I wasn't surprised when Peres stubbornly repeated his mistakes. He turned the call for an international conference into the main slogan of our campaign, in spite of the nation's reluctance, and in spite of the Intifada that had killed and buried the Jordanian option.

In July 1988 a major event occurred that should have made Peres change his mind. King Hussein, realizing the meaning of the Intifada, made a dramatic declaration announcing that he was definitely dissociating himself from the West Bank. In other words, the future of the Palestinians in the West Bank didn't concern him anymore; he was shelving his plans to reintegrate this territory into his kingdom.

Hussein's speech was followed by a series of practical measures, proving that the king was dead serious. But even this *coup de théâtre* didn't convince Peres, who continued talking about the London agreement, the Jordanian option, and the international conference. When I tried to remove the call for an international conference from the Labor platform, at a Central Committee session, I was outvoted by Peres and his supporters.

Peres's second mistake was the appointment of Ezer Weizmann as campaign manager. Weizmann had joined the Labor Party only recently, and was an outsider to its structure and methods. His main deficiency, however, lay in his dovish outlook, which was the worst position to hold in these days of Intifada. One day he declared he wanted to negotiate with PLO Chairman Yasser Arafat, the next that Peres's future government should rely on the support of the pro-PLO Progressive Peace Party, which was regarded by most of the nation as public enemy number one. On another occasion Weizmann wrote a friendly letter to an Arab Communist leader which made everybody mad.

Still, our main enemy in these elections was the Intifada. It had a tremendous influence on the public's mood. It polarized opinions, driving large portions of the electorate toward the extremes. The Israeli Arabs, deeply concerned by the plight of their brothers in the West Bank, had become restive; in many villages hostile slogans had been painted and PLO flags hoisted; cars driving through Arab-populated regions had been stoned occasionally. Many Arab voters, who traditionally supported the

Labor policy, were drifting away from our party. Abd el Wahab Darawshe, an Arab Knesset member, had quit the party in protest against Rabin's tough handling of the Intifada; now he had formed his own party, and many of our former supporters crossed the lines into his camp.

The Intifada had also influenced the country's economy. Tourism was at a record low, as people feared to approach what they wrongly conceived as a war zone. Many Palestinians didn't report for work in Israel, and the shortage of cheap labor rocked the economy. The export of Israeli merchandise and agricultural products to the West Bank had been halved, following UNC instructions to boycott Israeli goods. The crisis hit all the sectors of the economy, but most notably the Histadrut industry. The Histadrut economic empire was in bad shape already, as were many other industrial and agricultural sectors that had been affected by the thoughtless policies of the Likud; but the Intifada was the last straw. The huge Koor concern collapsed, triggering an unprecedented wave of criticism against its bad management. The accusations were justified, but as long as Koor had been making money nobody cared about the demands for urgent reform. As Labor controlled the Histadrut, it was swiftly dragged to the box of the accused.

But the main consequence of the Intifada was a wave of fear, mixed with hatred, that swept the country. The everyday confrontations with throngs of frenzied, firebomb-throwing Arabs throughout the West Bank, the long chain of assassinations and acts of terrorism, engendered fear and hatred in the Jewish society as never before. In the past, we had always prided ourselves on the fact that we didn't hate the Arabs. That was changing now. The Intifada had suddenly brought the danger to our homes.

Anybody who had a son in the army or was a reserve soldier himself could be hurt; anybody who drove a car in the West Bank could be attacked; and even those who stayed in their homes in Tel Aviv, Haifa, or Jerusalem were not safe. The Palestinians, more than one hundred thousand of them, were among us, working in our buildings, factories and restaurants, selling at our markets, walking our streets, entering our homes. At any moment one of them could pull a knife, which happened on a few occasions. Nobody was safe.

The only solution, of course, was what the Labor Party had been preaching for years: a territorial compromise, an immediate separation of the two nations. Only the restitution of most of the occupied territories to a Jordanian-Palestinian state or federation, and the demilitarization of the West Bank and Gaza, could guarantee our security.

But this was too logical an answer. In the early autumn of 1988 the Israelis reacted emotionally to the Intifada. They were not swept by Labor's complex solutions; they didn't want to give up the West Bank, which was a buffer zone against any Arab invasion from the east. But they weren't impressed either by the Likud's vague formulas that tried to gloss over the contradictions implied in its annexation slogans. The Likud leaders awkwardly evaded the crucial question: What would become of the Palestinians if the West Bank and Gaza were annexed to Israel?

People were worried by the demographic danger. There were roughly 3.7 million Jews and eight hundred thousand Arabs in Israel. In the West Bank and Gaza there were about 1.7 million Palestinians. These figures meant that any annexation might create a minority of 2.5 million Arabs vis-à-vis 3.7 million Jews; and because of the Arabs' higher birthrate, that meant the end of the Jewish state in a foreseeable future.

How, then, was Israel's security to be guaranteed while the demographic danger was eliminated? Many blindly groped for an overall, clearcut solution, a magic formula that would make the danger disappear instantly. They dreamt of waking up one morning to find out that the Palestinians had vanished into thin air. That's why they were drawn to the extreme right, which offered them radical solutions. Rabbi Kahane, the Israeli racist, was not in the running anymore: his party had been disqualified by Israel's Supreme Court. That had been the end of a long struggle we had waged against him since his election; I still remembered the police beating I had suffered two years before, when I had led a protest against a Kahane rally.

But instead of Kahane there was a new nationalist party called Moledet (Homeland), whose leader, General Zeevi, had launched the idea of transferring all the Palestinian Arabs across the Jordan River. As crazy as the scheme might seem, it responded to the nebulous yearnings of many to get rid of the Arabs once and for all. Moledet appeared to be gaining ground. And so were the other extremist right-wing parties, which preached an increase of the settlements, a strong-hand policy toward the Arabs, capital punishment for terrorists, mass expulsions, restrictions, and the use of radical measures to crush the uprising.

Two days before the election, an utterly gruesome massacre took place.

In the outskirts of Jericho some Palestinians attacked an Israeli bus with firebombs. The burning bottles penetrated inside the vehicle; a woman and her two children were burned alive in front of the other passengers, who had managed to escape the blazing bus. A soldier who tried to rescue the trapped family died later of the fumes he had inhaled during his attempt.

This shocking event certainly pushed some more undecided voters into the camp of the extremists.

The Intifada undoubtedly was one of the main factors in the 1988 elections. But a fascinating phenomenon of the campaign was that after two thousand years ultra-Orthodox Jews discovered television.

In former elections the rabbis of Agudat Israel, a non-Zionist, rigidly zealous party, had forbidden the use of that decadent and ungodly contraption to their followers. Many of them still regard the pictures moving on the screen as blasphemy, because the Bible explicitly forbids the making of images; the pious Jews conceal their faces whenever the evil snout of a TV camera is pointed at them.

In the past Agudat Israel had been reluctant to use the time allocated to its campaign broadcasts on state television. Its leaders had preferred instead to trade the precious TV time for longer radio broadcasts. But in 1988 they broke their own taboo and appeared on the screen, urging the pious Jews in Israel to vote for their list.

The religious parties, in general, made much better use of the mass media than the experienced secular parties. While Likud and Labor, which were advised by world-famous media wizards, strafed each other with sophisticated campaign ads and subtle punch lines, the Orthodox rabbis turned their broadcasts into a Jewish version of Sunday morning television. They just stood in front of the cameras and preached, mobilizing God on their side, promising the blessings of world-famous rabbis to those who voted for them, and predicting a sordid future for those who didn't.

The Labor and Likud campaign managers split their sides laughing at the stupidity of the rabbis who shouted, blessed, condemned, warned, prayed, sweated, and waved their fists in front of the cameras; they criticized the involvement of a Lubavitch rabbi, a Hasidic leader living in the United States, in the Israeli campaign; they ridiculed the use of the long-dead Baba Sali, a rather dubious saint of the Moroccan Jews, as an election asset; and mocked rabbi Itzhak Peretz, the leader of the Sephardi Orthodox party, Shas, who passionately declared in his broadcast: "A Jewish woman who lights her candles on Sabbath's eve is much more important than fifty professors who tell us that we descend from the apes."

"Primitives," one of our media wizards said to me that night at the G.G. Studios, "ridiculous, unprofessional, ineffective. They don't understand what television is all about." He couldn't have been more wrong.

The ultra-Orthodox broadcasts had a very deep influence on the masses. They threw into the race, beside Peres and Shamir, a third contender for the leadership of Israel: God. Try to imagine an observant Sephardi or Ashkenazi Jew, respecting the tradition, who goes to the synagogue once in a while without being necessarily ultra-Orthodox. In the past he might have voted for Labor or Likud, although they are nonreligious parties. He takes his seat in front of his television set every evening during the campaign and hears the parties' broadcasts. He sees Shimon Peres, "The Prime Minister That Israel Needs," and wrinkles his nose in distrust. He doesn't like Peres. Then he sees Shamir, a short, glowering, inarticulate man who seems pathetic in comparison with his predecessor at the head of the Likud, the charismatic Menachem Begin. "Only the Likud Can," the broadcaster announces. Our viewer stares at Shamir and shakes his head. No, he doesn't think Shamir can.

And here comes God. To the trumpeting of ram horns, on a background of Torah scrolls wrapped in blue velvet sleeves embroidered in golden thread, a rabbi's face fills the screen. The rabbi promises that if you vote for Shas (or Degel Hatorah or Agudat Israel) God will bless you and take care of you and protect you. And in the name of God the rabbi promises to preserve the beautiful Jewish tradition, and give a good Jewish education to your children, and strengthen the Jewish way of life, and defend the Jewish nation in the Land of Israel.

Well, on the one hand, you don't trust very much the other two contenders, who are far less charismatic than the Almighty. On the other hand, in these bitter days of the Intifada and terrorism and demographic perils and mounting criticism abroad, you feel confused, worried, and even somewhat scared. You need someone steady and permanent to rely upon, not some worn-out politician. So who can be better than God?

Therefore, you make up your mind: you'll vote for the Lord of Israel.

·   ·   ·

When the nation learned the results of the election on the night of November 1, it was stunned. Labor had fallen from forty-four to thirty-nine seats; Likud had lost only one seat, and with forty seats had become the largest party in the future Knesset. The religious parties had leapt from twelve to eighteen seats, an increase of 50 percent! It was clear that Labor couldn't form a coalition. The Likud could, but it would be an impossible government, including the most extremist right-wing and ultra-Orthodox parties. This would have become the darkest and most suicidal government in our history.

"What do you think is going to happen?" a television reporter asked me at our Dan Hotel headquarters.

"I think Labor should stay in the opposition," I said, "but what is going to happen is another government of National Unity."

The chances for such a government seemed slight. The Likud leaders didn't want Labor to share power with them. They pressed hard for a right-wing coalition. But Itzhak Shamir realized the frailty of a government that would depend on the goodwill of political or religious extremists. He understood that Israel would plunge into violent internal strife between right and left, and would be utterly isolated on the international scene as the confrontation with the Palestinians and the Arab world grew much worse. He also understood that the price the Orthodox parties would exact would be the amendment of the Law of Return, known as "Who is a Jew." That amendment would provoke a tremendous crisis between Israel and the majority of American Jews, who are either Reform or Conservative.

Therefore, at the last moment before signing the coalition agreement, Shamir backed off. In a bold move he imposed his will on his rebellious Central Committee and made it vote for a government of National Unity. Nobody spoke of rotation this time, and Labor joined the government as a junior partner. In my view this was a capitulation.

Itzhak Rabin became minister of defense again. Peres was offered the choice between foreign affairs and the treasury. The Histadrut and the kibbutz movement put a lot of pressure on him to take the treasury. The ruinous policy of the former finance ministers had brought them to their knees; they needed somebody who would help them survive. I met Peres a few hours before he made his decision. "Shimon," I said, "we might differ on quite a lot of matters, but we are friends. I urge you, don't take the treasury. It will wear you down. Take the foreign affairs. If you don't, you'll be excluded from any peace effort."

He shrugged. It seemed to me his decision had been made; his grim face showed that he had chosen the treasury and was utterly unhappy with it.

The next morning, the new Shamir government was sworn in.

I was back in the Knesset. My peers elected me chairman of the Education and Culture Committee and the Sports Committee. But in those days of early January 1989, I was not in a very festive mood. The country was in the worst shape ever. Israeli society was torn by bitter confrontations between religious and secular, Arabs and Jews, hawks and doves.

The gap between Sephardis and Ashkenazis had not vanished. True, as far as politics and administrative hierarchy were concerned, there was no difference between the two communities. Any Sephardi Jew could rise to the position of mayor, Knesset member, Chief of Staff of the Army, minister, premier, or president; but in the field of higher education the gap had grown since 1948. When the state had been created, most of the Sephardi Jews lacked a higher education; but the same was true of many Ashkenazi Jews, who had been simple blue-collar workers in their small East European towns. Today, though, most of their sons had a higher education, while most of the Sephardis going to a university were either dropping out during their first year or contenting themselves with a bachelor's degree. Few of them went on to get a master's or a Ph.D.

I saw this as a potentially explosive situation. A national effort to reform this inequality was urgently needed; we had to invest energy and means in a large-scale education program. The programs existed; we knew exactly what we had to do. But how could we raise the funds?

We also had to transform our economy. We didn't have cheap labor like Korea, Nigeria, or China. The textile factories we had built in the early fifties to absorb the unskilled immigrants couldn't compete with the Third World sweatshops. We didn't have natural resources either. Every time we dug for oil, we found ruins—another ancient city, another trove of menorahs, another mosaic. While marvelous, this became somewhat frustrating.

The only slot left for Israel on the world economic map was in high-tech and sophisticated industries. We had the brains, the original concepts, the aggressive approach. We had a magnificent young generation that could meet any challenge. Israel, in its short existence, had built ships, tanks, jet aircraft, and missiles, and had launched its own satellite into space. And according to the foreign press, nobody really knew what the Israelis were doing at the nuclear center in Dimona.

Our unique potential was there, although thousands of gifted Israelis were now leaving the country, bound for Silicon Valley in the United States and other world centers of sophisticated industries. We had to stop the brain drain and focus our efforts into developing our own ultra-modern infrastructure. But to transform our economy we needed an enormous investment. Once again, we knew exactly what to do. But what about the funding?

Sixty-two percent of our budget was earmarked for paying foreign debts and security expenditures; the education, health, and other social budgets were being cut, not increased. Until peace was achieved, Israel was unable to meet those challenges.

Yet in the early days of 1989 the chances for peace were rather grim. The right wing wouldn't hear of any territorial compromise. The left wing—parties like Mapam, the Civil Rights Movement, the doves of Labor—pressed for talks with Arafat's PLO, and for the establishment of an independent Palestinian state in the West Bank and Gaza. I believed both formulas were nefarious.

We couldn't annex the occupied territories, if only because of the demographic danger. We couldn't allow Israel to become a second South Africa. And a binational state meant suicide for the Jewish community.

But a Palestinian state, sandwiched between Israel and Jordan, was not less risky. Such a state, we all knew well, was not viable. Its size would be the same as the state of Delaware in the United States, with 40 percent of it covered by the Judean desert. It would have no economic resources; the refugee problem would get worse, not better. The Palestinians would demand that their capital be Jerusalem, which Israel had resolved never to give up. As soon as that state was created, the Palestinian extremists would launch their irredentist campaign for starting the next stage—the "liberation" of the whole of Palestine, including all of Israel.

Thinking of the Palestinians' aspirations, I always recalled that hot summer day in 1967 when I went touring the Gaza Strip with Moshe Dayan. We stood in the middle of an unpaved street, surrounded by high-ranking officers and reserve soldiers. From a dark doorway, a few children were peeping out at us, pointing at Dayan's black patch and whispering anxiously. One of them, the youngest and perhaps the boldest, stepped into the street and stood glowering at us. He was barefoot, six or seven years old.

Dayan noticed him. "Come here," he said in Arabic. The kid stepped forward, staring at us sullenly.

"Where are you from?" Dayan asked. He wanted to know which camp the boy came from. The Gaza Strip and North Sinai were full of refugee camps.

"I am from Jaffa," the child answered.

Dayan chuckled. "Nonsense. How old are you? Seven? You have never seen Jaffa in your life." This was 1967, and the last refugees had left Jaffa in 1948, nineteen years before.

The little boy took another step forward, thrusting his little chin up in the air. "I am from Jaffa," he repeated stubbornly, "and my brothers are from Jaffa, and my sisters are from Jaffa, and my mother and father and grandmother—we're all from Jaffa."

Dayan turned to me. His smile was bitter. "You see, Michael," he said, "the entire Palestinian problem in one single sentence."

And I thought to myself, Yes, indeed, that's the Palestinian problem. They don't want to return to Gaza and Nablus and Jericho. They want to return to where their homes had been, to Ramla and Lod, to Beersheba and Haifa and Jaffa. I felt a deep compassion for the little Arab child. I knew that if I were an Arab I wouldn't rest until I achieved that goal.

But I was a Jew; this was my land, and I had nowhere else to go.

I was not afraid of the Palestinians' military might. They could not challenge Israel, the strongest country in the Middle East. But I knew that if they obtained sovereignty, nothing could prevent them from concluding defense treaties with Iraq, Syria, Libya, or even the Soviet Union. Nobody would be able to prevent them from bringing sophisticated weapons and foreign armies to our very doorstep. Israel and Jordan would both be in mortal danger.

That was why I supported the idea of a Jordanian-Palestinian state or federation, with Amman as its capital. Such a state would be formed out of two autonomous provinces, one in the West Bank and Gaza, and the other, much larger in surface, on the East Bank of the Jordan River. The two provinces would be crowned by a federal government similar to that of the United States. I knew that King Hussein and many Palestinian leaders were in favor of such a solution.

I believed that we could reach an agreement with that state about the demilitarization of the West Bank and the deployment of the Israeli army along the Jordan River. The presence of our army in a security zone along the Jordan, as stipulated in the Allon plan, would prevent any Arab army from approaching our populated centers. By returning most of the occupied territories to Jordanian-Palestinian rule, I thought, we would satisfy the Palestinians' national aspirations. If any Palestinian wanted to serve in his national army, he would only have to pull up his trousers and cross that rivulet they call the Jordan River.

A good example of demilitarization and peace was the Sinai. We had given it back to Egypt when we signed the peace treaty, but it had practically no army units stationed there. Neither was Egypt allowed to keep even one single jet fighter in the seven air bases scattered throughout the peninsula. And the Egyptians didn't care, knowing that on the other side of the Suez Canal they could keep as many divisions, armor, and aircraft as they wanted.

I also believed that in the long run Jordan would become a Palestinian land. Even today the majority of Jordan's citizens—some say about 60 percent—are Palestinians. When King Hussein's era reached its end, the Hashemite princes would be easily evicted from power. They lacked the unique combination of charisma, courage, intelligence, and maneuvering skills that enabled Hussein to maintain himself on his shaky throne. After Hussein, Jordan was bound to come under complete Palestinian domination. As a result, the Jordanian-Palestinian federation that was going to emerge on our eastern border would turn into a Palestinian state, on both banks of the Jordan River. But this large state, with its capital in Amman, its economy, its army, and its vast territory, would be far less dangerous to Israel than a tiny, frustrated Palestinian state, crammed between Israel and Jordan, and governed by the PLO.

The question of that Palestinian state, confined to the West Bank and Gaza, was the main reason for my objection to negotiating with the PLO. I used to travel quite a lot, and I often saw the PLO executives rushing through airports in designer suits with elegant attaché cases. They had a good life in their villas in Tunis and their posh hotel suites throughout the world. They could keep going like that for many more years, fueled by the millions the rich Arab states were pumping into their coffers.

But when Arafat's aides, Jibril's officers, and Hawatma's lieutenants returned to Palestine, it would not be to become garbage collectors in Jenin, olive growers in Tubas, or sewage supervisors in Kalkiliya. The thousands of PLO terrorists living in exile for so many years didn't dream of returning to the poor Palestinian villages spread throughout the half-barren hills of the West Bank. They dreamt of the lush coastal plains, of Tel Aviv and Caesarea, Mount Carmel and Jerusalem, Lake Tiberias and the green mountains of Galilee. The Palestinian state on the West Bank would be only a first step.

Some of my friends were nevertheless convinced that we had to negotiate with Yasser Arafat. I had different views on that matter. Many Israelis loathed Arafat because his hands were covered with the blood of innocent victims. I understood but disagreed with them. I remembered my years as a correspondent in Paris during the Algerian War. I was there when President De Gaulle achieved a dramatic breakthrough by negotiating with the Algerian resistance, the *Front de Libération Nationale*. "How could you talk to those people whose hands are covered with blood?" a journalist had asked the president.

De Gaulle's answer was cynical, but so true. "*Le sang sèche vite sur les pages de l'histoire*," he replied. "Blood dries quickly on the pages of history." Which meant that we couldn't let our emotions prevent us from talking to yesterday's enemies.

It was not because of Arafat's past that I objected to negotiating with him. I had studied all his declarations carefully and had found that there were two goals he was very adamant about: the establishment of an independent Palestinian state, and the Right of Return of the Palestinians, from their diaspora, to the Land of Israel. As long as he adhered to those objectives, we had nothing to talk about. My objection, therefore, was not to the man, but to his positions, in which I saw a mortal danger to Israel.

But at the beginning of 1989, all these questions, and the internal, soul-searching Israeli debate that they reflected, seemed academic. There was nobody to talk to, and with our government of national paralysis, nobody could expect that situation to change in the near future. The general feeling was that we were in for another four years of immobilism that could lead to a new war.

All this was to change, suddenly, by the end of January.

Chapter 17

The Only Game in Town

"Out of the strong came forth sweetness," the Bible says (Judges 14:14). And out of the Intifada, at its bloodiest hour, came forth a slight, but encouraging glimmer of hope.

In October 1988, a few weeks before the general election, I secretly met with a Palestinian leader who said to me: "If Yasser Arafat doesn't change his policy toward Israel in the near future, he might cause a rift between the PLO in Tunis and the Palestinians in the occupied territories."

I was intrigued. We spoke for a long time that day. After I was elected to the Knesset I continued to meet with eminent Palestinians, far from the public eye; and I gradually realized that besides death and bereavement, the Intifada had produced what twenty years of Israeli rule had failed to create: an authentic Palestinian leadership that hated us but that nevertheless could become Israel's partner in the search for a solution to our feud.

As the Intifada raged throughout the occupied lands, new Palestinian leaders emerged. They were the real chiefs of the uprising. They fought against us. Some of them were wounded or beaten up; some were arrested and questioned; some spent time in our detention camps and our prisons. They made the Intifada what it was and carried the consequences in their flesh. They proclaimed their support of the PLO, and their total allegiance to Arafat and his Tunis-based organization. But even without realizing it themselves, they were on the quest for a different grail.

They had won. They had thwarted all our efforts to put an end to the Intifada. But they knew that if they wanted to reap the fruits of their success, and obtain something tangible for their people, they would have to negotiate with Israel.

211

Throughout our conversations I found them to be very realistic. They understood us, and knew what they could obtain from us and what they could not. They realized that the Intifada couldn't last forever. The Palestinians were becoming exhausted after a long year of protests, strikes, violence, and privation. The character of the uprising had changed: the mass protests had faded away, and the unrest consisted mainly of clashes between the army and smaller, more compact groups. That change did not affect the number of casualties, but certainly affected the number of people involved in the protests and the clashes. Even that restricted form of Intifada could come to an end, and the Palestinians' feeling of triumph could turn swiftly into acute frustration.

Another possibility was the shifting of media interest to a new focus —the troubles in the Soviet Union, in Afghanistan, in China. If the world got accustomed to the Intifada, and relegated it to the back pages of the newspapers, the Palestinians might lose their leverage on international public opinion and miss the opportunity of finding a remedy, even a partial one, to their plight.

Therefore, they had to start negotiating with us right away. But they couldn't do that as long as the PLO, their mentor and official representative, was waging an all-out war against Israel, which it had pledged to destroy. Nor could the Palestinians obtain the much-needed U.S. assistance in the negotiation while Arafat refused to renounce terrorism and make peace with Israel. Arafat would have to change to prevent the Palestinians from drifting away from him and his Tunis-based organization.

Arafat understood the Palestinian message, and on December 13, in the Palais des Nations in Geneva, he made his turnabout. He had come to Geneva to address the U.N. General Assembly. He had originally intended to attend the Assembly session in New York, but the U.S. State Department had refused him an American visa on the grounds that he was an accessory to terrorism. The U.N. delegates, therefore, had voted 154 to 2 to come to Geneva and hear Arafat. In a speech drafted with the secret assistance of an array of mediators—Swedish, American, and others—Arafat renounced terrorism and accepted U.N. Resolutions 242 and 338.

Still, his speech failed to satisfy the United States. The following day Arafat hastily called a press conference, and uttered the magic formulas transmitted by telephones and teleprinters from Washington: "We totally and absolutely renounce all forms of terrorism. . . . We respect the right of all parties of the Middle East conflict to exist in peace and security, including the state of Palestine, Israel, and other neighbors."

These were the words Washington wanted to hear. For thirteen years the United States had refused any contact with the PLO, following an agreement between then Secretary of State Henry Kissinger and Israel's Foreign Minister Yigal Allon. They had agreed that such talks couldn't be held unless the PLO renounced terrorism, and accepted the United Nations resolutions and Israel's right to exist.

These were the taboos that Arafat's speech now shattered. The reward followed immediately. Four hours after Arafat's press conference, Secretary of State George Shultz announced that the United States was now prepared for a substantive dialogue with the PLO representatives. At the end of the same week, U.S. Ambassador to Tunisia Robert Peletreau met the PLO representatives for the first time.

Israel reacted with fury and bitterness. Both Shamir and Peres called the decision a blunder, a mistake, and a bad judgment; it would not help the peace process, they said.

In my opinion, both Shamir and Peres were wrong. Once Arafat had met the American preconditions, Washington had no other choice but to talk to his representatives. We could not blame the Americans for behaving exactly as they had promised us they would.

But the U.S. decision placed Israel in an unpleasant position: suddenly Arafat was the champion of peace, while we, the Israelis, were labeled warmongers. I disliked the ecstatic manifestations of joy expressed by European leaders who had been urging Israel for years to talk to Arafat. The media called Arafat's performance a tremendous victory, and so did the French, the British, and many Americans.

Yet neither the Americans nor the Europeans understood the real meaning of Arafat's speech in Geneva. It had been a tremendous victory, indeed, but not for the PLO or the Palestinians. It was a victory for Israel.

For almost twenty-five years Arafat had been leading his nation along a road of hatred, destruction, and bloodshed. He had coined the slogan that the Palestinians would achieve their legitimate rights only by force. What had started as an amateurish attempt at sabotage on January 1, 1965, developed after 1967 into a veritable orgy of terrorism.

Attacks on schools and school buses, massacres of athletes and innocent travelers, assassinations of women and children, hijackings,
bombings of Western embassies, murderous raids on synagogues, summary
executions of American and European diplomats: everything was good
for the cause.

The bloody trail left by Arafat across Europe and the Middle East
hadn't prevented many European leaders from courting him, meeting
with his aides, and declaring that Arafat's PLO was the only representative of the Palestinian people. They continually pressured Israel to
engage in talks with Arafat. He was a good man, after all, our European
friends declared, and flocked to Tunis or Algiers to have their pictures
taken with the PLO leader. The good man showed a lot of goodwill
toward his distinguished guests, taking time out from planning his terrorist actions to embrace them before the cameras; once he even traveled
to New York and walked into the U.N. General Assembly carrying an
olive branch and a .38 revolver in a cowboy holster.

During all that time Israel held firmly to its position that terrorism
wasn't the means to achieve a just solution to the Palestinian problem,
and that peace could be obtained only through negotiations with representatives of the Arabs who didn't engage in terrorism. But our attitude
was severely criticized by many of our friends.

Then suddenly, at the Palais des Nations in Geneva, Arafat stepped
on the podium and made his *mea culpa*. He renounced terrorism in no
uncertain terms. These words of the PLO leader amounted to an admission that all that he had done for twenty-five years had been a tragic
error, that all the bloodshed had served for nothing, and all those thousands of people killed in Israel, in the West Bank, in Jordan, Lebanon,
throughout the Middle East and Europe had died because of a mistaken
conception. He didn't want to destroy Israel anymore, Arafat said; he
recognized Israel and accepted the Security Council resolutions.

With his speech, the PLO chairman actually justified Israel's positions
and accepted most of its demands. The U.N. delegates who wildly
cheered him didn't realize they were cheering a man who was admitting
defeat.

And the European leaders, the same ones who had been meeting with
Arafat while he was a full-time terrorist, had now the insolence to turn
to Israel and say: "You see, we told you all along that Arafat was a good
man. You should have agreed to talk to him long ago."

Good Lord, I thought while listening to the declarations of French, German, and Italian leaders, how dare you? You courted Arafat while he was a professional assassin, a terrorist with diplomas, and were not bothered in the least by his bloody activities. And now you come and blame us, the Israelis, for not having followed your example? If we had done what you asked us to do and recognized Arafat a year, six months, or even a week ago, he wouldn't have made that speech and wouldn't ever have denounced terrorism.

Even the Geneva speech didn't turn Arafat into Mother Theresa. By an ironic twist of fate, however, this speech was to play a role in the peace process that Arafat certainly had not foreseen. By his sensational appearance at the Palais des Nations, Arafat had unwittingly paved the way for the next act in the Arab-Israeli drama: the Rabin peace initiative.

Itzhak Rabin stepped onto the scene quite unexpectedly. We all knew that, aside from his routine duties as defense minister of Israel, he was busy with the never-ending Intifada. One morning, however, we were surprised by an item in the newspapers about a "peace plan" he had conceived and presented at a public meeting. We invited him to our caucus room at the Knesset to have him outline his plan before our parliamentary group.

It was January 30, 1989. The Intifada tracts had christened that day "The Molotov Day," ordering the Palestinians to attack Israeli targets with Molotov cocktails and firebombs. Rabin reported on the security situation, then presented his plan. It was based on the assumption that in the present political situation no step toward peace could be made without a consensus between the two main parties. Therefore, Rabin had conceived a project whose first stages could be carried out by the National Unity government; at a later stage Labor and Likud would have to bring their diverging views to the voters.

Jordan had left the Palestinian scene, Rabin said, creating a void that Arafat was trying to fill. But Arafat could not be a partner with us, because he stubbornly stuck to "the right of return" of the Palestinians and to the requirement of an independent Palestinian state. Therefore, we should turn to the Palestinians in the West Bank and Gaza. They should be our partners.

In his hundreds of meetings with Palestinians, Rabin would reiterate: "For the first time since 1948, the Palestinians living here are in charge of their national struggle. Why don't you take your life and your fate in your own hands? Why don't you take the driver's seat?"

At one such meeting with four Palestinians, one of them had said frankly: "Because the PLO will assassinate us."

The other three had protested, so the man had rephrased his answer. "If the PLO doesn't assassinate us, then you, Mr. Defense Minister, will throw us in jail."

"That's what I want to achieve," Rabin said to us. "Have them take the driver's seat without fearing that anybody will throw them in jail or assassinate them."

Rabin proposed to hold free elections in the West Bank and Gaza. These territories would be granted self-rule, and the Palestinians elected would become the Autonomy Council. Israel would let them run their own affairs, with the exceptions of security and responsibility for the Jewish settlements in the West Bank. The autonomy would last for a period of five years.

In a second stage, the elected Palestinian leadership would become our partner for a negotiation. Three years after the autonomy was established, talks for a comprehensive solution would start between Palestinian representatives and the Israeli government.

When we reached that stage, it was certain that Likud and Labor would differ. The Likud would probably insist on the incorporation of the autonomous territories into Israel; Labor would press for a far-reaching territorial compromise in which most of the West Bank and Gaza would be handed to a Jordanian-Palestinian state or federation. This would lead both parties to call for new elections and present their different plans to the Israeli voter.

After the meeting I went over my notes. Rabin's plan was hardly original; it was rather a well-mixed cocktail of the Camp David agreements and the Labor Party platform. But the defense minister had cautiously chosen only the ingredients that both sides could agree on.

Rabin knew that any effort to reach a quick solution, or immediate agreement on the final settlement, was bound to fail. The Palestinians would undoubtedly demand the establishment of an independent state in the West Bank and Gaza, a formula that would be rejected outright by Israel and the United States, and might put an end to the peace effort. Rabin's stage-by-stage approach was not a new idea, but it was the only way that allowed us and the Palestinians to make a start together and learn to live together. If we are given enough time, I thought, many of our taboos and fears might wane by the beginning of the following stage.

The proposed plan drove two wedges between the local Palestinians and the PLO in Tunis; they were both based on our common interests. One was the immediate need for the local Palestinian leaders to achieve some tangible results and prove to their people the Intifada served for something. We knew, and they knew, that Arafat and the Tunis PLO didn't feel the same sense of urgency. They could stay a few more years in their charming Tunis villas.

The second wedge concerned "the right of return." Although committed to the PLO slogans, the Palestinians in the West Bank wanted no more than we did the return of a million or two refugees. "Where shall I put them?" I recalled a Palestinian asking me shortly before. "In my courtyard? In my living room? In my bedroom?"

Rabin's plan made sense. It was based on totally free elections. It was not supposed to bring forward a leadership of Israeli stooges or quislings, but of authentic Palestinian leaders, even pro-PLO and Hamas figures. The success of the entire plan was based on their participation.

The plan also rested on the principles on which Israel and the United States agreed: elections and autonomy as specified in the Camp David accords, rejection of an independent Palestinian state. It also sketched an important role for U.S. diplomacy. As there could be no doubt that the pro-PLO Palestinians would ask for Arafat's approval, it was vital that U.S. diplomacy do its best to obtain PLO agreement to the plan.

Still, another reason for my support of the plan was the reaction I got from the Palestinian leaders I sounded out. Most responses were positive. "The plan is full of flaws," the Palestinians said. "It does not guarantee the independent state we desire, leaves many questions unanswered, excludes our leader, Yasser Arafat. . . . But it is a beginning."

Rabin's plan propelled him to the center of the political scene, crowning his astonishing comeback. Only days before he was being harshly criticized for his tough manner in dealing with the Intifada; all of a sudden he had become the man of peace. During the last few years the press had unanimously viewed Rabin as a man whose best times in politics were behind him. All of a sudden he became the most popular leader of the Labor Party. He had declared several times that he didn't envisage running for prime minister anymore. But his peace plan, complemented by his deep involvement in security matters, boosted his popularity inside and outside Labor to the point that it threatened Peres's position as the party leader.

On that day in January the Labor Knesset members unanimously adopted Rabin's plan. Several Likud ministers rejected it. Others, like Shamir, observed a stubborn silence. In any other situation, Shamir would have rejected the plan outright; but this time he was in a very delicate position.

Yasser Arafat's Geneva speech had suddenly placed Israel in the box of the accused. World opinion was highly critical of us, and we were accused of rejecting all the peace initiatives and killing the Intifada children while the PLO, a bloodthirsty terrorist organization, was now talking peace and begging to negotiate with us. Arafat traveled the globe making speeches on peace, oozed charm in press conferences with Israeli reporters, sent us messages urging us to open a dialogue, and declared he was in search of an Israeli De Gaulle.

We had to face the accusations of the international community alone, without the unconditional support of the United States. The new Bush administration was less friendly to Israel than the Reagan-Shultz team. Besides, a long series of blunders on our side had put a considerable strain on our alliance.

The Lebanon War was still remembered as the tragic Israeli adventure that had dragged the United States into a confrontation with the darkest forces of the Middle East, especially the Hizballah. Israel had been mentioned in connection with several Pentagon scandals. Senators and administration officials questioned the large amounts of foreign aid Israel was receiving from Washington. We had played a dubious role in the Iran-Contra affair; some of our representatives in the United States had got involved in the Pollard affair, a sordid espionage case concerning a Jewish employee of U.S. Navy intelligence who had been passing suitcases full of top-secret documents to his Israeli manipulators. We were drawing fire for our tough response to the Intifada; the expulsion of Dr. Mubarak Awad, a U.S. citizen of Palestinian origin, had infuriated Washington; the State Department had harshly criticized us in a report about human rights in the occupied territories.

Black leaders were adopting anti-Israeli positions; even Jewish organizations were openly criticizing our West Bank policy. Some Jewish circles had drifted away from Israel, which they didn't regard anymore as the symbol and the pride of the Jewish people; they spoke about America becoming the Jewish spiritual center. In general, it seemed that many influential groups in the United States, including the Senate, were getting fed up with our recalcitrant attitude. We were not very nice to look at. We were still America's ally, but a rather embarrassing one.

Against that background, with Arafat breathing down our necks, Israel couldn't afford to reject any peace initiative. Even the stolid Shamir understood that he had to come forth with something new, with a blueprint that might produce a breakthrough in the Middle East imbroglio. And when he finally came to Washington, in April 1989, he brought with him the Rabin plan, which had now become the Shamir-Rabin plan.

Shamir's proposals were received very favorably in Washington. The State Department, impressed with the idea of free elections and autonomy, immediately launched a diplomatic offensive aimed at convincing Arafat to accept the plan. Arafat was reluctant; he understood that the plan jeopardized his position. If the elections were held, the autonomy established, and the local Palestinian leaders put in charge of their people, would they still need Arafat in five years?

Besides, Yasser Arafat couldn't forget that he was the head of a terrorist organization whose extremists had only halfheartedly agreed with his recent initiatives. Another concession by Arafat could trigger a revolt of several PLO factions, eager to resume the armed struggle against Israel.

On the other hand, the local Palestinian leaders understood that the election plan was the best they could get. They watched the Likud right-wing ministers, led by Sharon, trying to sabotage the peace initiative with an explosive load of impossible conditions; they witnessed the response of the Labor Party, which threatened to leave the government if even one paragraph of the peace plan was modified.

They finally had to concede that Shamir seemed to take the plan seriously, as shown by his efforts to win the support of leading Palestinians to the plan. In July 1989, Shamir started meeting with well-known figures from the West Bank and Gaza. Some of his guests, like Jamil Tarifi from El-Bireh, were openly identified with the PLO. A few years before, even Rabin had refused to meet him because of his extremist positions.

I watched Shamir explaining and justifying his encounters with the Palestinian leaders and suspected that most Israelis did not understand the tremendous change that Rabin's plan had caused in the Likud. Shamir and Arens, the two tough Likud leaders who had rejected the Camp David agreements and opposed the peace treaty with Egypt, were now negotiating intensely with the Palestinians and offering them self-rule. It was not easy for them, and they hastily retreated when President Mubarak of Egypt offered to mediate between an Israeli and a Palestinian delegation in Cairo. Still, they were slowly moving away from the un-yielding positions that had become the trademark of their party. Sharon was right after all: the Likud was changing—grudgingly, reluctantly, but changing all the same.

I knew that at the last moment Shamir might back away from the plan, for fear that the projected autonomy would lead to the trading of territories for peace. He also could be defeated by the hard-liners in his own party. That could lead to a Labor government or to early elections. Those political changes, though, could merely delay but not thwart the establishment of autonomy in the West Bank and Gaza. A large number of Israelis understood that autonomy was the only practical solution.

Meanwhile, more and more signs of normalization could be seen in the West Bank. Palestinian workers were returning en masse to their jobs in Israel. As the schools remained closed, I decided to intervene and held a hearing of my committee with Rabin's chief assistants. We recommended the immediate reopening of the schools and got a positive response. Shortly afterwards, that promise was fulfilled. I learned there had also been considerable pressure to that effect from Washington, but Israeli defense experts had reached the same conclusion independently.

The operation of reopening the West Bank schools was carried out in July 1989, and crowned by the visit of the Education and Culture Com-mittee. We traveled to several schools in the West Bank. Students and teachers surrounded us, thanked us for our efforts, and assured us of their determination to resume their studies. I felt as if I were watching a surrealistic movie when I saw the children climbing all over the general in charge of the West Bank, while he, Shaike Etgar from kibbutz Shfayim, hugged them warmly.

And then a little boy produced a bullet he had found in the street and begged: "Please, don't shoot us anymore!"

This scene symbolized the utterly absurd reality in which we, Jews and Arabs, lived, in the second year of the Intifada. By then, more than 520 Palestinians had been killed, 330 houses blown up, thirty-five thousand

people imprisoned, fifty-one expelled. That situation had to be ended
as soon as possible. Even Yossi Sarid, the fiery member of the opposition,
declared from the Knesset podium: "The elections must be held. Everybody should understand that they are the only game in town."

A peaceful solution was as urgent for the Jews as for the Arabs. As 1989
neared its end, our society showed signs of strain that reached to its very
foundations. Forty percent of the high school students said to Ministry
of Education pollsters that they hated Arabs. West Bank Jewish settlers
violently assaulted Israeli soldiers and officers, claiming they didn't protect them adequately from Arab attacks; the cases of settlers shooting
civilians in Arab cities and villages, as a reaction to stone-throwing,
increased considerably; after several assassinations by Arab terrorists,
Israelis stoned Arab cars on the Ashkelon-Gaza road, severely wounding
Palestinian drivers.

Winds of upheaval swept Arab communities in Galilee and in central
Israel; summer camps were turned into "Intifada schools," where Israeli
Arabs taught their children how to throw stones and attack Jewish targets.
Left-wing leaders received threatening letters from right-wing organiza-
tions; a group of Rabbi Kahane's followers was suspected of gathering
arms for the creation of an independent state, Judea, in the West Bank.

After the worst incident, in which an Arab drove a bus down a ravine,
killing sixteen people, Israelis tried to lynch Arabs in some Jerusalem
streets. The crowd stoned Arab cars, then turned against the homes of
Jewish "traitors." On a scorching Saturday, a mob attacked the Jerusalem
home of Deddy Zucker, a Knesset member representing the Movement
for Civil Rights and Peace. Deddy was a friend of mine, in spite of our
divergent views. I phoned him to find out if he was all right.

His answer shook me deeply and has haunted me ever since. "Michael," Deddy said, "this is just the beginning. The movie has only
started."

No, I said to myself, I shall not accept that. We must do all we
humanly can to stop that movie before it reaches its end.

Epilogue

No Prisoners

On July 3, 1989, the 13th Maccabiah opened in the Ramat-Gan Stadium. The Maccabiah Games are the Jewish Olympics, held every four years in Israel. The flame-bearer was a young Israeli swimmer, an Olympic gold medalist, Hanoch Budin. In the balmy twilight of that summer evening, Budin circled the huge stadium, holding his torch high, then ran up a narrow flight of stairs and lit the Maccabiah fire. As I watched this tall, handsome youth, he seemed to me the symbol of Israel, so young, so capable, and still fighting for survival.

For Budin was maimed. He had lost his right arm in Lebanon and won his medals at the Disabled Olympic Games. We always won medals at the disabled athletic competitions; we had a lot of young maimed and mutilated people.

I recalled the face of Moshe Dayan, whom a journalist had described as representing Israel: the eye burning with life beside the black patch of death; the face of an Israel that was ready to die in order to survive.

A few months before, we had invited three hundred maimed and mutilated war veterans to the Knesset. I spent a few hours with them, listening to their conversation, awkwardly laughing at their private jokes ("Are you blind or what? You are . . ." "Come over, you one-armed bandit . . ." "I got off on the wrong foot, but I have no choice, I guess . . ."); I watched their hooks, stumps, and artificial limbs, their filmy eyes, their burned faces reconstructed with skin grafts. They were not bitter, and there was no frustration or suppressed anger in their behavior. They had given all they had to their land: their limbs, their eyes, their faces. They had been ready to give their lives.

But their sacrifice was not only to a land. Their sacrifice was to a unique society they had all wanted to create in Eretz Israel, a society they and their people could be proud of—a moral, just, humane Jewish society that not only could, but should, be judged by a different standard than any other.

I recalled the most important words of Ben-Gurion: "The fate of Israel depends on two things: on her strength and on her righteousness."

He had succeeded in giving Israel the strength to defend itself. Because of its strength Israel would survive, even if it were attacked by all the Arab states. But Ben-Gurion well knew that without the righteousness, without the model society, strength was worthless. Israel, he thought, would survive only as a just and moral society. When he toured the country, he preached the necessity for Israelis to become "a chosen people and light unto the nations." I remember how many of his listeners would dismiss his fiery discourses with a shrug and a forgiving smile. Those were nothing but clichés, they said.

But they couldn't have been more wrong. The vision of "a chosen people and light unto the nations" was a goal that Ben-Gurion had set before his people after a lucid analysis. The Promised Land where he had led his people was far from being a land of milk and honey. It was a faraway, desert land surrounded by enemies; nature had given it no bounty, no gold, mines, or oil; its economic hardships, the perpetual security tensions, generated tremendous pressures on its inhabitants. The Jewish people, whom centuries of humiliation and need had taught to frequently set sail for new horizons, could easily be tempted to abandon the harsh Israeli reality for the glittering cities of America and Western Europe.

Ben-Gurion knew that Israel would be able to offer its citizens neither the standard of living nor the feeling of serenity and calm that prevailed in the West. There was only one way to attach the people to their land permanently: that was to convince them that Israel is the only place where Jews could live a life based on superior humane and moral values—a life based on the "righteousness" of Israeli society and guaranteed by its "strength."

The intoxicating feeling of molding a better society, instilled with Jewish values, was the only defense against the temptation across the seas. That also was the only means to attract to Israel idealistic Jewish youths seeking new challenges, yearning to participate in the heroic enterprise of building a country.

That was Ben-Gurion's dream. But it still is a dream. During the last twenty years I feel that Israel has been retreating from Ben-Gurion's goals instead of advancing toward them. When the Israel of today looks in the mirror, it doesn't see a pretty image, but a lot of flaws and deviations from the road we had taken. In this mirror, however, we can also perceive the myths we should destroy, the sacred cows we should slaughter, and the changes we must carry out boldly.

We have to rebuild Israel. The structures, the rules, and the customs established forty years ago can no longer respond to the needs of our complex, dynamic society. We have to reform our ailing government system, elect our representatives and our prime minister directly. We desperately need electoral reform. Fifteen parties are represented in the Knesset today; more than half of them have between one and three Knesset members only. We must put an end to the fragmentation of our political parties and anchor the new system on fewer, larger forces.

We have to rebuild our Histadrut, which still sticks to the institutions created seventy years ago when the world was different, when 150,000 Jews lived in Palestine and Great Britain ruled over the Middle East. We have to turn high-tech industries and better education into the two great challenges at the end of the century, just as the return to Zion and to manual labor were the challenges of its dawn. We have to reform the obsolete Jewish Agency, our economic system, our social laws. . . .

This is a vast program, indeed, and to carry it out we need peace and leadership. We have progressed a lot toward peace, but not enough. The present leadership in both Labor and Likud is a tired, conformist group of people who are not inspired enough to imagine the reforms, not bold enough to propose them to the nation, not strong enough to carry them out.

Israel will overcome its present crisis only when the present leadership hands the torch to a younger generation. Both parties have produced a young and promising leadership. This is not a generation that, like its elders, has emerged from the giant shadows of the founding fathers, but a new leadership that has blazed its trail by its own dedication. These are young Israelis, raised in this country and deeply rooted in its complex reality; they are their own men, not the protégés of aging politicians. Only when they accede to power will Ben-Gurion's vision of "a chosen people and light unto the nations" come back to life.

Our younger generation is a source of justified pride and hope for all of us. They fiercely love the country, are intensely involved in its soul-searching debates, and readily volunteer for the elite army units, where they risk their lives for Israel's survival. Many young Israelis are stubbornly sticking to our moral values in spite of the destructive effect of forty years of war. With all the pain and fury the savage murders and massacres ignite in our hearts, we still have not executed even one terrorist in this country; we still recoil from the thought of firing squads and scaffolds. That's our way of trying to keep our sanity and our values in a region of hatred, bloodshed, and insane fanaticism.

In the summer of 1989, I met with a delegation of the United Negro College Fund that came to Israel as guests of the Anti-Defamation League. A member of the delegation, a distinguished professor of humanities, asked me frankly: "Don't you think you might be tempted to do to the Palestinians what the Nazis did to you?"

I started to explain, when an experience of mine from the Yom Kippur War flashed through my mind. "Let me tell you about that night in my life," I said, "when I, too, was screaming for my enemy's blood."

On the night of October 15, 1973, at the height of the Yom Kippur War, we launched our long-delayed attempt to cross the Suez Canal. I had joined the paratrooper brigade entrusted with that mission. Some of our half-tracks were late in arriving at the paratroopers' camp, so we had to leave one battalion behind and set out on our way, a rather small unit of reserve paratroopers. I had been assigned a place on the command half-track, together with the brigade commander. Night had fallen as we crossed the front lines and started our journey toward the canal.

Our convoy sped westward on the desert road. A black strip it was, narrow, frail and ravaged by the winds and the sun, spearing through the wavy dunes. In the pale moonlight the desert glowed with a dull-gray hue. I sat silent in my corner, staring ahead, as strange thoughts and images ran through my mind. The road stretched like a ruler toward a blurred horizon, whose center pulsated in a red, evil incandescence. It looked like the fringe of a huge ball of fire, a red sun tearing the night, its smoky glow expanding and shrinking in unison with the approaching thunder of cannon. The battle was there. Seen from above, I thought, our column must look like a convoy of damned souls heading to its doom.

Death was, in fact, much closer than we thought. We climbed a gently sloping hill similar to scores of others we had passed on the way. The low crest momentarily concealed the other side of the hill, which was bathed in deep shadow. By the time we saw the low, pale-yellow silhouettes of the Egyptian T-55 tanks lurking in ambush on both sides of the road, it was too late. The Egyptians' 105mm cannon had opened murderous fire on the company of Patton tanks that were moving five hundred yards ahead, protecting our convoy.

I was thrown forward as our half-track braked abruptly and the chains ground into the asphalt. The entire convoy stood still on the road. Word of the ambush spread along the column, and hundreds of paratroopers held their breath, trying to guess the outcome of the battle by the angry outbursts of cannon fire and the shattering explosions as an armor-piercing shell tore into a tank's magazine. I clumsily jumped out and stood beside the canvas-topped half-track, unnecessarily arming my Uzi. A spurt of fire, red and black and yellow, hissed toward the sky, and I felt the earth tremble. Then all of a sudden there was silence, followed by the hoarse rumble of tank engines. I saw two Pattons limping back on the side of the road. One passed quite close to us and I could distinguish an immobile body lying on its aft deck. I climbed back into the half-track. The two radio operators were whispering feverishly into their transceivers. "The Egyptians blew up five of our tanks, the bastards," my friend Ron* told me. He was pressing a bulky headphone to his ear.

I leaned toward him, the butt of the Uzi sticky in my grip.

"We're left without escort," Ron said. He chuckled hoarsely. "We'll have the medals all to ourselves."

"We're going ahead without escort?" I asked.

"Danny decided we'll carry on."

I stole a look at Danny Matt, perched on his high stool behind the driver. The bearded colonel had several maps spread on a wooden board before him and was studying them by the light of a portable lamp. Bent over his papers, he was nodding his head while pulling and ploughing his beard with his fingers, and he reminded me of a pious rabbi studying a page of Talmud. I knew him well; we had become friends in Paris and he had visited my home in Tel Aviv. Danny was a shy, stiff, soft-spoken man, and some of the younger officers openly aired their doubts about

---

*Except for the superior officers, all names have been changed.

his capacity to lead a paratrooper unit into combat. The old man was getting soft, they said. Still, I thought, this soft old man had just decided to carry out his mission in spite of the loss of his armor. Danny was going to break through the Egyptian lines unescorted.

The entire operation was an act of folly. Seven hundred and sixty paratroopers, carrying small arms, machine guns, and mortars, had to cross six miles held by tens of thousands of Egyptians, reach the Suez Canal, cross it on their launches, and establish a bridgehead on its African bank. And because it was pure folly, it had a chance of success. No sane Egyptian general would ever believe the Israelis would be so suicidal.

Still, even the folly had its inner logic. The road we had taken hadn't been chosen at random. It was the "stitch" between the positions of the Second and Third Egyptian armies. The day before I had ridden far into the desert aboard the half-track of Arik Sharon. On a tall sand dune we had met a gangly, blushing colonel who seemed to hide his shyness behind a fierce mustache. He was Amnon Reshef, the commander of the Seventh Tank Brigade. Reshef had assured Sharon: the Second and Third Egyptian armies were positioned quite close to each other, on our side of the canal. Still, there was that piece of no-man's-land between them, and the road, code-named Spider, went straight across the forgotten piece of desert to the canal.

"Let's check it," Sharon had said.

Reshef had whispered into his microphones and from a nearby hill a couple of dozen phosphor shells were fired across the Spider trail. We heard the explosions and clearly saw the wisps of yellow smoke rising in the limpid afternoon air like eerie, wavering mileposts. There was no reaction, and nobody fired back at us. The road was free.

Free it was indeed, I realized now, as we sped toward the canal. But at what cost! We drove past the grisly remains of the tank battle that had just ended. At a crossroads stood a half-track engulfed in flames; inside it, seven blazing torches, resembling the branches of a giant menorah, spat fire and smoke upwards. Only when we approached the blaze did I realize that the seven branches were seven soldiers, ours, who had been hit by an incendiary shell. "The bloody bastards," Ron muttered.

Then we were in the dark again, our lights off, and for a while we advanced in eerie silence, a caravan of shadows sneaking between the enemy bastions. But Sharon, who was watching us from the top of a hill, radioed Danny to flicker his lights, to signal his position. The Egyptians were watching the road, too, and the brief flashing of the half-track's lights triggered a fierce outburst of fire.

We didn't fire back and kept progressing, past the charred carcasses of Israeli tanks and supply trucks. The vehicles had been destroyed during the desperate battles of the first two days of the war. Some bodies were lying on the sand, ten or maybe twelve, in two parallel lines. "Our boys," Ron said. "Captured, disarmed, then shot."

I looked up, but Ron had retreated into the darkness. And from the dark came his low whisper. "We'll do the same to them. No prisoners." I found myself nodding back. No prisoners.

No prisoners, I heard some paratroopers mutter hoarsely. And the grim slogan spread like lightning inside our half-track, mysteriously reaching the other vehicles. "We'll do to them what they did to us," somebody said beside me. "Blow their heads off, that's all those sonofabitches deserve."

An eye for an eye and a tooth for a tooth. The cruel concept of biblical justice suddenly took possession of my mind, muffling, destroying, ridiculing all the formulas about humanity and fairness and "purity of arms" I had absorbed throughout the years. I felt as if a red-hot iron had torn into my gut, branding it with a determination to avenge my dead comrades, those teenage boys lying in the desert, bloated and stinking, with a slug in their hearts or in the base of their skulls. They hadn't been killed in combat; they had been captured, then coldly assassinated. The scary, yet thrilling anticipation of the forthcoming vengeance became my silent, faithful companion in the long hours ahead.

It was with me when the half-tracks stopped at the foot of a tall, steep dune. And it was with me when I waded, short of breath, in the ankle-deep powdery sand, hauling the rubber launch to the top of the dune with my comrades. Cold sweat poured under my helmet and stung my eyes, and the butt of the Uzi, slung on my neck, was beating against my chest, echoed by my thumping heart. But I forgot all that when from the narrow crest I saw, stretching at my feet, the silvery, oddly serene ribbon of water that was the Suez Canal.

On both my sides, all over the dune, paratroopers were busy hauling down their launches to the canal bank. The dispatchers were already standing by the water, flashing red and green lights with their torches. I started down the slope, when a quick succession of loud explosions made me stop. Ron furiously nudged me in the back. "What are you gaping at? Let's go!"

I trudged toward the water, pulling my load. In a matter of seconds the launch was afloat, and its small engine purred reassuringly. I waded in the water up to my knees and heaved myself into the launch. Danny Matt squatted beside me, whispering the code word into his transmitter. From Head Knight to Head Aurora, Aquarium, repeat, Aquarium, over.

The launch sped forth toward the African bank of the canal. Ahead of us, several fires were burning in a small eucalyptus grove, illuminating huge concrete bunkers. We were going to land in a fortified Egyptian compound; but we could see no soldiers, and nobody was shooting at us. The advance bombardment had driven the Egyptians away. I plunged my hand into the cold black water. My heart was pounding like a sledgehammer. The crossing was going to be the turning point of the war.

The launch bumped against a low stone pier. Ron was the first one out, followed by a sturdy, olive-skinned sergeant. I jumped and darted forward, while behind me the calm voice of Danny Matt flowed in the transmitter. Acapulco repeat Acapulco over. A burning tree on my left was crackling dryly, and sparks were dancing around its branches, like swarms of fireflies. I bent down and picked a twig off a low, small-leaved bush. It had a fresh, delicate scent. Behind me, the launch was already ploughing the waters back to the eastern bank, to pick up more men.

We were in Africa.

The oath of revenge burned in my heart all that night and the next day. The blazing menorah on the crossroads kept haunting me, as did the rows of rigid bodies lying cold and forlorn beside the road. I had seen so much death before, in Israel's former wars. I was seeing it again today, during the fierce fighting that started at dawn on the African bank of the canal; at the assault of the Purple compound, to the north of the bridgehead; at the desperate battle at Sarafeum railway station where our scout unit was attacked by throngs of Egyptian commandos; on the road to Ismailia.

But no death in battle, no pain for a fallen comrade, no feeling of helplessness under an air raid or a murderous artillery onslaught could be compared to the rage caused by the memory of the dead soldiers bathed by the cold moonlight. We had always gone to war to kill and be killed, to face an enemy in battle. But this was assassination. I felt that last night's grim discovery had released, deep in my soul, an un-suspected load of hatred and ugly determination. And only the certainty of the forthcoming revenge kept me going through this first day across the canal.

Sundown was near when Ron and I walked into a small enclosure a few hundred yards west of the bridgehead. It was surrounded by a half-ruined fence made of rough-hewn stones. About a dozen paratroopers were waiting inside, some of them lying on the ground, smoking, others leaning on the shoulder-high fence. In the far corner, behind two lengths of concertina wire, squatted about twenty Egyptian prisoners.

I approached them. I limped slightly, after a piece of shrapnel had torn through my pants and my thigh; another had left a deep scratch between my eyes. Most of the Egyptians wore crumpled uniforms: light tan shirts and trousers with large pockets, caps with soft visors, and heavy black shoes. Two of them had changed into fellaheen clothes, but had been easily identified. Two others were in their underwear, ankle-length baby-blue drawers. "The tall one, on the right, is a commando," a young, squat paratrooper said proudly. He had a Rumanian accent. "I caught him beside the ammunition dump. He said he wanted to surrender, but I found a hand grenade in his drawers. Want to see?" I shook my head. An Egyptian corporal was lying back apart from the group. His head was dressed with a dirty bandage, soaked with blood.

"Sonofabitches," a familiar voice muttered behind me. Ron walked briskly to the corner of the yard, pulled aside the barbed wire, and waving his Kalashnikov, ordered the Egyptians in broken Arabic to line up along the wall. The prisoners obeyed, dully watching the paratroopers who slowly advanced toward them, also forming a line. The wounded corporal leaned on the wall, unable to stand on his feet. The sun was no longer dazzling; it hung low in the west, touching the horizon, painting red the long strips of feathery clouds. Ron was back beside me, cocking his weapon.

"Let's get it over with, boys," he said, his voice unusually loud. "No prisoners, remember?"

I instinctively released the safety catch on my Uzi and heard the dry metal clicks all along the line. One of the Egyptians, suddenly realizing what was about to happen, fell onto his knees, and started wailing and screaming. Tears ran down his unshaven face. A bearded paratrooper was beside him in two strides and kicked him twice, none too gently.

"*Uskut!*" he yelled at him in Arabic, and the Egyptian folded up on the ground, in a position recalling the Muslim way of praying, his face buried in the dirt, his shoulders convulsing in repeated sobs.

"Let's finish the bastards and go away," the small Rumanian said. In the west, the sun sank behind the low hills, and dark shadows crept into the yard.

Nobody fired. Ron stirred, irritated. "What are you waiting for?" he asked.

A redheaded lanky paratrooper cleared his throat. "Listen," he started, gauchely shifting his weight from one foot to the other.

"What now?" the boy standing beside him said angrily.

"Listen," the redheaded soldier stammered. He seemed embarrassed, groping for words. "We should blow their heads off. I am all for it. Cut off their balls, too. Only I . . ." He looked about him, searching for help. "I can't do it."

"What's wrong?" Ron hissed. "You chicken now? Afraid?"

The redhead spread his arms helplessly. "No, I mean, I approve of the decision and I'll share the responsibility. If they throw you in jail, I'll go with you. But I can't do it, that's all. I've never killed somebody like that, in cold blood." He turned and walked to the opposite wall, trying to light a cigarette with unsteady fingers.

"You call that cold blood?" the Rumanian shouted at him. "After all that they did over there?"

"Leave him alone," Alex said. Somebody had told me Alex was a real killer; he had distinguished himself at the Battle of Jerusalem, in the Six-Day War. "The guy's right. We've never done it like that." He stepped forward and turned to face us. In the quickly fading twilight his features were blurred. The prostrated Egyptian raised his head. "Don't get me wrong," Alex said. "I am with you. You want to shoot them, go ahead. I agree. Only I can't do it. Never shot an unarmed soldier before."

"But they did," Ron grunted.

"Okay, so go ahead, what's holding you?" Alex stepped aside and slung his submachine gun on his shoulder.

Nobody moved.

"Well," a frail birdlike fellow standing beside me quipped, "till you make up your minds, I'll give some water to that sonofabitch over there. He's wounded." Without waiting for our approval, he crossed the yard, uncapping his canteen, and approached the wounded Egyptian.

"Fuck you!" Ron yelled after him. But the line had already broken, and a couple of others approached the prisoners. "Hey, Sabag, have you got any cigarettes?" somebody called and a voice answered "Sure."

"Fuck you all!" Ron muttered again, but his voice carried the ring of defeat. He turned and walked out of the yard.

Darkness was falling. Somebody pulled back the concertina wire around the prisoners. I couldn't see my comrades' faces anymore. A lump had formed in my throat and I swallowed painfully. All of a sudden I felt very proud. And very grateful to those boys, to the redhead, and to Alex and Sabag and the skinny one who had been next to me, for not trying to explain their behavior by some pompous nonsense about being Jewish and Israeli and humane and pure. Actually I was ready to bet that if asked, they wouldn't even be able to say why they couldn't pull the trigger. That's why I loved those clumsy, awkward, inarticulate boys and the land that had made them. I wanted to hug the kid who had spoken first. Only in the dark they all looked the same.

Index

233